# Engaging Children in Science

## THIRD EDITION

**ANN C. HOWE**
*North Carolina State University*

D1410058

Merrill
Prentice Hall

Upper Saddle River, New Jersey
Columbus, Ohio

**Library of Congress Cataloging-in-Publication Data**

Howe, Ann C.
   Engaging children in science / Ann C. Howe—3rd ed.
     p. cm.
   Includes bibliographical references and index.
   ISBN 0-13-040674-0
     1. Science—Study and teaching (Elementary)—United States. 2. Education,
Elementary—Activity programs—United States. I. Title.

LB1585.3.H69 2002
372.3'5044—dc21
                                                  2001032865

**Vice President and Publisher:** Jeffery W. Johnston
**Editor:** Linda Ashe Montgomery
**Production Editor:** Mary M. Irvin
**Design Coordinator:** Diane C. Lorenzo
**Production Coordination:** Carlisle Publishers Services
**Text Design:** York Production Services
**Photo Coordinator:** Valerie Schultz
**Cover Design:** Thomas Mack
**Cover Photo:** Corbis/The Stock Market
**Production Manager:** Pamela D. Bennett
**Director of Marketing:** Kevin Flanagan
**Marketing Manager:** Krista Groshong
**Marketing Coordinator:** Barbara Koontz

This book was set in Galliard by Carlisle Communications, Ltd., and was printed and bound
by R.R. Donnelley & Sons Company. The cover was printed by Phoenix Color Corp.

**Photo Credits:** Todd Yarrington/Merrill: 3, 102; Barbara Schwartz/Merrill: 13, 216, 231,
282; Scott Cunningham/Merrill: 23, 107, 138, 212; Anthony Magnacca/Merrill: 25, 35,
84, 114, 118, 127, 142, 156, 158, 180, 185, 190, 192, 195, 220, 222, 233, 242, 258, 260,
301, 311, 315; Copyright Sci-Link North Carolina State University, used with permission:
50, 58, 64, 75, 292; Anne Vega/Merrill: 79, 176; KS Studios/Merrill: 167; Tom
Watson/Merrill: 252; Robert Harangozo: 263; Ann C. Howe: 277.

Pearson Education Ltd., *London*
Pearson Education Australia Pty. Limited, *Sydney*
Pearson Education Singapore Pte. Ltd.
Pearson Education North Asia Ltd., *Hong Kong*
Pearson Education Canada, Ltd., *Toronto*
Pearson Educación de Mexico, S.A. de C.V.
Pearson Education—Japan, *Tokyo*
Pearson Education Malaysia Pte. Ltd.
Pearson Education, *Upper Saddle River, New Jersey*

Merrill
Prentice Hall

10 9 8 7 6 5 4 3 2 1
ISBN 0-13-040674-0

# *Preface*

*Engaging Children in Science* is a comprehensive guide to a course in science teaching methods for preservice and inservice elementary school teachers. This third edition maintains its constructivist approach but reflects subtle changes in emphases and priorities that have occurred in science education since the second edition was published.

- The idea that science should be fun has given way to the idea that science should challenge children to think.
- Today, there is greater emphasis on making science relevant to the lives of children and on including all children.
- Research on conceptual change has shown that change is gradual, that new learning must be built on what is already known or believed, and that this applies to adults, including teachers, as well as to children.
- Change in the power and availability of computers has been almost overwhelming, and we are still learning how to use them as tools in teaching science.

## NEW TO THIS EDITION

A new chapter, Chapter 3, integrates science content and processes in a series of investigations for students to carry out in class. Students will be able to experience some of the excitement of learning science through active engagement in investigations that model inquiry-based science teaching. For many students this may be their first opportunity to learn what it means to be a student in a class based on constructivist principles. These investigations challenge students to engage in thinking both about science and about teaching science. Some of the investigations were developed specifically for this edition. Others, used in previous editions as examples of lessons for elementary school pupils, have been rewritten for students and gathered together in this chapter.

Chapter 7, on assessment, has been revised by expanding sections on authentic assessment, alternative assessment, rubrics, concept mapping, and integration of assessment and instruction.

Chapter 10, on inclusion, recognizes that teachers have a responsibility to create a classroom climate in which all children are accepted and all have the opportunity to learn science. Students should be prepared to make science meaningful and interesting to both boys and girls, to children from diverse cultural groups, to children with disabilities, and to children living in poverty. Multicultural classrooms present opportunities and challenges for teachers to broaden their views of the relationship between science and culture. An important part of preparation to meet this challenge is understanding the influence of high, though reasonable, teacher expectations.

Other chapters have also been revised and updated in significant ways. Chapter 13, on computers, now incorporates current thinking about the use of computers as tools for thinking. Included are lessons that demonstrate ways to use computers that are compatible with, and supportive of, inquiry. The emphasis is not on learning to use applications such as spreadsheets and databases but on how to use them to support science learning.

## ORGANIZATION OF THE TEXT

Part I, A Framework for Teaching Science, establishes the scientific, theoretical, and practical foundations for the remainder of this textbook. The opening chapter gives a brief account of the modern view of science and its interpretation in the *National Science Education Standards.* This is followed in Chapter 2 by the theoretical basis for constructivism derived from the writings of Dewey, Piaget, Vygotsky, Bruner, and Kohlberg. As described earlier, Chapter 3 engages students in investigations that are practical applications of constructivist learning theory.

In Part II, Focusing on Instruction, there is a progression in Chapters 4 through 6 from direct instruction through guided inquiry to independent, or autonomous, learning. All three methods are based on active engagement of pupils, but the roles of both the teacher and pupils change as the pupils assume more responsibility for their own learning. These chapters provide step-by-step instructions and detailed plans for science investigations, illustrating each of the instructional methods described. Lessons in earth science, physical science, and life science—all tied to the *National Science Education Standards*—are included.

Chapter 7, on assessment, is included in Part II to emphasize the close connection between authentic assessment and meaningful learning. This chapter closes with an illustrative case study of a teacher who found that not all assessment ideas worked for her but that changing her methods of assessment transformed her teaching. The final chapter in Part II, Chapter 8, focuses on the processes of setting goals and planning for meeting them. A central theme of this textbook is the goal of helping children become autonomous learners by gradually giving them more control over and more responsibility for their own learning. A new feature of this chapter is a series of three lessons on the same topic—measuring area—taught first as direct instruction, then as guided inquiry, and finally as independent learning. This series of lessons demonstrates the three instructional methods described in the first three chapters of Part II and also demonstrates what is meant by providing for different degrees of pupil independence, or autonomy, in lesson planning.

Part III, Creating an Inclusive Science Program, begins with Chapter 9, on the physical and affective environment needed to promote inquiry. It covers some of the special considerations to be taken into account in managing science materials and in ensuring that children learn behavior appropriate for inquiry-based instruction. Following the chapter on inclusion, described earlier, the discussion in Chapter 11 considers reasons for integrating science with other subjects in the curriculum and how to do it. Chapter 12 includes outlines of lesson plans for seven science investigations to be carried out on or near the school grounds and suggestions for taking science beyond the classroom in the sense of considering the relation of science to society. The final chapter discusses using computers in new ways to meet instructional goals.

## SPECIAL FEATURES

The classroom conversations between Mr. Newman, a teacher in training, and Ms. Oldhand, an experienced teacher, are continued in this edition. Some former students found these conversations unrealistic, but others identified with Mr. Newman in his efforts to understand what Ms. Oldhand is doing and why she is doing it. This is one of the ways in which this textbook reflects what it means to teach science to real children in real classrooms.

Another important feature is the Material Resource Notes inserted throughout the textbook to alert instructors or students to sources of materials needed for lessons. Other significant features are the Questions for Discussion at the end of the chapter and Activities for the Reader. They are not afterthoughts but are central to the constructivist approach of the book. The Questions for Discussion are intended to stimulate independent thinking on the part of students and to model the kinds of questions they will ask their pupils. The Activities for the Reader suggest firsthand experiences that can lead students to construct new knowledge and gain understanding about learning and teaching science. These activities have been designed to be used as assignments to assist the course instructor in modeling the constructivist approach to teaching.

## ACKNOWLEDGMENTS

I am indebted to many teachers and colleagues who have shared their insights and experiences over the years and have enlarged my understanding by challenging my ideas. I am indebted beyond measure to Linda Jones, my colleague and friend, instigator and coauthor of the first two editions. I thank the teachers at Fuller Elementary School in Raleigh who have welcomed me into their classrooms so that I could be reminded of the realities of teaching inquiry-based science to a culturally diverse, inclusive group of children spanning several grade levels. I am also indebted to my grandchildren, Patricia, Sally, Nora, and Caroline, who are constant reminders of the importance of challenging and stimulating bright young minds. I am especially grateful to my husband, Charles, who has always offered steady encouragement and support with patience and good humor.

Special thanks are due to all the people at Prentice Hall who have been instrumental in bringing this book into being. I take this opportunity to express my deep appreciation to Linda Montgomery who brought fresh ideas of her own and gave support and guidance as I revised, reorganized, and added to the previous edition. Thanks go to Brad Potthoff who got the revision underway, to Mary Irvin who shepherded the manuscript through a series of problems, to Carol Sykes and Valerie Schulz who took special care to integrate photos and text, and to other members of the editorial staff who contributed their skills and expertise. I owe a debt to Jerry Moore who edited out my lapses of grammar and murky phrases, and to those at York Production Services and Carlisle Communications who worked to make the book what I wanted it to be.

I also thank the reviewers whose comments and suggestions were the basis for many of the revisions that make this book different from the previous edition: Lloyd Barrow, University of Missouri; Lawrence Bellipanni, University of Southern Mississippi; G. Nathan Carnes, University of South Carolina, Columbia; Richard Griffiths, California State University, San Bernardino; and Catherine E. Matthews, University of North Carolina, Greensboro.

# Discover the Companion Website Accompanying This Book

## The Prentice Hall Companion Website: A Virtual Learning Environment

Technology is a constantly growing and changing aspect of our field that is creating a need for content and resources. To address this emerging need, Prentice Hall has developed an online learning environment for students and professors alike—Companion Websites—to support our textbooks.

In creating a Companion Website, our goal is to build on and enhance what the textbook already offers. For this reason, the content for each user-friendly website is organized by topic and provides the professor and student with a variety of meaningful resources. Common features of a Companion Website include:

## For the Professor

- Every Companion Website integrates **Syllabus Manager**™, an online syllabus creation and management utility.
- **Syllabus Manager**™ provides you, the instructor, with an easy, step-by-step process to create and revise syllabi, with direct links into Companion Website and other online content without having to learn HTML.
- Students may log on to your syllabus during any study session. All they need to know is the web address for the Companion Website and the password you've assigned to your syllabus.
- After you have created a syllabus using **Syllabus Manager**™, students may enter the syllabus for their course section from any point in the Companion Website.
- Clicking on a date, the student is shown the list of activities for the assignment. The activities for each assignment are linked directly to actual content, saving time for students.
- Adding assignments consists of clicking on the desired due date, then filling in the details of the assignment—name of the assignment, instructions, and whether it is a one-time or repeating assignment.

- In addition, links to other activities can be created easily. If the activity is online, a URL can be entered in the space provided, and it will be linked automatically in the final syllabus.
- Your completed syllabus is hosted on our servers, allowing convenient updates from any computer on the Internet. Changes you make to your syllabus are immediately available to your students at their next logon.

## For the Student

- **Topic Overviews**—outline key concepts in topic areas
- **Web Links**—topic-specific lists of links to websites that feature current information and resources for educators
- **Electronic Bluebook**—send homework or essays directly to your instructor's e-mail with this paperless form
- **Message Board**—serves as a virtual bulletin board to post—or respond to—questions or comments to/from a national audience
- **Chat**—real-time chat with anyone who is using the text anywhere in the country—ideal for discussion and study groups, class projects, etc.

To take advantage of these and other resources, please visit the *Engaging Children in Science*, Third Edition, Companion Website at

www.prenhall.com/howe

# Brief Contents

# Contents

## CHAPTER 2

### CHILDREN'S THINKING AND LEARNING 23

## CHAPTER 3

### INTEGRATING SCIENCE CONTENT AND PROCESS 50

# PART II   FOCUSING ON INSTRUCTION     78

## CHAPTER 4

### TEACHING BASIC SCIENCE SKILLS     79

## CHAPTER 5

### TEACHING SCIENCE AS INQUIRY     107

# CHAPTER 6

## TEACHING SCIENCE TO PROMOTE INDEPENDENT LEARNING 138

# Chapter 7

## Enhancing Instruction through Assessment 167

# Chapter 8

## Planning for Achieving Goals 190

# PART III    CREATING AN INCLUSIVE SCIENCE PROGRAM        211

## CHAPTER 9

### SHAPING THE CLASSROOM LEARNING ENVIRONMENT        212

# CHAPTER 10

## INCLUDING ALL CHILDREN IN SCIENCE   231

# CHAPTER 11

## INTEGRATING SCIENCE WITH OTHER SUBJECTS                    252

# CHAPTER 12

## TAKING SCIENCE BEYOND THE CLASSROOM                    277

## CHAPTER 13

### LEARNING SCIENCE WITH COMPUTERS                                              301

# A Framework for Teaching Science

# *Science as a Human Activity*

■  Joe Newman, teacher candidate, is discussing elementary science with his cooperating teacher, Ms. Oldhand.

MR. NEWMAN:  I don't feel very confident about teaching science. I loved science in elementary school, but I'm nervous about teaching it myself.

MS. OLDHAND:  I'm glad to hear that you liked science in elementary school. What courses did you have in high school and college?

MR. NEWMAN:  I had all the required courses, and they were OK, but science wasn't my main interest, so I concentrated on other things.

MS. OLDHAND:  Well, it was about the same with me. Some of my teachers gave interesting lectures, but the theories weren't connected with anything I felt I had experienced. Fortunately, I later had some opportunities to learn about inquiry-based science for children. Now, I'm really enthusiastic about it.

MR. NEWMAN:  That's great. What happened to make you so enthusiastic?

MS. OLDHAND:  The children enjoy science activities and investigations so much. I use that built-in motivation to bring in as many other subjects as possible; it makes sense to integrate science into the rest of the school day. The experiences with materials are so meaningful for the children that they actually want to write about those experiences, read background material, and even use the computer for something other than games.

MR. NEWMAN:  OK, I'm convinced you've made it work. Now I just have to convince myself that I can do it, too.

MS. OLDHAND:  That's the first step. You know, you don't have to learn everything in one day. Watch me start a new unit this afternoon. Then I'll help you plan one of the lessons for next week.

MR. NEWMAN:  You make it sound so simple.

Science can be the most exciting subject in the elementary school for both children and teachers if science is an active, hands-on subject that children learn through doing, not just by listening or memorizing. In elementary school, when science is taught at all, it all too often is taught with reading as the main source of knowledge. The cognitive result is what has been called *dissociated learning,* that is, isolated facts having little or no connection to the learner's life. This result often leads children to have attitudes toward science that range from neutral to negative. In fact, children love learning when it is meaningful. Play is not just a childish pastime but the way children learn their world.

Young children learn best when they experience things themselves and then have time to think about those experiences as well as talk about what they have seen and done. Observing, measuring, collecting, and classifying—some of the ways of learning that work best in science—come naturally to most children. When you help children learn about the world through their own activity and thought, you reinforce their natural interests and curiosity.

# LEARNING TO TEACH SCIENCE

A beginning student teacher asked her university supervisor how to handle a particular situation. The supervisor replied that it depended on many factors and began to explain some of the various options. The student teacher grew restless and finally interrupted, "Don't confuse me with all that! Just give me the one-two-threes." The supervisor might have found a way to respond that would have been more directly relevant to the student teacher's needs; nevertheless, there are very few "one-two-threes" in learning to teach. Every successful teacher makes thousands of decisions every day. You may well respond, "That sounds impossible! How does anyone survive in that sort of pressure cooker?"

## An Analogy

Consider an analogy. Almost every adult in the United States drives a car. Driving is a complex and demanding skill. The penalty for too many mistakes can be death or a whole host of lesser evils. Yet, we are usually able to function as drivers without being paralyzed by fear and indecision. Try to think back to when you learned to drive. It did not all happen at once. First you learned and practiced the mechanical aspects of operating the controls of the car. Later you learned the rules of the road and practiced driving in street traffic. Only after you had developed these skills did you dare to enter the freeway and tackle tricky interchanges at rush hour. What was happening to the early skills as you progressed to the more advanced ones? Are you consciously thinking about how to steer, accelerate, and brake (and maybe even shift) while you maneuver through a freeway interchange? Probably not; probably you are able to manage these early skills in an almost automatic way, a sort of mental cruise control. A similar process allows you to move through all kinds of skill hierarchies. There is one difference, however: It is human nature to forget very quickly what it was like not to know something just as soon as you learn it. You will be much more effective as a teacher if you can retain the memory of that preknowledge state, because retaining that memory makes you able to relate to the learning process in your own pupils.

Learning to be an effective teacher is complex but not too complex to learn. You just need to think about what you're doing and not let the mental cruise control become too automatic. Just as many driving decisions are made as you drive along, many teaching decisions cannot be made in advance but depend on unforeseeable circumstances. On the highway, your decisions depend on what is happening all around you; on a busy highway you have to be alert at every moment. In the classroom, your decisions will also depend on what is happening around you, and you also have to be alert at every moment. These in-progress decisions that teachers must make include how to involve all the pupils in the class, whether to interrupt the lesson to correct misbehavior, whether to use variations in language or to stress repeatedly the same words, whether to accept an incomplete pupil response or to take time to probe for more depth, whether to make a major excursion from the planned lesson in response to unexpected pupil reactions, and many, many more. As you see, most of these decisions involve being aware of what is happening around you, knowing and reflecting on what you are doing, and modifying your own thinking and actions accordingly.

## TRUSTING YOUR OWN ABILITIES

As you become a teacher, it is important for you to learn to trust your own ability to learn and teach science. Richard Feynman, a Nobel laureate in physics, had this to say in a talk he gave to science teachers at a national meeting:

> You teachers . . . can maybe doubt the experts once in a while. Learn from science that you must doubt the experts. . . . When someone says, "Science teaches such and such," he is using the word incorrectly. Science doesn't teach anything; experience teaches it. If they say to you, "Science has shown such and such," you might ask, "How does science show it? How did the scientists find out? How? What? Where?" It should not be "science has shown," but "this experiment, this effect, has shown." And you have as much right as anyone else, upon hearing about the experiments (but be patient and listen to all the evidence) to judge whether a sensible conclusion has been arrived at. (Feynman, 1968, p. 319)

One reason that you can become a good elementary science teacher is that children love hands-on learning. That is the natural way to learn; your main job is to provide the situation and teach them how to function within its boundaries. In such a context, science ideas will be concrete rather than abstract, and your role will be to guide a learning experience rather than to tell about or explain concepts.

Another reason that you can become a good teacher is that this book, and your instructor, will help you construct the knowledge and acquire the skills you need to be successful. As you develop knowledge of how to guide students through activities and discussions of the kind described here, you will gain confidence in your own ability to have a positive effect on student learning.

Self-efficacy, the sense that what you do can make a difference, is one of the few teacher characteristics shown to be related to student achievement (Woolfolk & Hoy, 1990). To be effective, you must believe that what you do will have an effect. You must also help children believe that what they do will have an effect. Particularly with girls and with minority children, you will need teaching strategies that give each child a sense of self-efficacy, a belief in his or her own ability to learn science as well as the motivation to be an active and responsible learner.

# CHILDREN'S KNOWLEDGE CONSTRUCTION

The kind of science program described in this book is one in which children build their own knowledge from their own experiences, from both doing and thinking. "Hands-on" must be accompanied by "minds-on." Having interesting things for the children to do is not enough; thinking and talking about what they have done must be part of the science program, too. In this way children build their own knowledge from their own experiences.

Research of cognitive psychologists and science educators has shown that real understanding of science concepts, as well as other concepts, occurs only when people participate fully in the development of their own knowledge. That is, they must construct their own knowledge. This idea that people must build their own knowledge from their own experiences and thought is called *constructivism*. A great deal has been written about constructivism over the past few years, and you may want to read more about it (see, e.g., Fosnot, 1989; Marin, Benarroch, & Gomez, 2000; Solomon, 1994). However, the main idea is that knowledge is not transmitted directly from one person to another but is actively constructed by the learner. Learning is an active process that requires both action and reflection on the part of the learner. Knowledge and understanding grow slowly, with each new bit of information having to be fitted into what was already there. Contrast this idea of learning with the opposite idea, that children's minds are like sponges that absorb what they are told without any mental action on their part. In one case the learner is active, engaged; in the other case the learner is passive, unengaged.

You may be thinking that there are certain things that a pupil simply must be told and then asked to remember, and you wonder how the memorization of facts fits into this idea of learning. Undoubtedly, some things have to be committed to memory without explanation, such as your telephone number, the name of the street you live on, and the names of trees, birds, and flowers. Everyone needs a mechanism for remembering and retrieving these kinds of numbers and words, and you will want your pupils to be able to do so. But learning of this kind is a lower level mental function; although some may be necessary, it should not be the main emphasis or even an important emphasis of your teaching. Science teaching should lead to a deeper understanding of relationships and interrelationships, of causes and effects, of how we as human beings know what we know and how we can find out more. These concepts require higher level thinking and should not be treated as facts to be memorized. All learners must construct this kind of knowledge in their own way.

# CONSTRUCTING YOUR OWN KNOWLEDGE

Just as children must construct their own knowledge of science, you will have to construct your own knowledge of how to teach science. For you, too, knowledge and understanding will grow slowly, with each new bit of information having to be fitted into what is already there. This textbook includes science activities for you that can only be effective if they are accompanied by reflection, discussion, and independent thinking. Knowledge that is useful in your life is not built up by memorizing facts and adding them all together but by thinking about the facts, ideas, and experiences that you encounter—and connecting them to each other and to other things we already know. Your ideas of what constitutes good teaching, and what science is, have developed over all the years you have been a student, and you may find that some of those ideas will change as you focus on trying to become a good science teacher. As a student in college or university science courses you weren't often required to think about science in the basic way that children think about the world around them. Some of your assumptions may have to be revised as you learn to help children interpret their experiences of the world in a way that leads to greater knowledge.

## WHAT SCIENCE IS

Science is both knowledge, or understanding, and a way of arriving at knowledge. Remember that science is not the only way of knowing; people can also gain knowledge in other ways, including intuition, art forms, and faith. Science cannot answer all questions; questions about values, good and evil, and the meaning of life cannot be answered by the methods of science. What science can do, and has done, is to achieve an ever-increasing understanding of the natural world, including all of us as human beings, and the rules that govern the patterns and interrelationships found in nature.

The desire to know more about the natural world has probably always been a part of human life and has certainly been present since the beginning of recorded history. However, the systematic study of natural phenomena in more recent times has produced an explosion of scientific knowledge that has changed almost every aspect of the way people live and think. Many ideas that once seemed farfetched and even ridiculous are now part of general knowledge. For example, it would be hard to find a person today who does not believe that bacteria and viruses exist and cause disease and that it is possible to obtain energy from splitting atoms—ideas that were hotly debated and denied by intelligent people a little over a century ago.

To study science is to learn about what other people have found out and to learn about the methods that allowed them to arrive at this knowledge and then to convince other people to accept it. To be scientifically literate, a person needs to have knowledge of concepts and theories of science and, in addition, to have some understanding of how this knowledge has been obtained in the past and is still being learned. Let's look at some of the distinctive aspects of science.

### Scientists' View of the World

Scientists believe that the world is understandable and can be understood through the careful, systematic application of human intelligence. A look back through the history of the last hundred years shows how much has been learned about all aspects of plant and animal life, the particles that are the basic forms of matter, the history and composition of the earth, the parts of the solar system, and the complex workings of the universe beyond. As scientific work continues to probe these areas, unexpected observations will surely force scientists to revise their current ideas and develop theories that give better explanations than the ones they now have. Science will never be a finished body of knowledge because new ideas and theories are always being proposed, new discoveries are being made, and some things that were taken for granted turn out to be different from what they were thought to be. Students sometimes get confused when they hear that scientific knowledge is subject to change and ask, "Then why am I learning all of this science if it may not be true?" One answer is that *science* is not the same as *truth;* science is the sum of the best explanations, we as human beings, now have for all the complexities of nature. This knowledge has been built up over thousands of years, and much of what has been learned endures; change comes slowly, and major theories or principles may be revised but are rarely overturned. However, as teachers, we always have to leave a little room in our minds for the possibility that some new observation may force us to change our ideas or that a new theory will be a better explanation for old observations. And, as teachers, we strive to introduce our students to the scientific world view of the time we live in.

## Science as the Search for Knowledge

Scientists use many strategies and techniques in their search for greater knowledge and understanding, but at some point they rely on observations that can be repeated or verified by others. Scientists use their own senses and instruments—sometimes very complicated ones—to make the observations that form the data on which they base the theories and hypotheses that explain what they have found. When important new observations are published, other scientists will try to verify them. If observations, or data, can't be verified, they aren't accepted. When observations have been verified, other scientists still may not accept the original scientist's explanation for them. Arguments may go on for years about how to interpret the observations, with other scientists proposing different hypotheses to explain the observations.

## Scientific Theories and Hypotheses

The advancement of scientific knowledge depends as much, if not more, on the hypotheses or theories scientists propose as it does on the data they collect. In fact, hypotheses and theories usually determine what data will be collected because isolated facts by themselves can seldom be interpreted. The process may work something like this: A scientist is interested in something that isn't well understood. By a combination of extensive knowledge, intuition, and imagination, the scientist thinks of a possible explanation, states it as a hypothesis and determines what data will be needed to support or refute the hypothesis. The next step is to develop a plan for collecting the necessary data in such a way that others will be convinced that the data are reliable. When the observations have been made, the scientist examines the data to see whether the hypothesis has been supported; if so, the scientist publishes the results and offers the original hypothesis as the explanation for the observations.

## Methods That Scientists Use

The various branches of science tend to use different methods for collecting the evidence needed to support hypotheses or theories. The popular picture of a scientist is of someone carrying out an experiment in a laboratory with an imposing array of esoteric equipment. That is one important way that observations are made, but it is by no means the only way. Astronomy, paleontology, and geology are some of the fields of science in which laboratory experiments are not possible. Scientists who cannot carry out experiments in a laboratory have to find other ways to collect evidence for their hypotheses. Knowledge of animal behavior is advanced by scientists who leave the laboratory and go to where the animals are. Astronomers make observations when stars or planets are in certain positions relative to each other. Geologists travel to places where rock formations "tell a story."

## The Social Nature of Science

Few scientists work alone or in isolation from other scientists, but those who are not surrounded by other people on a daily basis communicate regularly with colleagues, even when widely scattered. Scientists work in research institutes, universities, industry, government, and hospitals all over the world. Although scientists everywhere make every effort to be unbiased in their work and to hold to the same ethical standards, science, like all human endeavors, is influenced to some extent by the culture of the country where it is carried out. The subjects chosen for study, the freedom accorded scientists, and the prevailing views of the meaning and purpose of life all may have an effect on scientific endeavor. In the United States, for example, the cultural climate is reflected in the way government allocates various amounts of money for research in space exploration, medicine, new weapons, and environmental science. As women have become more vocal in seeking equality, more funds have gradually been allocated to the study of women's diseases. And as acquired immune deficiency syndrome (AIDS) has become a terrible health problem, money has been redirected to research on that disease. Although science is correctly said to be international, it cannot be said to be entirely culture-free.

## Science and Technology

As science helps people understand the world, technology helps people shape the world. From the earliest crude tools of cave people to the World Wide Web of today, technology has been a force in the development of civilization. Applications of science continue to profoundly affect people's lives everywhere, from the control of infectious diseases to the pervasive use of computers. Thinking of technology as applied science is too simple a view of technology. The relation between science and technology is not a simple one-way street. Technology, like science, is a complex human endeavor that has often made its own discoveries and advances without the benefit of scientific knowledge. For example, ancient Egyptian and Mediterranean civilizations developed technologies that allowed them to preserve the bodies of their dead, extract metals from ores, and make beautiful glass without knowing the chemical reactions involved in these processes.

Today science and technology contribute to each other and depend on each other in many ways. The application of scientific discoveries, for example, has led to technologies for using atomic energy, the control of many diseases, improved methods of food production, and space travel. Conversely, the electronic computer has led to scientific advances in understanding gene structure, weather, and other complex systems. Thus science and technology are inextricably linked. As a result, although the emphasis in this book is on science, technology will also play an important part in the science activities in your classroom.

## SOURCES OF KNOWLEDGE

Several sources of knowledge have a place in successful science teaching. Understanding the differences between them will help you decide which teaching methods or strategies to use in any particular case.

Some science concepts come from direct experience or observation and are sometimes called *concrete concepts*. For example, a child can directly observe the life cycle of a butterfly. No sequence of logic or leap of insight is required to understand that interesting changes take place along the way from egg to adult. A child can also notice that beetles go through similar changes in their life cycles. The child might then overgeneralize that all insects have larval and pupil stages. This misconception could easily be refined by providing some additional insect cultures to observe, such as crickets or mantises. That refinement is also based on concrete experience.

Other situations appropriate for direct experience require the child to think about the observation or experience in order to understand it. An example is sinking/floating. Anyone can observe that some objects float and some sink when placed in water. Observing the sinking/floating behavior of objects is a concrete experience. Certain conclusions about sinking and floating also can be drawn at a concrete level. For example, metal things sink and wooden things float. But as more and more exceptions to these conclusions become apparent, the firmness of the early understanding begins to slip. For example, some kinds of wood sink, and waterlogged wood also sinks; but metal cups float. An aircraft carrier, weighing hundreds of tons, floats. An adequate concept of sinking/floating—one that will explain and predict any floating/sinking system—requires abstract thinking that coordinates the density (weight per unit volume) of the object to the density of the liquid. Not all elementary-school pupils will be able to understand sinking/floating in this way, but initial experiences will give them a background to return to later.

Some science ideas are quite abstract and are not easily presented in any concrete way. The growth of knowledge about the spherical shape of the earth is an interesting example of the use of explanatory concepts in science. Before anyone actually sailed around it, many thinkers had proposed the idea that the earth was round, though everyday experience told them, as it tells us, that the earth is flat. Thinking of the earth as a sphere was at first a scientific theory that explained many puzzling things that were not explained by the flat-earth idea, and it supported a variety of predictions. For example, Columbus predicted that he could get to the Orient by sailing west and that he would not fall off the edge of the earth, because a sphere has no edge. His voyages supported the second prediction, but the first prediction was not borne out until Magellan's crew sailed around the world.

All the thinking that originally went into formulating the idea of the round earth was based on indirect evidence. And even though the idea had proved to be correct, it was not until the last half of the twentieth century, some 500 years later, that people actually saw the earth as a sphere. The famous photograph taken by the Apollo astronauts on their way to the moon was literally an eye-opener. Many people, including news commentators, remarked that they always knew that the earth was round, but they never really believed it until they saw that picture.

By the time children are old enough to go to school they have acquired an amazing stock of knowledge, not all of which has been acquired in the same way. For instance, a six-year-old might know the alphabet, know that ice is cold, and also know why shadows are longer late in the day than at noon. That same child might know how to play well with other children. But the way the child arrived at knowing is different in each of these cases. A child learns the alphabet by memorization, learns that ice is cold through experience, learns about relationships in the natural world through thinking about experiences, and learns about getting along with others through interaction with other people. (For a more detailed discussion of kinds of knowledge, see Kamii and DeVries, 1978.)

## Arbitrary Knowledge

Some knowledge is arbitrary in the sense that someone, at some time, decided that this is the way something would be. Included in this category are names, symbols, conventions, rules, and procedures. They have been defined by certain people—or by society as a whole—and are learned from those people, either directly by being told or indirectly by reading or from watching television.

The names of animals and plants, the planets around the sun, and units of measurement are examples of the kind of knowledge that children cannot discover on their own; they need information from a teacher, a book, or some other source. This kind of knowledge remains a part of science education, but it should not be the main emphasis.

## Physical Knowledge

Physical knowledge arises from direct experience and observation of objects and events. People really know that ice is cold only if they have experienced ice. Examples of physical knowledge include the knowledge that rocks sink in water and that wood floats, that water runs downhill, and that caterpillars turn into moths or butterflies. This kind of knowledge can be discovered by each person but universally rings true. Learning experiences that lead to physical knowledge are the heart of sci-

*Physical knowledge comes from direct experience.*

ence in the primary grades (Kamii & DeVries, 1978). Much necessary arbitrary knowledge can be learned in the context of science activities of this kind.

If your goal is for children to learn some form of arbitrary knowledge, such as names of rocks and minerals, you have to supply the information either by telling them or assigning reading. But, if your goal is for them to understand the way magnets interact (or fail to interact) with objects, you have to give them opportunities to explore and discover.

## Logical Knowledge

Logical knowledge encompasses concepts, conclusions, and higher order ideas derived from thinking about observations or experiences. This kind of knowledge must be constructed by the learner. It cannot be acquired by observation alone, and it cannot be learned from being told; it has to be constructed in the mind of the learner. Young children think that a ball of clay broken into pieces will weigh more than it weighed before it was broken up. Weighing the clay before and after will not convince them; they think that the scales are wrong. Eventually, however, they come to understand that, logically, the amount of clay cannot change when it is broken up and thus that the clay has to weigh the same. Most children in the upper elementary grades are ready to begin to think logically about some of their experiences.

## Social Interactive Knowledge

Social interactive knowledge is gained through interaction with other people, including how to get along with others, how to understand the feelings of others, and how to work cooperatively. Children have to grow into the knowledge of others that allows them to see something from another's point of view. This knowledge is not of rules of behavior but a deeper understanding of the ways of compromise and cooperation.

# SCIENTIFIC LITERACY

Scientific literacy, which has been declared to be a national goal, has been defined in many ways. At the most basic level it includes understanding key concepts, principles, and processes of science and the ability to use this knowledge in making personal and societal decisions. It encompasses the first three of the kinds of knowledge just described and is the central overall goal of K–12 science education. Few of your students will become scientists, but all of them will live in a world shaped by the outcomes of scientific research and the products of research-based technology.

One of the purposes of education in the United States is to prepare students to participate in the discourse and debates about important public issues that are the hallmark of a democratic society. Today few important public issues do not involve science or technology in some way at some level. Whether the issue is one of the environment, public health, weapons production and control, or any of many others, all are linked in some way to science and/or technology. Thus all citizens need to have enough knowledge of science to understand the main issues facing society.

Scientific literacy includes knowledge of science processes and content, both of which are needed increasingly in the workplace. Many jobs require specific skills or knowledge of science; few jobs are so routine that they do not require workers to understand what they are doing and to recognize problems and seek ways to solve them. The United States needs a scientifically and technologically literate workforce to compete in the global market.

Beyond our duties as citizens and our need for work to do, an intangible benefit comes with scientific literacy. To learn about and understand the natural world enhances the personal lives of all of us. An interest in science and technology developed during childhood and adolescence can last a lifetime and make life more interesting and fulfilling for each individual.

# NATIONAL SCIENCE EDUCATION STANDARDS

To promote the achievement of the goal of scientific literacy, the National Research Council (NRC) called on a group of teachers, administrators, curriculum developers, parents, scientists, engineers, and government officials to develop standards, or criteria, for all aspects of science education. The result of their work was the publication in 1996 of *National Science Education Standards,* (NSES), a volume that presents broad criteria for science teaching, the professional development of teachers, assessment in science education, science content, science education programs, and science education systems.

The chapter of NSES devoted to Science Content Standards outlines "what students should know, understand and be able to do in natural science" (NRC, p. 103) for physical science, life science, earth and space science and science and technology, for Grades K–4, 5–8, and 9–12. As children move through the grade levels they build on what they have already learned and are introduced to more and more complex and demanding concepts in all categories. In addition to the usual science content areas, there are standards for science in personal and social perspectives and the history and nature of science.

## Unifying Concepts and Processes

The science content to be learned is set within a framework of unifying concepts and processes that cross disciplinary boundaries and form the underlying foundation for all science education from kindergarten through high school. You might think of these as themes that are always present in the teacher's mind as instructional goals and classroom activities are planned. These concepts and principles are listed and explained in the following section.

## NSES Unifying Concepts and Principles

- *Systems, Order, and Organization.* The world is too large and complex to be understood without some way of ordering and organizing knowledge. Thus one goal of this standard is for pupils to think in terms of systems rather than trying to learn and remember isolated facts, concepts, and processes. Another goal is for pupils to learn that there is order and regularity in nature and that knowledge can be organized in ways that help them make sense of the world. Children are learning that there is order and regularity in nature when they learn about the solar system or the phases of the moon; they are learning to organize knowledge when they learn to classify objects or organisms.

- *Evidence, Models, and Explanation.* In all content areas it is important not only to collect data, or evidence, but also to use that information to build models that explain the evidence. The term *model* is used broadly by scientists. It may be a physical object or a diagram or a mathematical equation.

- *Constancy, Change, and Measurement.* The natural world is characterized by both constancy and change. Organisms change as they grow and the landscape is always changing, but the earth moves around the sun in the same way year after year. When a ball of clay is flattened into a pancake, the shape of the material changes but the amount of clay remains the same. Measuring change is an important part of science that is emphasized at all grade levels.

- *Evolution and Equilibrium.* Evolution is not only a biological theory, but it also is the idea that the world as it exists today has emerged and continues to emerge from forms and materials that existed in the far distant past. For example, those who live near the ocean can observe the reshaping of the shoreline after a major hurricane. Equilibrium is a state in which forces are acting in opposite directions so that no apparent change is occurring. Think of two teams of children pulling on a rope in opposite directions; if the teams are equally matched, neither team can move the rope and a state of equilibrium is achieved.

■ *Form and Function.* Form and function are interrelated aspects of organisms, objects, and systems. The form of a fish allows it to live and move—that is, to function—in water, whereas the form of a bird allows it to live and move in air.

## Science Content Standards

Content Standards for Grades K–4 and Grades 5–8 are shown in Tables 1.1 and 1.2. Note that the eight categories are the same in both tables and that the topics for the first two and last two categories are similar, though not exactly the same, for the two grade ranges.

**TABLE 1.1**  *National Science Education Standards:* **Content Standards for Grades K–4**

| Content Standards, Grades K–4 | | | |
|---|---|---|---|
| *Unifying Concepts and Processes* | *Science as Inquiry* | *Physical Science* | *Life Science* |
| Systems, order, and organization | Abilities necessary to do scientific inquiry | Properties of objects and materials | Characteristics of organisms |
| Evidence, models, and explanation | Understandings about scientific inquiry | Position and motion of objects | Life cycles of organisms |
| Change, constancy, and measurement | | Light, heat, electricity, and magnetism | Organisms and environments |
| Evolution and equilibrium | | | |
| Form and function | | | |
| *Earth and Space Science* | *Science and Technology* | *Science in Personal and Social Perspectives* | *History and Nature of Science* |
| Properties of earth materials | Abilities of technological design | Personal health | Science as a human endeavor |
| Objects in the sky | Understandings about science and technology | Characteristics and changes in populations | |
| Changes in earth and sky | Abilities to distinguish between natural objects and objects made by humans | Types of resources | |
| | | Changes in environments | |
| | | Science and technology in local challenges | |

*Source:* Reprinted with permission from National Science Education Standards. Copyright 1996 by the National Academy of Sciences. Courtesy of the National Academy Press. Washington, DC.

**TABLE 1.2  National Science Education Standards for Grades 5–8**

| Content Standards, Grades 5–8 | | | |
|---|---|---|---|
| *Unifying Concepts and Processes* | *Science as Inquiry* | *Physical Science* | *Life Science* |
| Systems, order, and organization | Abilities necessary to do scientific inquiry | Properties and changes of properties in matter | Structure and function in living systems |
| Evidence, models, and explanation | Understandings about scientific inquiry | Motions and forces | Reproduction and heredity |
| Change, constancy, and measurement | | Transfer of energy | Regulation and behavior |
| Evolution and equilibrium | | | Populations and ecosystems |
| Form and function | | | Diversity and adaptations of organisms |
| *Earth and Space Science* | *Science and Technology* | *Science in Personal and Social Perspectives* | *History and Nature of Science* |
| Structure of the earth system | Abilities of technological design | Personal health | Science as a human endeavor |
| Earth's history | Understandings about science and technology | Populations, resources, and environments | Nature of science |
| Earth in the solar system | | Natural hazards | History of science |
| | | Risks and benefits | |
| | | Science and technology in society | |

*Source:* Reprinted with permission from National Science Education Standards. Copyright 1996 by the National Academy of Sciences. Courtesy of the National Academy Press, Washington, DC.

Each of these standards is described in more detail in the text of the NSES. For example, the Content Standard for Life Science for Grades K–4 is as follows:

> As a result of activities in grades K–4, all students should develop understanding of
>     The characteristics of organisms
>     Life cycles of organisms
>     Organisms and environments (NRC, p. 127)

These objectives are followed by several paragraphs of general comments about teaching life science to children and an explanation of the fundamental science concepts that underlie each part of the standard listed. Thus the reader is provided with general guidelines for teaching science in Grades K–4, 5–8, and 9–12, general recommendations for how to teach each subject at the different levels, and the basic science concepts that the teacher needs to know.

The lesson plans that you will find later in this book are all tied to one of the standards listed in *National Science Education Standards* and, in some cases, also to

*Benchmarks for Science Literacy.* Most of the standards and benchmarks are broader than the objectives of a single lesson; thus a lesson plan will describe a lesson that goes only part way toward meeting a standard or benchmark.

## Science as Inquiry

Science as inquiry is the guiding principle in the vision of science education presented in the NSES. *Inquiry* refers to a systematic investigation of something of interest; thus "science as inquiry" emphasizes the investigative nature of science. Inquiry-based instruction engages children in investigations appropriate to their ages with the goals of developing both understanding of science concepts and the skills necessary to become independent learners. Processes of science are not taught in isolation but are used as a means of acquiring scientific knowledge. They are learned as children plan and carry out investigations that require observation, data gathering, planning, problem solving, and critical thinking. Teaching science as inquiry is similar in some ways to teaching science as discovery, but there are important differences that you will see as you carry out the activities and discuss the questions posed in this book. One of the most useful features of the NSES is the imaginative examples of teaching science as inquiry that show how the standards can be carried out in practice.

## An Example of Science as Inquiry

This example, adapted from the NSES (NRC, 1996, pp. 124–125), starts with an observation by a second grader. He complained that the watering can didn't contain enough water to water the plants in the classroom, although it was almost full when he left it on the windowsill on Friday. He wanted to know who had taken the water. All the children said that they hadn't touched the watering can. Someone said that maybe Willie, their hamster, drank it. The children decided that that was what had happened, but their teacher suggested that they test that idea.

The children decided to cover the watering can so that Willie couldn't get to it while they were gone. The next morning the water level had not changed, so they decided that they had been right: Willie had been getting out of his cage and drinking the water. But the teacher asked, "How do you know Willie gets out of his cage?" "We'll prove it", they said. So they put the cage in the middle of the sand table and left it overnight. After several days there were no footprints in the sand. "The watering can is still covered and Willie can see it, so why would he get out?" asks one of the children. That afternoon before school was out they took the cover off of the can and left the cage in the sand table. The water level began to drop but there were no footprints in the sand. So Willie didn't drink the water.

The teacher suggested that they place a can of water with a wide top on the windowsill and measure the water level every day. They found that the water level went down every day but not always by the same amount. This result led to the question of whether water disappears faster when it is warmer. And that launched a whole new investigation.

## The Standards and You

There are several reasons why you should have a basic knowledge of the NSES. The first is that it gives a concise but comprehensive list of the science concepts and processes that its authors believe should be learned at each level of schooling. The science courses that you have taken at the college level are specialized and leave many gaps in your knowledge. The NSES will help you to sort out what you have learned and what you still need to learn—and to fit the pieces together.

Another reason for familiarizing yourself with the NSES is that it emphasizes inquiry as the basis for science teaching and learning and gives many examples of inquiry-based lessons. A careful study of those examples will help you understand what inquiry-based teaching is. Another reason is that many state education departments in the United States have used this document as a basis or guide in revising their own science curriculum guidelines and standards. A basic knowledge of the NSES will help you understand and interpret the state guidelines wherever you are teaching.

# OTHER GENERAL RESOURCES FOR ELEMENTARY-SCHOOL SCIENCE

The American Association for the Advancement of Science has published two volumes that take a far-ranging look at science goals and curriculum for Grades K–12.

*Science for All Americans,* published by the American Association for the Advancement of Science (AAAS) in 1990, is a book-length report that defines scientific literacy as (a) the awareness that science is a human enterprise with strengths and limitations, (b) an understanding of the key concepts and principles of science, (c) a familiarity with the natural world and recognition of its diversity and unity, and (d) the ability to use this knowledge for individual and social purposes. The report recommends that schools teach less and teach it better and teach for broader understanding rather than to cover material. Its authors state their belief that elementary-school science should enhance childhood; that is, science should be taught not only for some future benefit but also to make life richer and more rewarding for children as they experience it.

*Science for All Americans* identifies broad areas of knowledge that can be taught at many levels and in many ways. Details and facts are not important in themselves and are useful only to the extent that they lead to understanding of the principles involved. The focus is on depth of understanding and on using knowledge of science in the choices everyone makes in daily life. Topics that are considered important include knowledge of the universe, the earth, the forces that shape the earth, the structure of matter, energy transformations, motion and forces, diversity of life, heredity, cells, interdependence of life, flow of matter and energy, evolution, human identity, life cycles, and the basic functions of organisms. As you study this textbook, you will see many examples of lessons and activities that teach simple concepts related to these basic scientific ideas. They aren't ideas that children, or anyone else, can learn by memorization or by listening to the teacher. People have to build knowledge and understanding gradually from their own experiences and from their own thinking.

*Benchmarks for Science Literacy* (AAAS, 1993) is a companion volume to *Science for All Americans* and breaks its broad themes into specific science objectives for students of Grades K–2, 3–5, 6–8, and 9–12. The same themes and topics are carried throughout, and the objectives for each level build on those for the earlier level. For example, one of the goals of instruction is for students to learn about the structure of matter. The main objective for second graders is to describe objects in terms of their basic characteristics; by the end of fifth grade, children should know about changes caused by heating and cooling, that its weight stays the same when an object is broken into parts, and that materials may have parts that can only be seen with a magnifying glass. Designed as a guide rather than a prescription for teachers and curriculum builders, *Benchmarks* can give you many good ideas for your teaching.

## GOALS FOR SCIENCE IN ELEMENTARY SCHOOL

Although details and specific lesson objectives may vary, there is remarkable agreement among scientists and educators about what an elementary-school science program should be and about the kinds of activities that children should engage in. From these sources, as well as from my own experience, I believe that the important overall goals for children in elementary-school science are to

- develop and maintain curiosity about the world around them,
- observe and explore their environment and organize those experiences,
- develop the technical and intellectual skills needed to make further study of science possible,
- build an experiential basis for understanding important concepts in science,
- relate what they learn in school to their own lives, and
- enjoy science and develop positive attitudes about school; children who enjoy school and see their needs met there are more likely to become active learners and successful students.

## TEACHING METHODS

This textbook will help you develop the knowledge and skills you will need to help children reach these goals. You will learn to

- promote independent thinking,
- encourage children's creativity and curiosity,
- build on children's ideas,

- reduce the amount of material covered so that more time can be devoted to developing thinking skills,
- make connections between science and other areas of the curriculum,
- start with questions rather than with answers, and
- focus on the needs of all children, including those from various ethnic groups and those with special psychological or physical needs.

These methods are appropriate at all ages, and they apply to your own learning as well. This textbook was written to promote your independent thinking, encourage your creativity and curiosity, and stimulate you to build new ideas and knowledge. It should also help you connect what you learn here with what you are learning in other courses.

## ■ SUMMARY

You will find that children enjoy science, and you will enjoy teaching it if you learn to guide children through activities that engage their hands and minds. Science is both knowledge of the natural world, including humans, and the way that this knowledge has been produced. Scientists believe that the phenomena and patterns observed in nature can be understood through the application of human intelligence, and they work to make the world understandable by developing theories that explain observations made by themselves or others. Because science is a human endeavor, it is part of the culture in which it is embedded, and it both influences and is influenced by that culture.

When children come to school, they already know a great many things, but that knowledge has not all been acquired in the same way. The four kinds of knowledge described are arbitrary knowledge, physical knowledge, logical knowledge, and social interactive knowledge. A teacher should be aware of the knowledge that children have, as well the misconceptions they have acquired, in order to guide them in constructing knowledge that will be meaningful to them.

The *National Science Education Standards* is an important resource that outlines what children should know at different grade levels and provides guidance in learning to teach science as inquiry. Chapters on professional development and assessment are also included in the Standards. Two other useful books are *Science for All Americans* and *Benchmarks*. These books encompass all areas of science and provide recommendations on what should be taught and how to teach it at different grade levels.

Science goals for elementary-school children are simple and straightforward and are not designed to intimidate you as a future teacher. The purpose of this book is to help you have a better understanding of science and how to teach it so that you will become an enthusiastic and effective science teacher. In Chapter 2, you will find some ideas that will help you understand how children's minds develop and how they learn.

# ■ QUESTIONS FOR DISCUSSION

Write your answers to the following questions and come to class prepared to discuss them with the whole class or in a small group.

1. How would you define science to someone from a totally different culture?

2. How could you incorporate four kinds of knowledge in a lesson? Give a simple example.

3. If you are going to explore the environment with children, you will be studying animals. Is there anything you are squeamish about? If so, how will you get over your squeamishness so as not to pass it on to your pupils?

4. What is your reaction to Feynman's statement to teachers?

5. What potential do you see for using science to help children become more responsible? In what ways, if any, is this potential different in science than it is in other school subjects?

6. Many children decide that they dislike science. Maybe you were one of them. What experiences might cause such an attitude? How might a person's life be different if a more positive attitude had developed?

# ■ REFERENCES

American Association for the Advancement of Science. (1990). *Science for all Americans.* New York: Oxford University Press.

American Association for the Advancement of Science. (1993). *Benchmarks for science literacy.* New York: Oxford University Press.

Feynman, R. P. (1968). What is science? *The Physics Teacher, 7*(6), 313–320.

Fosnot, C. (1989). *Enquiring teachers. Enquiring learners. A constructivist approach for teaching.* New York: Teachers College Press.

Kamii, C., & DeVries, R. (1978). *Physical knowledge in preschool education: Implications of Piaget's theory.* Upper Saddle River, NJ: Prentice-Hall.

National Research Council. (1996). *National science education standards.* Washington, DC: National Academy Press.

Marin, N., Benarroch, A., & Gomez, E. (2000). What is the relationship between social constructivism and Piagetian constructivism? An analysis of the characteristics of the ideas within both theories. *International Journal of Science Education, 3,* 225–238.

Solomon, J. (1994). The rise and fall of constructivism. *Studies in Science Education, 23,* 1–19.

Woolfolk, A., & Hoy, W. (1990). Prospective teachers' sense of efficacy and beliefs about control. *Journal of Educational Psychology, 60,* 327–337.

# Children's Thinking and Learning

The study of children's thinking and learning has occupied some of the most original minds of the twentieth century and continues to be a subject of intense interest to psychologists, cognitive scientists, and teachers. This chapter gives a brief summary of the main ideas of five twentieth century thinkers who have influenced thinking about how children learn science. They share the view that learning is not a passive activity but one that requires the active participation of learners in constructing their own knowledge. You may have studied in other courses some or all of the thinkers you will encounter here, but this chapter will help you understand how their ideas may be useful to you in teaching science and thus give you a basis for making instructional decisions. At the end of the chapter, a short section on recent research highlights several issues of current interest to researchers in science education.

# JOHN DEWEY (1859–1952)

Although Dewey's life spanned the nineteenth and twentieth centuries, he cannot actually be called a *constructivist* because the term was not used in his time. He is included here because he believed, like the constructivists of today, that "no such thing as imposition of truth from without, as insertion of truth from without, is possible. All depends upon the activity which the mind itself undergoes in responding to what is presented from without" (Dewey, 1902/1956, p. 31). In his view, the schools of his day were too rigid and programmed, with little opportunity for children to express their own interests and curiosity. Instead, he emphasized using the child's experience as the starting point for instruction, a process of "continuous reconstruction, moving from the child's present experience out into that represented by the organized bodies of truth that we call studies" (p. 11).

## The Dewey School

In the 1890s, while a professor at the University of Chicago, Dewey founded a school that was used as a laboratory to test his ideas. The school was an expression of his belief that the curriculum should grow out of and deepen children's experiences— that the lives and experiences of children should not be sacrificed to follow a curriculum devised by specialists in the various fields of formal knowledge. In the school that Dewey founded, children's interests and activities therefore were the starting point that teachers used to guide their pupils toward greater knowledge and understanding. "If children can retain their natural investigating tendencies unimpaired," he wrote, "gradually organizing them into definite methods of work, when they reach the proper age, they can master the required amount of facts and generalizations easily and effectively" (quoted in Mayhew & Edwards, 1936, p. 34). The social value of having children work together as they carried out classroom activities was an important consideration in the overall plan of the school.

Symbols or words are meaningful, Dewey believed, only when they represent something in the child's own experience. When subject matter is presented to children as something known by experts but outside their own experience, the words and symbols, whether in arithmetic, grammar, or history, have no meaning. They are like hieroglyphics, unrelated to anything encountered outside the classroom, and useless. Thus the activities in school should be those that will help the child acquire experiences that can then be summarized or represented by symbols.

Dewey did not advocate basing the whole curriculum on children's current abilities and interests; they were only the starting points for development of knowledge and understanding of the subjects taught. He knew that some activities occupy children's time and interest but lead nowhere. Nor were children to be left to their own devices to figure everything out for themselves without stimuli to guide their instincts and impulses into higher levels of thinking and understanding.

A practical application of these ideas can be seen in the description by a science teacher of the way science was taught to children in the school Dewey founded in Chicago. The guiding principle in selecting an activity, she explained, was its use in carrying the child on beyond the activity itself to an understanding of relationships. The important question about an activity was whether the processes and procedures to be carried out could be related in the child's mind to important general ideas about natural processes. For example, children learned at an early age to identify the notion of weight, which they already possessed, with the pull of the earth's gravity and to measure and control it. Observations of the effect of force of gravity on plants and animals began in kindergarten. The child's interest and curiosity about

*Learning is meaningful when it grows out of children's own interests and experiences.*

plant life and animal life led naturally, over the years, into a continually enlarging course of study dealing with the life processes of plants; with plants' relations to animal life; with the influences of moisture, soil, and environmental conditions; and with the influence of plants on environmental and geographic conditions. Leaves, stems, and flowers were regarded as important only in relation to function and processes. Observation and experiment were both important, and always there was the teacher to stimulate children's thinking by asking questions, suggesting things to try, and helping them develop and learn to use the symbols and tools that would advance their thinking (Mayhew & Edwards, 1936, pp. 271–296).

As you study the ideas of the other thinkers presented here, you will find many echoes of Dewey's philosophy of education.

# JEAN PIAGET (1896–1983)

The person whose ideas probably had the greatest impact in science education in the second half of the twentieth century was Jean Piaget, who acknowledged Dewey's influence on his own thinking. Piaget, who was born in Switzerland and spent most of his life there, was interested in finding out what goes on in children's minds as they try to make sense of the world around them. His research method was simply to sit down with a child and ask a series of questions. The questions of most interest to teachers were designed to find out how a child thinks about or understands something encountered in daily life. From the results of interviewing a great many children, Piaget concluded that young children do not think logically by adult standards and that it takes many years for children to grow to think about things in a logical way. Many of Piaget's ideas were developed in collaboration with Barbel Inhelder, a woman who worked with him throughout much of his career.

Although Piaget was not an educator, his work has been of particular interest to science teachers. The following classroom scene will help you understand how knowledge of children's thinking can improve your teaching of science and why teachers turn to Piaget for insight and help in understanding some of the problems they encounter.

## ■ A CLASSROOM SCENE

Mr. Newman discovered that his first-grade children got upset if they thought that he wasn't absolutely fair about everything. They got particularly upset if they thought that one person got more juice than another did at juice time. After several such episodes, Mr. Newman planned a lesson to convince his pupils that he was always fair, even though it might appear that one child got more than another. He looked around his apartment and found five small glass jars of different sizes and shapes and took them to school. The next day he set the jars in a row on a table and had the children sit on the rug where they could all get a clear view of the demonstration. He carefully measured out 100 milliliters of colored water and poured it into the first jar. Then he called one of the children up to

**FIGURE 2.1  Mr. Newman's Jars**

help him measure out exactly 100 milliliters of water and pour it into the second jar. Figure 2.1 shows what the children saw after 100 milliliters of water had been poured in each jar.

Mr. Newman explained that each jar had exactly the same amount because he had measured very carefully. Even though the amounts did not look the same, they were the same.

The children didn't appear to be very interested in what Mr. Newman was trying to explain. Because they didn't ask questions or show much interest about the amounts in the jars, Mr. Newman thought that it was obvious to everyone that all the jars had the same amount of liquid. Actually, the children seemed to be more interested in the jars than in the amounts of liquid in them and asked questions about where the jars had come from and what they had originally contained.

Juice time came soon after this lesson, and Mr. Newman was prepared with two different kinds of plastic drinking cups and a measuring cup to portion out the juice. He could not believe it when an argument broke out between two children with different-sized plastic cups. One of the things that was most puzzling to him was that these were two of the brightest children in the class; both of them were reading well above grade level. The one with the larger cup started to cry because he thought he had less juice.

Mr. Newman was at wit's end over this episode and could hardly wait until after school to talk with Ms. Oldhand about what had happened. He just couldn't understand why the children didn't believe their own eyes when he thought he had made it all so clear and logical. He couldn't understand why his lesson didn't work.

[*Can you think of reasons why Mr. Newman's lesson didn't work?*]

When Mr. Newman found Ms. Oldhand and told her what had happened, Ms. Oldhand explained that Mr. Newman had presented the children with a task that is similar to one of the tasks devised by Jean Piaget to study children's thinking. She suggested that Mr. Newman would understand why his lesson hadn't had the outcome he had expected if he learned more about Piaget's ideas about children's thinking.

You will get a better idea of Piaget's work and how it relates to science teaching from examples of children's responses to the questions he asked when he interviewed them. Recall that Chapter 1 contains descriptions of four kinds of knowledge that children may acquire: arbitrary, physical, logical, and social interactive. In the following example, logical knowledge is of interest.

## Conservation of Quantity (Liquid)

The word *conservation* is used in science to denote the principle that a substance or an object remains the same, regardless of changes in form or appearance, provided nothing is added or taken away. For example, when a glass of water freezes, it changes in appearance, but the weight remains the same. A ball of clay can be flattened to the shape of a pancake, but the amount of clay stays the same. The following example, taken from The Child's Conception of Number (Piaget, 1965) summarizes responses from children who were asked questions about conservation of liquid, a concept Mr. Newman assumed that his children understood.

An interviewer shows a child two identical glasses containing equal amounts of lemonade and says that one glass belongs to Mary and the other to Laura. The interviewer then pours the lemonade in Mary's glass into two smaller glasses and asks the child whether Mary and Laura still have the same amount of lemonade. Then the interviewer pours the lemonade from Laura's glass into two smaller glasses and repeats the question. As the interviewer pours lemonade back and forth between glasses of different sizes, the child is always asked whether Mary and Laura have equal amounts to drink (see Figure 2.2).

The typical reaction of a four-year-old is that the amounts are the same if the glasses are the same size and different if the glasses are of different sizes. As the liquid is poured back and forth, the child continues to say that the amounts are equal or unequal, depending on the size and number of the glasses, with no apparent awareness of any contradiction. Then there comes a transition period when the child is not quite sure; finally, usually around the age of six or seven, the child realizes that pouring the liquid back and forth, regardless of the shape or size or number of

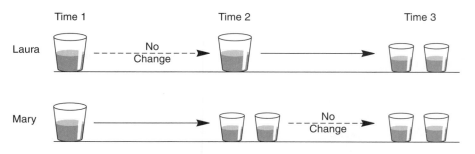

**FIGURE 2.2    Mary's and Laura's Glasses**

glasses, does not change the amount. When asked at this time, "How do you know?" the child answers "I just know. Once you know you always know."

One of the important things Piaget discovered is that children have their own reasons for thinking the way they do about the things they see happening around them—and it isn't easy to convince them to change their minds. Children construct their own realities, and there is a certain logic in the frameworks they construct. For young children, appearance is what matters. If something looks smaller, in the child's mind it *is* smaller.

Piaget believed that children's ability for logical thinking develops gradually, just as many of their other abilities do. First graders aren't expected to have the hand–eye coordination that will allow them to produce the kind of handwriting expected of sixth graders. In the same way, first graders shouldn't be expected to have the same degree of mental coordination that will allow them to "put two and two together" to arrive at a logical conclusion about the relative amounts of liquid in two glasses.

Piaget used the idea of "stages" to describe the way that children's logical thinking progresses from infancy through adolescence. When Piaget's work first became widely known to science educators, they thought it was important to test children to pinpoint the "Piagetian stage" of each child. Today, however, the emphasis has shifted. Most educators and psychologists now believe that development tends to be a continuous process rather than one of stops and starts, although experience shows that growth is more rapid at some times than at others. Moreover, what students can learn in any area depends on how much they already know in that area. Piaget's system of stages is now considered by most educators to be a useful shorthand for describing the capabilities that may be expected of children within a given age range rather than a rigid system with no exceptions or gray areas.

Piaget's central concern was with the question, "How do we come to know what we know?" His answer was that people must construct their own knowledge and understanding through logical thinking. He believed that knowledge cannot be transmitted intact from one person to another. It was his view that children can memorize facts and be taught how to do many things, but they cannot really understand a phenomenon or a relationship except by thinking about it and putting the pieces together in their own heads. This process is the essence of Piaget's theory of mental development and is the basis for the constructivist view.

In the preceding example, you saw how one kind of knowledge, logical knowledge, develops. The following example involves both physical knowledge and logical knowledge.

## Children's Ideas about the Moon

This example is excerpted from *The Child's Conception of the World* (Piaget, 1965). Responses given by children of different ages to the same questions give insight into how children think about the things they observe in the world around them.

Piaget asked children aged 6–12 the question, "When you go for a walk at night, what does the moon do?" The interviews that follow contain responses that are typical of children at three stages of development.

### Jac, Age 6 (First Stage)

*What does the moon do when you are out for a walk?*
It goes with us.
*Why?*
Because the wind makes it go.
*Does the wind know where you are going?*
Yes.
*And the moon too?*
Yes.
*Does it move on purpose to go* where you are going or *because it has to?*
It comes so as to give light.

### Lug, Age 8 (Second Stage)

*What does the moon do while you are walking?*
It follows us.
*If you and I were walking in opposite directions which of us would the moon follow?*
It stays still because it can't follow two at the same time.
*When there are a lot of people in the town what does it do?*
It follows someone.
*How does it do that?*
It stays still and its rays follow us.

### Kuf, Age 10 (Third Stage)

*When you go out for a walk at night what does the moon do?*
When you're walking you'd say that the moon was following you, because it's so big.
*Does it really follow you?*
No. I used to believe it followed us and that it ran after us (but I don't believe that any more).

(Piaget, 1965, pp. 216–220)

In this example note the progression from (a) the idea that the moon's role and function are to be helpful to us to (b) an unresolved contradiction (the moon "follows us" but "always stays in the same place"). Finally, the child understands that the moon is independent of the people on earth, an idea that requires both physical knowledge and logical thinking. Because he found that many children gave similar answers, Piaget believed that these ideas arise spontaneously, based on direct observation and the child's own thinking.

This example of how children think about a natural phenomenon that everyone has experienced gives a science teacher a lot to think about. If children have these misconceptions or alternative frameworks about the moon, what do they think about the sun, clouds, wind, and rain? Is it possible to change their beliefs just by explaining things to them? You've seen that this method didn't work in the case of the juice and the glasses. Is it any more likely to work in the case of objects as far away and as mysterious (to them) as the moon, the sun, and the wind?

From a Piagetian perspective, the task of the teacher is to provide the learning environment, the materials, and the tasks that will stimulate and encourage children to construct knowledge for themselves. Talking to children, or even demonstrating, will not teach them that the amount of water remains the same when it is poured from one container to another; they have to construct this knowledge for themselves through their own experience of acting on objects and through their own thinking. Seeing is not always believing for children; they have to experience things for themselves.

Although Piaget's work is no longer thought of as an infallible guide to teaching science, it has inspired a tremendous amount of research by others. Perhaps the most important research outcome based on Piaget's work was stated by Confrey (1990) as "the belief that teaching is most effectively improved when the teacher learns to listen to students' thoughts and to interpret students' actions and thoughts from their perspectives as children" (p. 11). Our understanding of the importance of listening to children and seeking their explanations for what they say and do is probably Piaget's most enduring legacy.

One way to construct for yourself a better understanding of how children think is for you to have experience in presenting Piaget tasks to children and hearing their responses firsthand. A representative sample of Piaget tasks is given at the end of this chapter.

# JEROME BRUNER (1915–    )

Piaget's chief interest lay in discovering the origin and nature of knowledge as it develops in the mind of the child, but he had little to say about what outside forces or experiences, other than natural growth and maturation, might propel a child from one stage to another. Acknowledging a debt to Piaget, Jerome Bruner tackled this problem by going beyond a description of stages to consider not only how children think but also how children learn (Bruner, 1966; Bruner & Haste, 1987).

## Problem Solving

Bruner noted that children may encounter two kinds of problems in school. The most important problem for many children is that of finding out what the teacher wants. When a child is confronted with a problem in arithmetic, for example, the first thing that pops into the child's mind is not "What is the best way to tackle this problem?" but, instead, "What did the teacher say about this kind of problem? How does the teacher want me to work this problem?" The child is focusing on pleasing the teacher rather than on solving the problem.

Children who have never had experience in school with problems that require independent thinking are at first nervous and uncertain about how to proceed. The teacher has to reassure them that their ideas and suggestions will be accepted and that there are more ways than one to solve the problem and that the teacher is not going to show them the "correct solution" at the end.

## Modes of Representing Knowledge

Bruner identified three ways of representing experience and knowledge: The child begins with the *enactive mode,* then develops the *iconic mode,* and finally arrives at the *symbolic mode*—but at all stages of life, people can and do use all three modes.

*Enactive representation* is experience translated into action. Anyone who has tried to teach a child to ride a bicycle or to play tennis, as Bruner points out, has become aware of the inadequacy of words. In those cases we represent what we know through action, not words. In many instances, the old axiom "actions speak louder than words" can be applied in teaching. Some things cannot be taught except by showing what we want children to learn. How to use equipment, such as a balance or a microscope, is one thing that comes to mind, but many things are best taught by action or example rather than words. This principle is accepted in sports and in music and art education, but it also applies to many aspects of science teaching.

*Iconic representation* depends on visual or other sensory means of organizing information. Just as many things are best taught by showing how to do them, others are best taught by using a drawing, a picture, or a diagram. In science teaching, it is important for children to learn to use this method of representing their own experiences. For example, children who have set up an electric circuit are more likely to remember what they have done and to understand it if they then represent the system by making a diagram or drawing of it.

*Symbolic representation* is the use of words or mathematical symbols to express experience or ideas, the past, the present, and the hypothetical future. It is the most powerful, as well as the most advanced, mode of representation. Facilities with language and with mathematics are two of the chief goals of science teaching, but children must develop these abilities over time. Because of younger children's lack of facility with symbolic representation, other forms of representation will be more effective for most of the science taught in elementary school.

## The Spiral Curriculum

In Bruner's view, the curriculum should involve the mastery of skills that in turn lead to the mastery of more powerful skills. This progression is in itself motivating and rewarding. He asserts that there is an appropriate version of any skill or knowledge that can be taught at any age and that the curriculum should be built as a spiral. In other words, teacher and learner come back again and again to the same topic, each time increasing and deepening understanding (see Table 2.1). Let's see how this might work in a science class.

Let's take, for example, the idea of acceleration, an important concept in physics. How do young children get the "feel" of acceleration? Think of riding a sled or roller skating down a hill or running down a steep bank or watching a ball rolling down a hill, farther and farther out of reach. Such learning occurs through the senses, in the enactive mode. As a teacher, you can ask the children to recall their experiences and talk about how it feels to go faster and faster. If there is a hill

**TABLE 2.1  The Spiral Curriculum**

| Elementary | Middle School/Junior High | Senior High |
|---|---|---|
| Experiences with objects that float or sink | Measuring mass and volume; calculation of M/V | Calculation of specific gravity; Archimedes Principle |
| Observing changes in colors of acids and bases using indicators | Neutralization of acids and bases by mixing measured volumes | Titrations; using volumes, moles, etc. |

nearby, you can take the class outside to watch objects accelerate as they roll down the hill.

A few years later, the children will be given the materials for performing an experiment with cylinders rolling down an inclined plane. They will learn to measure how fast the cylinder rolls and be taught how to represent that action on a chart, as a means of iconic representation and a way to advance their understanding. They will now be given a word, *acceleration,* to describe what happens, so they will now have used enactive, iconic, and symbolic means to represent the same concept.

Now, let's step into a physics class in high school. Because of the spiral curriculum adopted by the school, the physics teacher is confident that pupils in the class have had experiences with and performed simple experiments about acceleration, so now they are ready to carry out more complex, detailed experiments and to learn a formula expressed in mathematical symbols. After these experiences, they will have constructed an understanding of acceleration through Bruner's three modes—the enactive, the iconic, and the symbolic. But if (as often happens) acceleration is an idea that has never been discussed or represented in school, for most pupils the formula will have little relation to their own experiences. They will learn to work problems by memorizing the formula for computing acceleration.

The situation will be different for those pupils whose experiences have included talking about, thinking about, and representing acceleration from time to time throughout their school years. For them the formula will represent a concept that they can now understand in a deeper and more meaningful way because the new learning builds on what they have already learned. Some of them will turn and say to each other, "Do you remember when Ms. Oldhand took us out to the hill behind the elementary school and showed us how a basketball went faster and faster as it rolled down the hill? I've always remembered that." Other examples of concepts that are returned to in this way throughout the years will be given in later chapters.

To carry out Bruner's ideas, the teacher has to be an active problem solver with an attitude of openness to pupils' ideas and the expectation that pupils will be active and enthusiastic learners. No formula or set of rules for inquiry teaching can capture the essence of Bruner's ideas. For him, the important thing is the process, not the product. Both teacher and learner must become involved in the process.

# LEV VYGOTSKY (1896–1934)

Lev Vygotsky was a Soviet psychologist who was born in the same year as Piaget but died when he was in his late 30s. His work was little known in the United States for many years after he died, but now that it has become better known, educators can see that he had some very interesting and stimulating ideas that are relevant to science teaching. He was familiar with Piaget's early work and wrote one of his early books (Vygotsky, 1926) in response to some of Piaget's ideas about the role of children's language in mental development. Vygotsky, like Piaget, believed that the learner constructs knowledge. In other words, what children know is not a copy of what they find in the environment but is, instead, the result of their own thought and action, mediated through language.

Both of these thinkers focused on the growth of children's knowledge and understanding of the world around them but with different emphases. Piaget placed more emphasis on the child's internal mental processes, whereas Vygotsky placed more emphasis on the role of teaching and social interaction in the development of science concepts and other knowledge. He also believed that language plays a central role in mental development. In this way, perhaps, Vygotsky had more in common with Bruner, and Bruner has, in fact, written that Vygotsky influenced his own thinking (Bruner, 1985).

## Development of Mental Function

Vygotsky believed that development depends on both natural or biological forces and social or cultural forces. On the one hand, biological forces produce the elementary functions of memory, attention, perception, and stimulus–response learning. On the other hand, social forces are necessary for the development of the higher mental functions of concept development, logical reasoning, and judgment. Through social interaction, including interaction with teachers, children become conscious of their basic mental functions and able to use them in their growth toward self-control, self-direction, and independent thinking and action. As you will see shortly, a good science program helps children develop the characteristics of self-control, self-direction, and independent thinking—along with the knowledge of science concepts and processes.

## The Growth of Scientific Concepts

Vygotsky studied the development of scientific concepts with the specific purpose of improving instruction in schools. He distinguished between the concepts that children develop on their own, which he called everyday concepts, and those learned in school, which he called scientific concepts. *Everyday concepts* are developed from

*Children learn by working with others on interesting problems.*

experience and are tied to specific instances; *scientific concepts* are taught in school as part of a hierarchy or general theory and are remote from children's experience. Conceptual change is an ongoing process in which children integrate their everyday concepts into the system of related concepts taught in school. For example, most children know a good deal about animals as pets and have seen other animals in the zoo or on a farm, but their knowledge is unorganized and random. When they are taught a hierarchical system for classifying and labeling animals, they have to fit what they already know into the system. In doing so, they have to give up their own classification schemes, which may label animals as those that are pets, those in the zoo, and those on the farm. This process can only take place over time, as children start with everyday concepts and gradually expand them to be more inclusive, to apply to more cases, and to become integrated into a system (Howe, 1996).

## Zone of Proximal Development

Vygotsky believed that children should be given tasks that are just beyond their present capability but which they can perform with guidance from a teacher or more advanced peer. He described a "zone of proximal development" (ZPD) as an area just beyond a child's current level of ability. It is the area in which children need help at first to perform a task but gradually learn to do it on their own. At first, students must depend on the teacher to be shown what to do, but gradually they master the task and gain control over a new function or concept. Bruner suggested that this process is analogous to the process in which a builder constructs a scaffold to support the workers who erect a building. As the building takes shape, the scaffold is no longer needed and can be removed. Scaffolding in the context of science education refers to a process in which the teacher, parent, or tutor structures a task so that students are supported as they move from the beginning point to a higher point through a series of small steps.

It's easy to see how this works in teaching a physical skill, like riding a bicycle. The parent holds the child on and guides the bicycle until the child gets the "feel" of riding and gains confidence. Then the parent gradually lets go until the child can keep the bicycle up and guide it without help. The main point to remember is that the teacher has the responsibility to choose learning tasks that are just beyond children's current level but within their reach and then to help them move ahead to the new, higher level of performance. If tasks are too easy, children become bored and restless; if tasks are too hard, children become frustrated and anxious.

A Vygotskian perspective suggests a classroom where active exchanges between children themselves and between children and teacher are an ongoing part of daily life. Children have opportunities to work together, to give and receive verbal instructions, to respond to peer questions and challenges, and to engage in collaborative problem solving. The teacher sets tasks that are just beyond the learners' current levels of competence and provides the help that they need to reach those higher levels. From these exchanges and interactions, children construct meaning and knowledge.

# LAWRENCE KOHLBERG (1927–1987)

Lawrence Kohlberg was another constructivist who built on the foundation laid by Piaget. His field of interest was the development of moral reasoning rather than logical reasoning. He, like Piaget, based his theory on studies of the responses of children and adolescents to questions asked during individual interviews. He presented situations in which a choice had to be made between conflicting ethical or moral values—situations in which a person wants to do what is right but can't avoid undesirable consequences. A simple example of a situation that children find themselves in is whether to report it if they see a good friend cheating on a test. From responses to situations of this kind, Kohlberg (1969, 1981) arrived at a developmental theory of moral reasoning.

Kohlberg has been criticized, notably by Carol Gilligan, a former student and colleague, for basing his work on a masculine point of view and not taking into account differences between men and women in their responses to moral dilemmas. Despite this blind spot, Kohlberg's insights can help you establish a classroom that promotes children's moral development.

By including Kohlberg in the short list of thinkers in this chapter, I am expressing my belief that science at the elementary level cannot be taught in a moral vacuum. The years in elementary school are a time of growth in all dimensions, including the moral dimension. The children you teach will live in a world of many real moral dilemmas, not a few of which will be brought on by the uses and misuses of science. They will be better able to make these hard choices if their moral development has kept pace with their increasing knowledge and understanding of science.

## Stages of Moral Development

Kohlberg sought to show that children's development of a sense of right and wrong and the ability to make moral choices and to act on them are slow processes that take place over many years. He, like Piaget, defined stages of development, each of which has characteristics that differentiate it from the other stages.

In the *preconventional stage,* children accept the right of authority figures to exercise power and try to obey rules to avoid punishment. They are very concerned about fairness and may be quick to point out other children's infractions of rules. It is very upsetting to children in this stage if they think they have been treated unfairly or punished when someone else has escaped punishment.

In the *conventional stage,* children want to do what is right and try to live up to the expectations of parents and teachers. They want to be loyal, truthful, and honest. They may sometimes be torn between conflicts in values as, for instance, between telling the truth and being loyal to a friend.

In the *postconventional,* or *principled, stage,* behavior is based on awareness of the variety of opinions and values held by other people and recognition that most values and rules are relative to a group or culture. Finally, a person reaches the *belief in the validity of universal moral principles stage,* including the equality of human rights and respect for the dignity of individuals, and has a sense of personal commitment to them.

Just as Piaget believed that children must construct their own logical knowledge, Kohlberg believed that children must construct their own moral knowledge. It was his view that children cannot become moral people by memorizing rules of behavior any more than they can become logical thinkers by memorizing ways to work problems. Trying to teach children to be "good" by admonishing them to obey a set of rules is equated by Kohlberg to giving them a bag of tricks to pull out at appropriate moments and is a method that has had notably poor results. Kohlberg's ideas can be put to practical use in several ways, but always keep in mind that children are at a lower stage of development than you are.

Children must pass through the earlier stages before they can progress to the later stages. Class discussions that center on what is the right thing to do in situations that may arise in the classroom must take into account the level of the children. Remember that they do not have an adult point of view, but you can help them to see things from other children's perspectives and to construct for themselves the principles that they will live by.

## Classroom Atmosphere

It is important to establish a classroom atmosphere in which each child is respected and where you as a teacher are scrupulously fair to all pupils. Again, fairness is extremely important for children in elementary school. They become uncertain and anxious in a situation in which they cannot depend on the adult in charge for fair treatment. Recall the classroom scene at the beginning of this chapter. The teacher was motivated to have a lesson on conservation because the children thought that he was not being fair in giving out juice. When children are concerned and upset about lack of fairness, their attention is diverted from the lesson. Take care to be fair in assigning duties, in allocating equipment to groups, and in the amount of time you spend with individual children or groups. Fairness is especially important when a class is made up of children from different ethnic groups or has children with handicapping conditions. A more extensive discussion of this point can be found in Siegal (1982).

Kohlberg's ideas are important in the context of science teaching because of the guidance they can provide in establishing a classroom where the interactions between you and your pupils, both as individuals and as a group, are guided by moral and ethical considerations. One consideration is fairness: being fair and letting children know that you will be fair in all your dealings with them. Another consideration is respect: letting children know that you respect them and expect them to respect each other. Science cannot be well taught when children's social and emotional development are not taken into account. At a higher level, Kohlberg reminds us that the advance of science can lead to difficult moral issues.

# RECENT RESEARCH ON THINKING AND LEARNING

Recent research has built on and extended the work described so far in this chapter and has brought new insights and ideas to the study of children's thinking. One focus has been the study of children's naive or spontaneous ideas about natural phenomena. It has led to efforts to design instruction that will bring children's ideas in line with accepted scientific knowledge. Research has also examined the social contexts of learning, focusing on children's experiences both within the classroom and in the home and larger community.

## Children's Misconceptions

An extensive and rich literature describes how children think about physical phenomena and biological processes and the explanations they create as they try to make sense of the world and of their lives. These explanations and ideas have been called misconceptions, naive ideas, alternative conceptions, and alternative conceptual frameworks; Vygotsky called them everyday concepts. All of these terms refer to children's ideas that are not congruent with accepted scientific concepts. Misconceptions may come from inside or outside a child's mind. They may develop from a child's own private reflection and thought, or they may come from another child or from misunderstanding something heard from an adult, even a teacher.

Although Piaget's interest was in cognitive development rather than misconceptions, his work is full of descriptions of children's ideas about physical phenomena.

He also studied children's ideas about living and nonliving things (Piaget, 1951). Studies in various countries, including the United States, have found that children develop ideas similar to those of Piaget's Swiss children about living and nonliving things. Many very young children believe that anything that moves is alive, including automobiles and the wind and that plants, which do not move, are not alive. Studies have shown that children develop their own ideas about many physical phenomena including shadows, light, heat, and electricity (Carey, 1985; Confrey, 1990; Eylon & Linn, 1988). In the section on Piaget you saw children's ideas about the moon. In some cases children have expressed their ideas by answering interviewers' questions orally; in other cases they have responded in writing or by drawing. All three methods also can be useful to teachers.

The following example describes children's misconceptions about the shape of the earth. Ask yourself whether their misconceptions arose from not paying attention to lessons on the shape of the earth or because they were ingenuous in reconciling their own experience with what they have been told by adults.

## Children's Ideas about the Earth

Several studies of children's ideas about the earth, carried out in different places, disclose some of their misconceptions, show how they may misinterpret what they hear in class, and how difficult it is to change their thinking. In the first of the studies (Nussbaum & Novak, 1976), children from two second-grade classes were individually asked a series of questions designed to elicit their beliefs about the shape of the earth. When first asked about its shape, all the children said that, of course, the earth is round like a ball. On further questioning, it became clear that almost two thirds of the children actually believed that the earth is flat. They had been taught in school that the earth is round "like a ball," but their experience told them that the earth is flat. Because what they were taught was contradicted by their own experience, they had to work out a way to reconcile the two opposing ideas. Subsequent studies conducted in Israel (Nussbaum, 1979), Nepal (Mali & Howe, 1979), and California (Sneider & Pulos, 1983) yielded similar results. Figure 2.3 illustrates what children in Nepal were thinking when they said that the earth is round while actually believing that it is flat.

The following notions correspond with the numbered drawings in Figure 2.3:

1. The hills and mountains are round; that's why we say the earth is round.
2. The round earth is in the sky somewhere; we are on a different earth.
3. The earth is a flat disk, shaped like a pancake.
4. The earth has a flat plane through the center with the sky above and rocks, water, and dirt underneath.

Audiotutorial lessons were given to the children with the objective of changing their ideas, but at the end of the series of lessons, the number who still believed in the flat earth was almost as large as before instruction. Not only in this case, but in many others as well, researchers have shown that children hold onto their beliefs

**FIGURE 2.3   Children's Notions of the Earth**

*Source:* Adapted from figure in "Development of Earth and Gravity Concepts among Nepali Children" by G. Mali and A. Howe, 1979, *Science Education 63*(5), p. 687. Copyright © 1979 by John Wiley & Sons, Inc. Adapted by permission.

tenaciously, changing them only reluctantly and over a period of time. It's easy to see that telling children what you want them to learn will have little effect when the ideas they already have are strongly held. Adding a new fact to what they already know is not enough to bring about a conceptual change. To understand a new concept, children have to restructure their thinking

## Difficulty of Changing Misconceptions

Most children grow up with some cultural beliefs that they cling to even when those beliefs contradict their experience. Many of the Nepalese children in the preceding example said that four elephants held up the flat earth. Did you grow up in a culture that fostered belief in Santa Claus? If you did, did it trouble you that Santa was supposed to go all over the world in one night and squeeze in and out of chimneys? When you noticed that not all children lived in houses with chimneys, you accepted your parents' explanation that Santa could just as easily enter houses through doors. Finally, you began to wonder how anyone could get around the world in one night, and you noticed some other very strange things as well.

One six-year-old carefully examined a foil-wrapped chocolate Santa from her Christmas stocking, noticed a bar code on the bottom, turned to her mother and said "Santa must buy some of his things in stores. I don't think his elves have time to make everything." She was trying to reconcile her belief in Santa's elves with her knowledge that bar codes are placed on items sold in stores.

## Teaching for Conceptual Change

A goal of science teaching is to help children build on or abandon their misconceptions as they construct science concepts appropriate to their ages and cognitive abilities. This process is called conceptual change and is currently an active subject of study and discussion. (For a review of recent literature see diSessa and Sherin, 1998.) The situation that students find themselves in is explained by MacBeth (2000) as follows: "Students enter into their science instruction with understandings of the natural world that already have the deep recommendations and evident good sense of life experience, and then encounter a curriculum whose foundation seemingly cannot be found in their experience" (p. 229). Vosniadou and Ioannides (1998) believe that conceptual change is a "slow revision of an initial conceptual system through the gradual incorporation of elements of the currently accepted scientific explanations" (p. 1222) and that children's representations of the physical world undergo both spontaneous and instructionally based changes. The important question for a teacher is, "What can I do to help children change or give up their naive concepts, that is, their misconceptions, and construct more acceptable scientific concepts?" If you were teaching children who held the ideas about the earth described earlier, what could you do or say that would persuade your pupils to change their concepts?

The place to start is with children's ideas. In an article that summarizes current thinking about conceptual change, Hewson, Beeth, and Thorley (1998) emphasize the importance of having children make their ideas explicit and intelligible to others. They are encouraged to explain their ideas, compare ideas, and respond to each other's ideas. The process of explaining and discussing different ideas is ongoing throughout the activities and investigations that form the basis for teaching for conceptual change. The focus is not only on facts and knowledge but also on how knowledge is acquired, validated, and accepted.

This approach will be a new experience for children who are accustomed to trying to decipher the teacher's mind and giving the answers they think the teacher wants. The teacher has to encourage children to think of themselves as learners who construct their own knowledge. Getting them to do so isn't always easy, a point illustrated by Beeth (1998) who cites a conversation between two fifth graders and their teacher:

> "We see what all of this is about now. You are trying to get us to think and learn for ourselves," said the first student.
> "Yes, yes" said the teacher, heartened by this breakthrough. "That's it exactly."
> "Well", said the second student "We don't want to do that." (p. 1092)

It's clear that these pupils will have to have an "attitude adjustment" before they can participate fully in the teacher's efforts to bring about conceptual change. Persuading children to participate openly and actively may be the first hurdle in teaching for conceptual change.

## The Role of Social Context in Learning

Recognition of the central role of social interaction in knowledge construction is bringing about a shift in emphasis in elementary-school science education. This understanding owes much to Vygotsky's influence, but others have also contributed to it (e.g., Moll, 1990). As teachers we no longer think of children as essentially solitary individuals trying to understand the world by applying logic to the results of their actions. Rather we view them as participants in an ongoing dialogue with children of their own age, with older and more knowledgeable children, and with parents and teachers. The importance of hands-on science is not in the manipulation of objects or the observation of phenomena but in the explanation and discussion of the experience that stimulates thinking and leads to understanding and knowledge.

Research in this area treats the classroom as a sociocultural system and studies the talk that goes on in the classroom between teacher and students and between students themselves as a way of understanding the development of knowledge (Forman, Minick, & Stone, 1993). The model is a classroom in which teachers use interactive teaching methods, which include scaffolding learning for students, supporting student's involvement in their own learning, and encouraging students to work and learn together.

Learning is now understood to depend more on context than science educators once thought it to be. That is, knowledge tends to be embedded in a specific situation, and the skills learned and used in one context may not be—and often aren't—transferable to another situation or context (Rogoff & Lave, 1984). Young children may do poorly on memory tasks in a psychology laboratory but remember the names and locations of objects at home without difficulty. Children who learn to make inferences or control variables in the context of a science lesson may not use these processes at all when confronted with a problem in their everyday lives. Children who have learned a skill in math class but can't use the skill in science sometimes baffle teachers. "That's math, not science" is what the teacher hears the pupils say.

Recognition of the importance of context has also influenced educators' thinking about the importance of developmental stages in learning science. Many researchers have tried to show that specific science concepts can be understood only after a child has reached a certain stage of development. This view implies that the teacher has to wait until the child has reached a certain stage before a concept can be introduced. Research has failed to provide strong evidence for that point of view and suggests, instead, that multiple factors, including developmental level or stage, play a part in what children can do and learn (Metz, 1995). What a child can learn at any particular moment about animals, for example, depends both on past experience with animals and on the ability to reason at a certain level (Inagaki, 1990). In one subject, a child may operate at the concrete operational level and in another subject at the formal operational level (see, e.g., Linn, 1983; Lawson & Wollman, 1976). Developmental levels cannot be ignored and science processes are still important, but they do not occupy the central place they occupied at one time.

## ■ SUMMARY

The five thinkers whose ideas were presented in this chapter came to their conclusions from different intellectual backgrounds and perspectives and studied different aspects of children's development and learning. What ties them together is the belief that meaningful knowledge is not acquired by passive listening; rather, it is constructed through mental activity on the part of the learner. Recent research on teaching and learning owes something to each of them.

Table 2.2 summarizes the main ideas in this chapter and suggests the implications of these ideas for you, as a teacher. In the chapters that follow you will work through many examples of practical applications of these ideas and will find that constructivism is not so much a theory as an approach to teaching and learning.

## ■ ACTIVITIES FOR THE READER

The following activities are included as a reality check on the theories and ideas presented in this chapter. You will get more from these activities if you compare and discuss your results with classmates.

### PIAGET TASKS

The best way to understand Piaget is to present several Piaget tasks to children and reflect on their responses. Find several children of different ages between 5 and 12 and administer these tasks to each child. Record their answers and your observations and come to class prepared to discuss them. A less satisfactory alternative is to prepare answer sheets for pupils and demonstrate the tasks to a whole class with pupils using the answer sheets at their desks.

**TABLE 2.2   Constructivism in Science Teaching**

| Scholar | Major Ideas or Themes | Implications for Science Teaching |
|---|---|---|
| Dewey | Learning is meaningful to children when it grows out of their own experience. The school curriculum should be built around constructive and practical activities that extend children's experience and stimulate their thinking. Symbols are important as a means of representing experience and advancing thinking. | Establish a classroom environment in which children can express their own interests and curiosity. Select science activities that start with children's experience and lead beyond their experience toward larger ideas and concepts. |
| Piaget | Children acquire knowledge by acting and thinking. Knowledge is classified as physical, logico-mathematical, or social. Development of logical thinking is a maturational process. Understanding of natural phenomena depends on logical thinking ability. | Provide an environment to encourage independent action and thought. Distinguish between kinds of knowledge in planning instruction. Be aware of children's level of logical thinking. |
| Bruner | Children learn by discovering their own solutions to open-ended problems. Knowledge is represented in enactive, iconic, and symbolic modes. Appropriate ways can be found to introduce children to any topic at any age. The process of learning is more important than the product. | Use open-ended problems in science regularly and often. Use all three modes of teaching and testing for understanding. Emphasize processes of science. Teach concepts and processes that will lead to further learning. |
| Vygotsky | Children learn through interaction with peers and adults. Knowledge is built as a result of both biological and social forces. Language is a crucial factor in thinking and learning. Children need tasks just above their current level of competence. | Encourage pupils to work together and to learn from each other. Encourage children to explain what they are doing and thinking in science. Set tasks that challenge children to go beyond their present accomplishments. |
| Kohlberg | Children learn moral and ethical behavior by example rather than by teaching. Moral development is a slow, maturational process. Moral dilemmas that have no easy solution are part of life. | Set an example of fairness and honesty in your own behavior. Guide discussion of problems as they arise and allow children to suggest solutions. Include science-related ethical issues in class discussion. |
| Recent research | Children bring many ideas and concepts to class; some of these can interfere with new learning. Learning is more domain-specific and less easily transferred from one area to another than was once thought. Social interaction and the context in which a cognitive skill is learned and used are important factors in the construction of meaning. | Probe to find out what misconceptions children bring to class. Expect greater competence in familiar topics than in unfamiliar ones. Recognize that developmental level is only a rough guide to children's abilities. |

## CONSERVATION OF SUBSTANCE

*Materials*

Two equal-sized balls of modeling clay, about the size of Ping-Pong balls

*Procedure*

1. Let the child handle the balls of clay. Ask whether the balls are the same size and, if not, how the child can make them equal. Continue until the child is satisfied that the balls are equal.

2. Ask the child to flatten one ball into a pancake shape and to leave the other ball unchanged.

3. Ask, "Does the pancake have the same amount, less, or more clay than the ball? Can you tell why you think that they are the same (or that the pancake has more or that the pancake has less)?"

4. Now press the pancake back into a ball, and ask the child to make a snake with one of the balls. Repeat the procedure and the questions that you asked about the pancake.

## CONSERVATION OF LIQUID AMOUNT

*Materials*

Colored water (orange and green)
Two glasses or beakers (100 milliliters)
One tall thin glass
One low wide glass or jar
Two smaller glasses or jars (25 milliliters)

*Procedure*

1. Fill the two glasses about half full, one with orange water and the other with green water. Be sure that the child believes that the two glasses have the same amount of liquid.

2. Ask the child to pretend that she has the glass of "orangeade" and her friend has the glass of "limeade." Pour the orange water into the tall thin glass and ask the child whether she has the same amount to drink as the friend. If the answer is no, ask the child whether she can say which child has more or less. Ask the child to explain why she answered as she did and record the answer.

3. Pour the water back into the original container. Ask the child again to verify that the amounts are the same. Now pour the orange water into the low, wide

dish and repeat the questions and the request for justification. Record the answers.

4. Repeat the process, pouring the water into the two small containers this time. Ask the same questions and record the answers.

## CONSERVATION OF AREA

*Materials*

Two sheets of green construction paper
20 to 30 identical one-inch cubes or squares
Two small toy horses (or cows)

*Procedure*

1. Show the child the pieces of paper, and say that they are the same size. Show the cubes or squares and say that they, too, are all the same size. If the child questions this statement or seems unsure, allow time for him to verify it.

2. Point to the pieces of paper and ask the child to pretend that these are fields of grass and that the horses are grazing in the fields. Each field has the same amount of grass for the horses to eat. Now the farmer builds a barn at one corner of one field and a barn of equal size in the middle of the other field. Ask the child whether the two horses still have the same amount to eat. Ask the child to explain his or her answer and record it.

3. Repeat as in step 2, adding a barn beside the first one in the first field and a barn at a distance from the first barn in the second field. Repeat the question and record the answer.

4. Repeat as in step 3, adding the third barn beside the first two barns in the first field and at a distance from the first two barns in the second field. Ask whether the horses now have the same amount to eat. Ask the child to explain his or her answer and record it. If the child thinks that the amount of grass is different after you have placed a few cubes, you can stop. If, however, he or she thinks that the amount of grass is the same, continue adding cubes. Children who are transitional in their ability to conserve area will often change their minds when more "barns" are added.

5. If the children in your sample are not familiar with horses or cows and their eating habits, the task can be changed in one of the following ways:

    a. A sheet of cookie dough replaces the two fields, and cutout cookies replace the barns.

    b. The fields become lawns to be mowed, and the barns become flower beds.

## TASKS FROM MISCONCEPTIONS RESEARCH

### I. CONCEPT OF A RIVER

This task is to be presented to fifth or sixth graders who have already had some classwork on rivers and river basins. Try it with a classmate first to work out the details and be sure that your instructions are clear.

Tell the children that you want to discover their own ideas about rivers and that their work will not be graded or used for grading. Give each child a piece of plain paper. Ask the children to draw a picture of a river, showing where the river starts and ends and adding an arrow to show which way the river flows. They may add other features if they want to. Limit the time allowed for the task to 10–15 minutes to minimize children's borrowing ideas.

Study the drawings and classify them by level of understanding, depending on where the river is shown to begin and end, whether it is shown as widening as it flows, whether tributaries are shown, and whether the river is shown as straight or meandering toward the sea. You may question the children individually about their drawings (Dove, Everett, & Preece, 1999).

### II. SHAPE OF THE EARTH

Collect data about children's belief about the shape of the earth, as in the example given in this chapter. Practice first with a classmate.

Explain to the children that this is not for a grade—only to let you know how they are thinking. Ask them to draw the earth and each child to draw (a) himself or herself standing on the earth, and (b) to draw a child standing on the earth in Australia (or at the South Pole). Now ask them to suppose that they, as well as the child in Australia (or at the South Pole), are each carrying a bucket of water and to draw where the water would go (a) if they spilled the water and (b) if the child in Australia spilled the water. (Many children will show the water falling into space rather than pulled by gravity toward the center of the earth.)

Study the drawings and classify them by level of understanding of gravity.

### III. MEANING OF (1) ANIMAL AND (2) LIVING

This task is for children in the first through fifth grades or individual children aged 5–11.

Make cards with a picture on each one and show the cards, one by one, to the children as you ask the questions or just use the indicated words. Each question is to be answered "yes" or "no."

1. *Animal.* (a) Is a cow an animal? (b) Is a person an animal? Continue with (c) a whale, (d) a spider, and (e) a worm.

2. *Living*. (a) Is a fire living (or alive)? (b) Is a person living? Continue with (c) a moving car (d) a mountain, and (e) a tree.

Make a chart showing the percentage of children giving the correct answer for each item. If you questioned individual children, show the number of correct answers by age.

## ■ QUESTIONS FOR DISCUSSION

1. You have probably studied Piaget's and Vygotsky's theories, and perhaps those of Dewey, Bruner, and Kohlberg, in another course. How are the interpretations of their thought in this chapter similar to or different from your previous understanding of their ideas?

2. If you had to add a summary of one other person's ideas to this chapter, whose ideas would you add? Discuss others who have influenced your own thinking about something related to teaching.

3. In his book *Toward a Theory of Instruction*, Bruner stated that "there is an appropriate version of any skill or knowledge that may be imparted at whatever age one wishes to begin" (1966, p. 35). What do you think he meant by that statement? Try to defend or refute the statement with examples. Select one important process or concept in science and discuss appropriate versions for primary-school children and for upper elementary-school children.

4. What does it mean to create an answer to a problem? Give an example of a problem that has more than one answer.

5. Give an example of and explain

   a. something you learned in the enactive mode.

   b. something you learned in the iconic mode.

   c. something you learned in the symbolic mode.

6. Can you remember a time when you felt that a teacher or other adult did not treat you fairly? Looking back on it, can you understand the adult's point of view, or do you still think the treatment was unfair?

7. Describe a misconception that you had at one time about a scientific or other concept. What made you change your mind?

## ■ REFERENCES

Beeth, M. (1998). Teaching science in fifth grade: Instructional goals that support conceptual change. *Journal of Research in Science Teaching, 35*(10), 1091–1101.

Bruner, J. (1966). *Toward a theory of instruction.* Cambridge, MA: Harvard University Press.

Bruner, J. (1985). Vygotsky: A historical and conceptual perspective. In J. Wertsch. *Culture, communication and cognition: Vygotskian per-spectives* (pp. 21–34). Cambridge, England: Cambridge University Press.

Bruner, J., & Haste, H. (Eds.). (1987) *Making sense. The child's construction of the world.* New York: Methuen.

Carey, S. (1985). *Conceptual change in childhood.* Cambridge, MA: MIT Press.

Confrey, J. (1990). A review of research on student conceptions in mathematics, science and programming. In C. Cazden (Ed.), *Review of Research in Education* (pp. 3–56). Washington, DC: American Educational Research Association.

Dewey, J. (1902/1956). *The child and the curriculum. The school and society.* Chicago: University of Chicago Press.

diSessa, A., & Sherin, B. (1998). What changes in conceptual change? *International Journal of Science Education, 20*(10), 1155–1191.

Dove, J., Everett, L., & Preece, P. (1999). *International Journal of Science Education, 21*(5), 485–497.

Eylon, B. S., & Linn, M. (1988). Learning and instruction: An examination of four research perspectives in science education. *Review of Educational Research, 58*(3), 251–301.

Forman, E., Minick, N., & Stone, C. (Eds.). (1993). *Contexts for learning.* New York: Oxford University Press.

Hewson, P., Beeth, M., & Thorley, N. (1998). Teaching for conceptual change. In Fraser, B., & Tobin, K. (Eds.), *International handbook of research in science education.* Dordrect, The Netherlands: Kluwer.

Howe, A. (1996). Development of science concepts within a Vygotskian framework. *Science Education, 80*(1), 35–51.

Inagaki, K. (1990). Young children's use of knowledge in everyday biology. *British Journal of Developmental Psychology, 8,* 281–288.

Kohlberg, L. (1969). Stage and sequence: The cognitive developmental approach to socialization. In D. A. Goslin (Ed.), *Handbook of socialization theory and research* (pp. 118–140). Chicago: Rand McNally.

Kohlberg, L. (1981). *Essays on moral development* (Vols. 1 & 2). San Francisco: Harper & Row.

Lawson, A., & Wollman, W. (1976). Encouraging the transition from concrete to formal operational functioning: An experiment. *Journal of Research in Science Teaching, 13*(5), 413–430.

Linn, M. (1983). Content, context and process in adolescent reasoning. *Journal of Early Adolescent Reasoning, 3,* 63–82.

MacBeth, D. (2000). On an actual apparatus for conceptual change. *Science Education, 84*(2), 229–264.

Mali, G., & Howe, A. (1979). Development of earth and gravity concepts among Nepali children. *Science Education, 63*(5), 685–691.

Mayhew, K., & Edwards, A. (1936). *The Dewey school.* New York: Appleton-Century.

Metz, K. (1995). Reassessment of developmental constraints on children's science instruction. *Review of Educational Research, 65*(2), 93–127.

Moll, L. (Ed.). (1990). *Vygotsky and education. Instructional implications and applications of sociohistorical psychology.* Cambridge, England, Cambridge University Press.

Nussbaum, J. (1979). Israeli children's conceptions of the earth. *Science Education, 63*(1), 83–93.

Nussbaum, J., & Novak, J. (1976). An assessment of children's concepts of the earth using structured interviews. *Science Education, 60*(4), 535–550.

Piaget, J. (1965). *The child's conception of the world.* London: Routledge and Kegan Paul.

Piaget, J. (1965). *The child's conception of number.* New York: W. W. Norton.

Rogoff, B., & Lave, J. (1984). *Everyday cognition: Its development in social context.* Cambridge, MA: Harvard University Press.

Siegal, M. (1982). *Fairness in children.* New York: Academic Press.

Sneider, C., & Pulos, S. (1983). Children's cosmologies: Understanding the earth's shape and gravity. *Science Education, 67*(2), 205–221.

Vosniadou, S., & Ioannides, C. (1998). From conceptual development to science education: A psychological point of view. *International Journal of Science Education, 20*(10), 1213–1230.

Vygotsky, L. (1926). *Thought and language.* Cambridge, MA: MIT Press.

# Integrating Science Content and Process

If you have never experienced inquiry-based science it may be hard for you to picture yourself planning and carrying out the kind of science activities described in Chapter 1. The purpose of this chapter is to help you get over that hurdle. The investigations in this chapter are for you to carry out in class with your fellow students. You will experience science as both content and process, using science processes as you consider some basic science concepts. Science content and process are two sides of a coin; sometimes you may look at one and sometimes at the other, but the two sides are tightly bound together.

## SCIENCE CONTENT

The content of science includes concepts, understandings, and theories, along with established factual knowledge about the natural world and ways to represent that knowledge. This content formed the core of your high school and college or university science courses, and it is the background that you will draw on as you learn to teach science. Examples of the science content of the elementary curriculum from the Content Standards of the *National Science Education Standards* were given in Chapter 1.

## SCIENCE PROCESSES

Science processes are the methods scientists use as they systematically investigate the natural world. They make observations, try to explain the observations, and invent concepts and theories. In the 1960s, psychologist Robert Gagne observed scientists at work and made a list of the processes that he thought they used as they went about their work. These processes were incorporated in an elementary science program, *Science. A Process Approach,* (AAAS, 1967) and have been widely used in textbooks and curriculum materials. These processes are as follows:

- *Observing.* Using one or more of the five senses to notice characteristics of objects or events.
- *Communicating.* Conveying information through language, pictures, or other means of representation, including graphs.
- *Classifying.* Putting things into categories according to certain characteristics, including creating and using new classification systems as well as using other people's systems.
- *Measuring.* Making quantitative observations by comparing things to one another or to a unit of measure.
- *Relating objects in space and time.* Using the relationships of space and time in describing and comparing shapes, locations, motions, and patterns.
- *Predicting.* Using previous observations to make an educated guess about a future event or condition.

- *Inferring.* Making a tentative or trial explanation for a set of observations.
- *Controlling variables.* Identifying attributes or factors that could vary in a system and holding all but one constant.
- *Defining operationally.* Setting specific limits to the meaning of a term for the purpose of dealing with a particular situation.
- *Experimenting.* Applying all the science processes, as needed, to design, carry out, and interpret a test of a question or hypothesis.

Science processes are still considered an important element of elementary science but focusing on processes without regard to content is not sufficient at any level, even at the youngest age group. Both scientists and educators recognize that the curriculum should be built around both important science concepts and science processes. In the classroom, science processes should be learned in the context of studying important ideas and concepts.

## STANDARDS FOR SCIENCE AS INQUIRY

The *National Science Education Standards* (NRC, 1996) does not make a distinction between content and process but has a standard for science as inquiry that includes, but is broader than, the processes in the preceding list. There is also a standard for science and technology that includes abilities needed to design a solution to a problem. Standards for science as inquiry for Grades K–4 are that children are expected to develop skills and abilities to

- ask a question about objects, organisms, or events;
- plan and conduct a simple investigation;
- use simple equipment and tools to gather data;
- use data to construct a reasonable explanation; and
- communicate investigations and explanations.

At Grades 5–8 children are expected to have skills and abilities to

- identify questions that can be answered through scientific investigation;
- design and conduct a scientific investigation;
- use appropriate tools and techniques to gather, analyze, and interpret data;
- use evidence to develop descriptions, explanations, predictions, and models;
- think critically and logically to connect evidence and explanations;
- communicate procedures and explanations; and
- use mathematics in all aspects of scientific inquiry.

As you study the second list, remember that it was developed for Grades 5–8 and that children may not attain many of these abilities and skills until they reach the seventh or eighth grade.

Standards for science and technology for Grades K–4 are that children will develop abilities to

- identify a simple problem;
- propose a solution;
- implement proposed solutions;
- evaluate a product or design; and
- communicate a problem, design, and solution.

For Grades 5–8 the standards are similar but go a little further, with children expected to be able to

- identify appropriate problems for technological design;
- design a solution or product;
- implement a proposed design;
- evaluate the completed design or products; and
- communicate the process of technological design.

A science lesson can start with a question to be investigated or with a problem to be solved.

## Science Processes as Aids, Not Goals

Individual science processes are highly interrelated and different authors have dealt with them in various ways. Science processes can serve as tools for the teacher in planning and carrying out science activities, and the standards can serve as guides. To interpret the processes or standards as individual packets of knowledge that must be transmitted to learners would be to misunderstand their purpose. They are only aids to thinking about science instruction.

# LEARNING TO INTEGRATE CONTENT AND PROCESS

The activities that make up the remainder of this chapter are intended to be carried out by you in class. They apply many of the ideas about science, about teaching, and about learning that have been presented up to this point. Most of the content of these investigations will not be new to you. However, you may never have thought about the concepts and processes at the basic level that is needed for teaching science to children.

At one level you will be a student as you experience the excitement of expanding and clarifying your ideas and perhaps understanding a science concept that you never really understood before. At another level, you will begin to think of yourself as a teacher or future teacher and reflect on your own experience as a guide in planning lessons for children.

You will need a bound notebook for recording data, observations, and reflections. It is important for you to keep an orderly record of these investigations for future reference in this course and for your own use when you are teaching. Each of these investigations can be adapted for use with children. The corresponding NSE Standard is given for each investigation to help you in future planning, but none of the investigations are actually limited to the ability or knowledge of one standard. Good teachers think much more broadly than that.

### INVESTIGATION 3.1

## THE PENDULUM

In this activity you will investigate the behavior of a simple pendulum, controlling one variable at a time.

### NSE STANDARD

(5–8) Think critically and logically to make the relationship between evidence and explanations (NRC, 1996, p. 145).

### QUESTION TO INVESTIGATE

Does weight of bob or length of string, or both, determine how fast a pendulum swings?

### MATERIALS

Simple pendulum
Clock or watch with second hand

### APPARATUS CONSTRUCTION

There are many possibilities for constructing a simple pendulum. All that is needed is a suspended weight that can swing freely. Two suggestions follow.

1. A simple apparatus made from easily available materials is illustrated in Figure 3.1. You will need several washers.
2. A more stable apparatus can be constructed with string, two weights (say, 100- and 400-gram weights) on hangers and a laboratory stand with ring or steel bar attached, as shown in Figure 3.2. Clamp the base of the stand to a table if necessary.

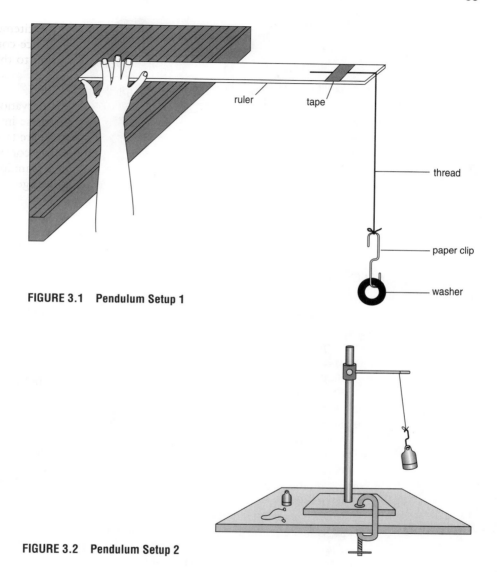

FIGURE 3.1　Pendulum Setup 1

FIGURE 3.2　Pendulum Setup 2

## THE INVESTIGATION

*Step 1.* Work with a partner to set up your pendulum. For the setup shown in Figure 3.1 cut a piece of thread somewhat longer than a meter. Open a paper clip into a hook and tie it to one end of the thread. Put one washer on the hook. Measure the desired length of the entire pendulum, from the bottom of the washer to the pivot point of the string. Tape the string at the pivot point to the end of a ruler. Hold the ruler steady against a tabletop or other stable platform, with the thread hanging over the end of the ruler.

Pendulum Data Sheet

| Length | Weight | Number of Swings | | | |
|--------|--------|---------|---------|---------|---------|
| | | Trial 1 | Trial 2 | Trial 3 | Average |
| Long | Heavy | | | | |
| Short | Light | | | | |
| | | | | | |
| | | | | | |

**FIGURE 3.3   Pendulum Data Sheet**

For the setup shown in Figure 3.2 be sure that the support is firm. Then cut two lengths of string and tie a loop on each end so that the loop-to-loop distance of one is about 70 centimeters and of the other is about 35 centimeters.

*Step 2.* Make a data sheet similar to the one shown in Figure 3.3.

*Step 3.* Now you can begin to collect data. Attach the long thread or string to the support and attach three washers to the thread (Setup 1) or attach the heavy weight to the string (Setup 2). Now one partner pulls the weight back gently and lets it go while the other partner starts the stopwatch. Count the number of swings in 15 seconds. A swing is counted from the point at which the bob was released back to the same point. Record your results in the appropriate space in your data table. Repeat twice, using the same weight and length and letting go of the weight gently.

Now remove the string and weight and attach the short string and the light weight. Use the same procedure and record the results of three trials.

*Step 4.* Can you say from these trials which variable determines the number of swings? What is your guess? In Steps 4 and 5 you can learn the answer.

*Step 5.* Change only one variable of the last setup (short string, light weight). You may change either variable but only one. Repeat three times and record the data.

*Step 6.* Change the other variable, repeat three times, and record the data.

*Step 7.* Now you have enough data to answer the question.

## ASSESSMENT

Identify the variable that determines how fast a pendulum swings.
Use your data to explain the answer in writing.
Suggest other variables that you could test. How would you test them?

## CLASSIFYING THINGS

Classification is both a concept and a process. As a concept it is very powerful and is basic to all of science. Biologists, physicists, chemists, and scientists in all other fields classify the objects or concepts that they work with. When a biologist discovers a new organism or an astronomer discovers a new object in the sky, the first question he or she asks is, "What is it?" or "To what class does it belong?" To answer such questions scientists use the process of classification.

The *concept of classification* is an invention of the human mind rather than a discovery of something that existed in the natural world. Because of the way classification is often taught, pupils sometimes get the notion that classification systems have some internal logic that was simply "discovered" by scientists of the past and is now passed on in school. Many systems and names of things in science change over time as new knowledge becomes available, as old knowledge is reconsidered, or as the animals or other things being classified change. The main reason that systems of naming and classifying animals, plants, rocks, and other things have been devised is to make it easier for scientists to communicate with each other.

Three important concepts are involved in classifying: (a) classification is arbitrary, (b) any group of objects can be classified in more than one way, and (c) classification is meant to be useful.

The following investigation uses ideas from "Treasure Boxes," one of the Teacher's Guides in the GEMS series of science and mathematics units (listed in the Appendix). The activities were designed for children in the early grades and are simple to carry out. However, they should stimulate your thinking about classification itself and about ways to teach the concept and process to children.

### NSE STANDARD

(K–4) Properties of Objects and Materials. Objects can be described by properties and those properties can be used to sort a group of objects (NRC, 1996, p. 127).

### QUESTION

In what ways can a collection of objects be classified?

### MATERIALS

Zip bags
Yarn or string

Collections of small objects such as buttons, old keys, earrings, small shells, small rocks, plastic figures, and bottle caps. Students are asked ahead of time to bring in whatever they may have or can find that can fit on a 1.5-inch by 1.5-inch

*Prospective teachers investigate the behavior of live organisms.*

square. The items should be of no value  because they usually will not be returned. The instructor will have additional items to add to whatever students bring.

## THE INVESTIGATION

*Step 1.* Sort your own objects and then work with other students to combine similar items and place them in labeled bags or small boxes. When you've done this, there will be, for example, a bag of buttons, a bag of old keys, and so on. Each labeled bag should have about 15 to 20 objects; other bags can hold miscellaneous objects. There should be enough bags for each pair or group to have one.

*Step 2.* Work with a partner or a small group. Examine the items in your bag, noting as many differences as you can. Select one attribute that you can use to sort them (e.g., color, shape, or size). Sort the items and record the name of the attribute, how you decided where to put an object that was questionable, and the number of objects in each category. Repeat this process. Then exchange bags with another group and repeat the process.

*Step 3.* One of the class members, or the instructor, will list on the board all the attributes used and allow time for students to compare observations and discuss problems encountered in classifying the objects.

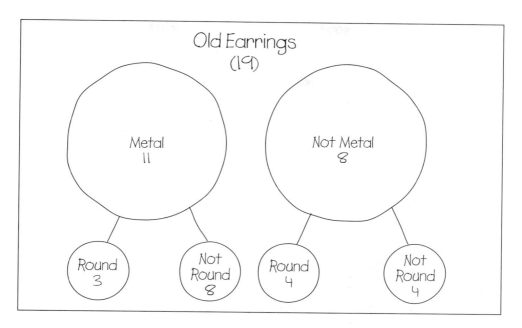

**FIGURE 3.4   Two-Level Classification**

*Step 4.* Sort the objects in a bag into two classes (e.g., round and not round or smooth and rough). Now divide the objects in each class into two classes. Figure 3.4 shows the classification system devised by two students for a collection of old earrings.

Record the classification system you used in a similar diagram.

Now classify your objects again, using different attributes. Record your results in another diagram.

*Step 5.* All pairs or groups will display their diagrams. Take time to see how others sorted their objects. (Observing what they've done will give you ideas that had not occurred to you.)

*Step 6.* Now sort the objects in a different way. Select two attributes that are not mutually exclusive (e.g., round and rough or dull and shiny). Make two circles with yarn or string, lay them side by side, label them with your two attributes, and place your objects in one circle or the other. Set aside objects that do not fit in either circle. You will find that some objects belong in both; that is, you will have an intersection. Figure 3.5 shows how the same earrings were reclassified, resulting in intersecting groups. Note that some earrings were left out.

Draw a diagram to represent your sort. Some students will recognize this as an intersecting *Venn diagram.* If your chosen attributes did not give an intersection, try again. Repeat, using different attributes and draw a second Venn diagram. If time permits, exchange bags with another group and sort a different set of objects.

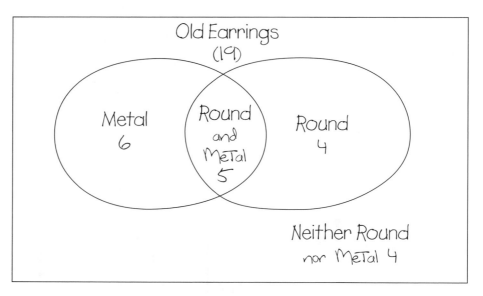

**FIGURE 3.5    Venn Diagram**

*Step 7.* Participate in a class discussion that focuses on the uses of these methods by scientists and how to introduce these ideas to children.

## ASSESSMENT

You will be given a set of keys.

(a)  Devise and diagram a two-level classification system for the keys.
(b)  Sort the keys into two intersecting groups and draw a Venn diagram to represent this way of organizing the keys.

## ADAPTING THIS ACTIVITY

These and related activities can be used at all grade levels, with increasing complexity at higher levels. Children enjoy handling interesting objects, so these activities have built-in motivation as well as being important learning experiences.

Kindergarten children can sort items by color, shape, and other obvious attributes, but some children have difficulty changing from one attribute to another. For example, they often pick color as the first attribute. If they are then asked to sort by shape, they may start with shape but switch to color midway through the activity. Learning to focus on one attribute at a time can be an important step in their cognitive development. Venn diagrams will be a challenge for second and third graders and should not be pushed if many children find it too difficult to select intersecting attributes.

How many ways can you classify these animals into two groups?

<u>Rules</u>: (a) There can be only two groups and (b) every animal has to be in a group. Label the groups and list the animals that belong in each group.

<u>Hint</u>: 1. Animals with fur and animals without fur.
2. House pets and not house pets, etc.

**FIGURE 3.6    Classifying Animals**

One way to introduce classification to third or fourth graders is suggested in Figure 3.6.

INVESTIGATION 3.3

## ELECTRIC CIRCUITS—PART 1

Electricity is the subject of this investigation and Investigation 3.4. This subject was chosen because it is included in almost all elementary-school science curricula, it is one of the units provided in most commercial science programs, and it is a subject that many preservice teachers have had little experience with.

### NSE STANDARD

(K–4) Electrical circuits require a complete loop through which current can pass (NRC, 1996, p. 127).

### QUESTION

**Resource Materials Note.**
These materials can be obtained at a hardware or electrical supply store. An old-fashioned store is best because individual items, not wrapped in plastic, can usually be purchased there.

How does current flow in a simple electric circuit?

### MATERIALS

*For each student or pair of students:*

One and a half–volt cell
Flashlight bulb
Bulb holder
Two 1-foot lengths of insulated wire

## MATERIALS

*For the class:*

    Ammeters
    Wire strippers
    Additional wire

## THE INVESTIGATION

    *Step 1.* You and a partner will receive a one and a half–volt cell (a battery), a small bulb, a bulb holder and two pieces of insulated wire. Your task is to make the bulb light up and to draw a diagram of each attempt, whether successful or unsuccessful. After about 15 minutes, your instructor will ask you to display your diagrams, look them over carefully, and determine how many different models you tried.

    *Step 2.* Take the diagram of your successful model and draw arrows showing the direction of current and whether the current in two wires (if you used two wires) is the same. Display your model by drawing it on the board or in some other way. All models will be displayed and discussed by the class. Consider these questions.

Does current go from the battery to the bulb in both wires?
Is electric current used up when it goes through the bulb?

    *Step 3.* Now you will find answers to those questions.

    Figure 3.7 shows four models of a complete circuit. Study the diagrams to be sure that you understand each one.

**Resource Materials Note.** Ammeters can be obtained at electrical supply stores.

    Write in your notebook your prediction of which is the correct model. To check your prediction you will need an instrument that gives the direction and amount of current in an electric circuit. This instrument is called an *ammeter.*

    Place an ammeter in one part of your circuit (you will need an additional wire to insert the ammeter into the circuit), take a reading, record it on your diagram, and predict what the reading will be in the other wire. Write your prediction in your notebook. Compare your prediction with those of your classmates.

    *Step 4.* Place a second ammeter in the other wire (again, you will need an additional wire) and record the direction and amount of current on your diagram. (Correct your diagram if necessary.) What does this result tell you about current in an electric circuit?

## ASSESSMENT 1

    Select the correct model in Figure 3.7 and explain why you selected that model.

## ASSESSMENT 2

    What was the content objective of this lesson?
    What was (were) the process objective(s) of this lesson?

A Battery is connected up to a flashlight bulb as shown in the diagram. The bulb is glowing.

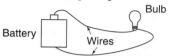

In the way you think about it, the *electric current* in the wires is best described by which diagram?

There will be *no* electric current in the wire attached to the base of the battery.

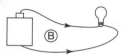

The electric current will be in a direction *toward* the bulb in *both* wires.

**FIGURE 3.7   Models of Electric Current**

From *Learning in Science. The Implications of Children's Science* (1985) by R. Osborne and P. Freyburg. Auckland, New Zealand: Heinemann, p. 25.

The direction of the electric current will be as shown. The current will be *less* in the "return" wire.

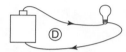

The direction of the electric current will be as shown. The current will be the *same* in both wires.

## ADAPTING THIS ACTIVITY

This activity can be adapted for Grades 4–6. Electricity has been a popular topic for developers of comprehensive curriculum projects for elementary science and is included in most curricula, often at Grade 4. It is one of the units in the *Science and Technology for Children* series (see the Appendix).

The topic continues to be of interest in science education as evidenced by two recent research reports. Shepardson and Moje (1999) traced fourth-grade children's development of the concept of electric circuits; Borges and Gilbert (1999) studied secondary school pupils' mental models of electricity.

**Note to Instructor.**
Start this investigation by demonstrating how to construct and use a circuit tester. This activity includes several places for class discussion and demonstrations of circuit boards, either by you or students.

This investigation builds on Investigation 3.3 and requires students to make inferences based on the data they collect.

INVESTIGATION 3.4

## INFERRING HIDDEN CIRCUITS

### NSE STANDARD

(5–8) Recognize and analyze alternative explanations and predictions (NRC, 1996, p. 148).

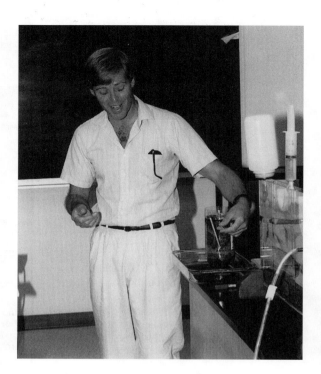

*A student in a methods class gives a demonstration to classmates.*

## MATERIALS

*For each pair or group of students:*

Materials from Investigation 3.3 (battery, bulb in holder, wires)
Brass paper fasteners
Pieces of sturdy cardboard, approximately 15 centimeters by 20 centimeters
Insulated copper wire
Wire cutter
Data sheets
Scotch tape

## THE INVESTIGATION

*Step 1.* Your instructor will demonstrate how to construct and use a circuit tester. Use your materials from Investigation 3.3 to construct a circuit tester, as shown in Figure 3.8. Try your circuit tester with several metal objects to be sure that it works.

*Step 2.* Your instructor will assign to each pair or group one of the circuit boards shown in Figure 3.9.

Construct the assigned circuit board as follows. Make four evenly spaced holes in a piece of cardboard. Insert a brass fastener in each hole on the top side and open the ends of the fastener on the reverse (under) side of the cardboard.

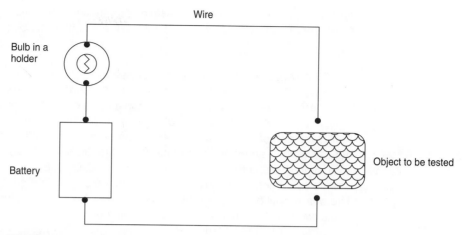

**FIGURE 3.8  Circuit Tester**

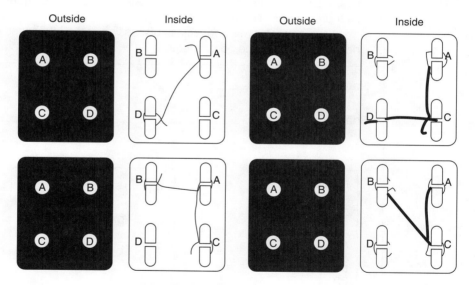

**FIGURE 3.9  Four Circuit Boards, Outside and Inside**

Cut two pieces of wire. Use the wire cutter to strip the ends of the wires to expose the copper. Fasten the wires to the brass fasteners on the underside, as shown in Figure 3.9. Label the fasteners on the top side as shown. Now you have an open circuit board. Draw a diagram of both sides of it in your notebook.

Use your circuit tester by touching one wire to A and the other wire to B (the "buttons" of the fasteners). If the light comes on, a current is flowing between A and B. Repeat for each of the possible combinations: AB, AC, AD, BC, BD, and CD. Record your results as − or + for each combination. For example,

AB +      AC −.

Exchange your board with another pair of students and test their board in the same way. Draw a diagram of that board and record your results as before.

*Step 3.* Class discussion and demonstration of the four circuit boards.

*Step 4.* Construct two closed circuit boards. These boards will have six fasteners instead of four. Make the boards as before, using either two or three wires, but use tape to attach a piece of cardboard to the back of each so that the wires are covered. Label the points of contact as A, B, C, D, E, and F. Identify your boards by putting your initials and 1 or 2 in the upper right corner of both boards. The boards will be collected by the instructor, who will then give each pair of students two boards constructed by other pairs of students.

*Step 5.* Test the boards that you receive, recording your results for each board on a data sheet like the one shown in Figure 3.10.

Mark a diagram for each board, showing the connections that you *infer* from your testing. If there is more than one logical possibility, mark as many diagrams as there are possibilities.

Your instructor will lead a class discussion of the inferences drawn, using demonstrations of the boards tested.

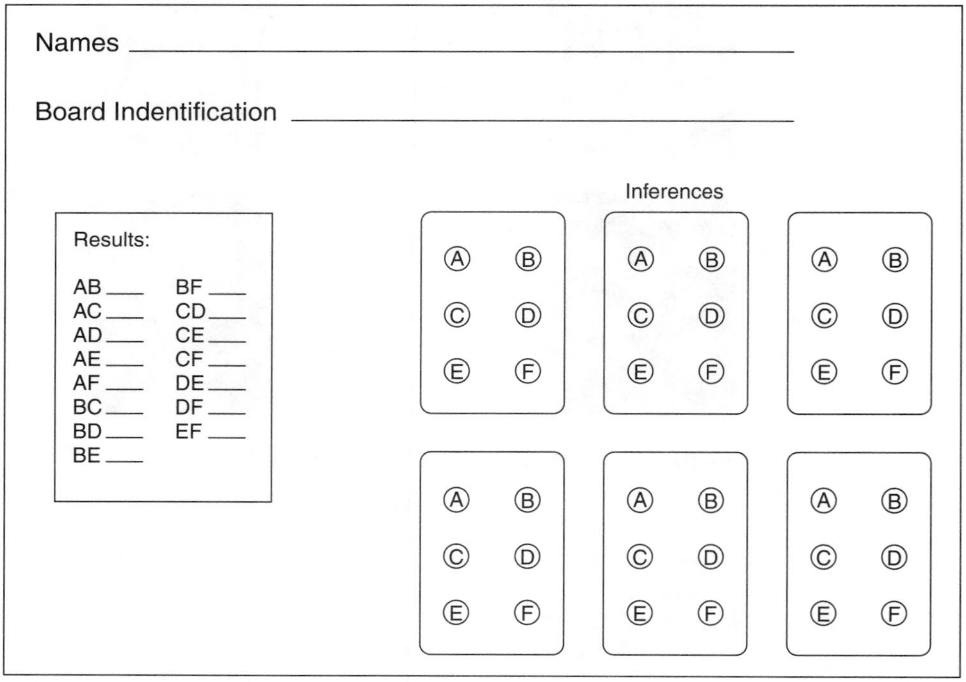

**FIGURE 3.10   Circuit Board Data Sheet**

## ASSESSMENT

Open the boards that you have tested and check you inferences.

## ADAPTING THIS ACTIVITY

This activity may be adapted for your use in fourth, fifth, or sixth grade. You will have to spend more time demonstrating and explaining how to test the boards to your students than the instructor of your class spent with you. Prepare transparencies to use on the overhead projector to help you do so. The first part of the lesson may be taught using direct instruction methods, particularly with fourth graders.

If you use this activity with elementary-school pupils, you may decide not to allow them to look inside the circuit boards. This variation is similar to what scientists do in real scientific research. This is called a *black box problem*. There is usually no way to look into a "black box" in nature to check on inferences, so scientists build models of their inferences and then compare the models to operation of the black box. Whether you allow pupils to open the circuit boards is your decision. Motivation runs high until the contents of the boards are seen. After that, the window of learning opportunity slams shut. Many science educators feel strongly that to simulate a real science situation learners should not be allowed to open the boards. This approach may seem hard, but consider the possible benefits of at least deferring the revelation for a day or more.

## ■ TALKING IT OVER

PROFESSOR SMITH: The next investigation is one in which the teacher as well as the pupils can be a learner.

MS. LEE, STUDENT: But how can I be a teacher and a learner at the same time?

PROFESSOR SMITH: That's an important question. It always concerns me when I occasionally hear a teacher say, "Oh, I'm learning science along with the kids." The teacher doesn't have to know everything and can't know everything but there are some things that a teacher must know.

MS. LEE: Can you give me some examples?

PROFESSOR SMITH: A teacher must know how to plan lessons that will engage the pupils in learning and to guide pupils through them. A teacher must have a firm knowledge of basic science concepts that underlie the science curriculum and the processes involved in scientific inquiry. In the shortest day lesson, the teacher would have to have facility with graphing and know how to guide pupils in making and interpreting graphs.

MS. LEE: There's so much to learn; it makes me wonder if I will ever become a good teacher.

PROFESSOR SMITH: There *is* a lot to learn. That's why good teachers never stop learning.

**Note to Instructor.**
This investigation is to be studied as an example of how scientists conduct experiments rather than an actual investigation to be carried out.

# AN EXPERIMENT WITH FERTILIZER

This experiment is too complicated for most elementary-school children, but it is included as a model to show how to plan, set up, and follow through on a scientific experiment. Most of the processes listed earlier in this chapter are used. When you understand the basic design of an experiment you can plan simpler ones for whatever age group you are teaching.

## NSE STANDARDS

The NSE Standards that apply to this investigation are

(K–4) Organisms and Their Environments (NRC, 1966, p. 129) and
(K–4 and 5–8) Abilities Necessary to do Scientific Inquiry (NRC, 1996, p. 122).

The question, "Is this fertilizer any good?" is one that might arise spontaneously in a conversation between gardeners. Before it can be tested, however, some critical thinking is needed. What is meant by "any good?" What is fertilizer expected to do? And how can you decide whether it performs this function "well"? When people buy fertilizer, they must expect some kind of improvement in their plants; otherwise, why buy it? Actually, different kinds of fertilizer correct different kinds of plant problems or improve different aspects of plant growth. Consider one function for study—whether a fertilizer causes plants to grow faster. The question could be restated more specifically:

How does Fertilizer X affect the growth of corn plants?

This investigation illustrates one way to use the science process *hypothesizing*. A hypothesis is a formal statement of the experimental question. It is similar to a prediction, but it is stated more formally and is in a form that can be tested. It is stated as a declarative sentence rather than a question. An example of a hypothesis for a plant study is:

Corn plants treated with fertilizer will grow taller than untreated corn plants during the same length of time.

The experimenter does not know yet whether the hypothesis is true. The purpose of a hypothesis is to guide an investigation. If the corn grows taller with fertilizer than without it, the experimenter can conclude only that the hypothesis is supported. "Proving" that the hypothesis is true would entail testing every kind of corn plant with every kind of fertilizer. Obviously, that would be impossible. In fact, no one can ever say that a hypothesis is proven—only that it is supported or not supported. If lots of corn plants and lots of fertilizers are tested and the corn grows taller in every case, the experimenter can have strong confidence in this hypothesis. Theoretically, it would take only one experiment in which the fertilized corn did not grow taller to disprove the hypothesis. Actually, when negative results occur, scientists usually use the new data to modify the old hypothesis rather than throw it out and start all over.

Formulating a hypothesis is more abstract than simply stating a question. A clearly stated experimental question is often sufficient to guide the relatively simple experiments appropriate for elementary children. You can be the judge of whether to include formulating hypotheses in your pupils' experiments.

Next, consider identification of variables. By stating the question clearly, you have already identified the variable you will change (fertilize or not) and the variable you will measure (growth of corn plants). Does either of these variables need operational definitions? To simplify the experiment, compare the size of plants that were given the amount of fertilizer recommended on the label to the size of plants that were given no fertilizer. You have operationally defined fertilizer as Fertilizer X in the amount recommended on its label.

What about "growth of corn plants"? Growth sounds like something that should be measured. How could you do so? There are a number of different ways, but as corn plants generally grow straight up and fairly stiff, it should be easy to measure the height of the plants with a ruler. If a different kind of plant had been chosen, you may have needed a different way to define "growth of corn plants" operationally. For a vine or a shrubby branching plant, you might decide to count leaves or measure in some way the total surface area of the leaves. In any case, you would need an operational definition for growth.

Now think of other variables that you are not especially interested in so that you can be sure that none of them are factors in any plant growth differences you may see later. These other factors include amount of light, amount of water, temperature, type of corn plants used, type and size of containers for the plants, and kind and amount of soil. Your list may also include other factors. Such a list is never complete because there is no end to other factors that might be involved. The best you can do is to identify those that you think may be important and try to keep them the same for all plants. These factors are called *controlled variables*. The more variables you control, the more certain you can be that they do not influence any differences you may observe later in the growth of plants.

The next step of the procedure is to design a test to answer the experimental question. There is no formula that tells how to design a test. You must consider the variables and make a number of judgments. How many plants are needed? What kind of containers, soil, and so on? How often should you water? How should the fertilizer be applied? Should you start with seeds or purchase some corn plants at a nursery? How often should the seedlings be measured? Perhaps you can think of other decisions to be made.

Before deciding on the details of the experiment, keep in mind that one or more corn plants will receive fertilizer and that one or more corn plants will not receive fertilizer. Conditions for both groups should be as much the same as possible except for the fertilizer. All plants should have the normal amount of the other factors (e.g., water and light) because you want to test normal plants. If the plants were stressed by lack of water, for example, they might react differently to fertilizer. Thus you need to know how to provide normal care for the plants. You might ask an expert or get information from a resource book about how best to maintain the plants in normal good health. Both sets of plants should receive all this good, normal care in exactly the same way, except for fertilizer.

Sometimes plants die for reasons no one can control. Also, plants receiving exactly the same care may not all grow exactly the same. It is usually a good idea to have several trials or multiple data to provide a more typical result by averaging. The following is one way to design the experiment; others could be equally valid.

If you were actually carrying out this investigation, you would proceed as follows. Plant several shallow boxes (flats) of corn seeds—say, about 100 seeds. When the seedlings had grown to a height of about 10 cm, choose 20 seedlings that are as much alike as possible. Carefully transplant these seedlings to individual one-liter containers, each having equal amounts of potting mix from the same bag. Place all the containers on the window sill, and give each 100 milliliters of water. After three days, eliminate any plants that do not look healthy. Divide the remaining plants equally into the fertilizer group and the no-fertilizer group (also called the experimental group and the control group, respectively). Decide on a watering schedule; how much and how often will depend on what you learn from the resources you consult. All plants should be given the same amount of water at the same time. In the water for the fertilizer (experimental) group, dissolve the recommended amount of fertilizer.

You would set up the experiment physically the way you planned. Measure and record the height of each plant periodically—say, every Monday, Wednesday, and Friday for a month. Design a data table to record the measurements. Figure 3.11 is an example of a data table; we will use these data to continue.

The data shown in Figure 3.11 were plotted to produce the graph shown in Figure 3.12.

What conclusions can you draw? Do the graphs give any information not provided by simply comparing the final average heights of the two groups? The data table and the graphs show no consistent difference between the growth of the two groups of plants. This conclusion could be stated in two ways, depending on whether it is in response to the question or the hypothesis. To the question, "How does Fertilizer X affect the growth of corn plants?" the conclusion could be stated in this way: "Fertilizer X does not seem to have any effect on the growth of corn plants." To the hypothesis, "Corn plants treated with fertilizer will grow taller than untreated corn plants during the same length of time," the conclusion could be stated in this way: "The hypothesis is not supported." A report of the experiment is shown in Figure 3.13.

| Day | Fertilizer | No Fertilizer |
|-----|-----------|---------------|
| 1 | 10 | 10 |
| 3 | 10 | 10 |
| 5 | 12 | 13 |
| 8 | 18 | 17 |
| 10 | 25 | 25 |
| 12 | 33 | 31 |
| 15 | 45 | 44 |
| 17 | 55 | 55 |
| 19 | 68 | 69 |
| 22 | 84 | 83 |
| 24 | 89 | 91 |
| 26 | 92 | 93 |
| 29 | 95 | 95 |
| 31 | 95 | 95 |

**FIGURE 3.11   Average Height of Corn Plants (cm)**

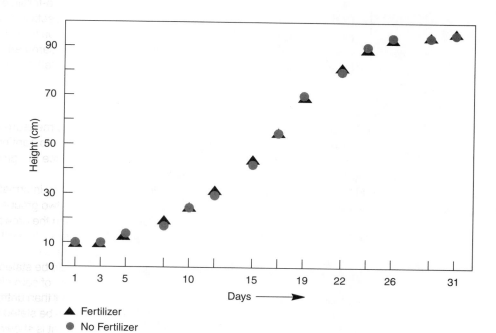

**FIGURE 3.12
Growth of Corn
Plants**

▲ Fertilizer
● No Fertilizer

---

**TITLE**

A Study of the Effect of Fertilizer on Corn Plants

**THE QUESTION**

How does Fertilizer X affect the growth of corn plants?

**THE HYPOTHESIS**

Corn plants treated with fertilizer will grow taller than nontreated corn plants during the same length of time.

**VARIABLES**

manipulated = fertilizer or no fertilizer

responding  = height of corn plants

controlled    = soil, light, temperature, type of corn plant, type and size of
                      container, water

**DESIGN AND PROCEDURE**

Twenty young healthy corn plants 10 cm tall were selected from a flat on basis of looking alike. Each plant was transplanted into equal volumes of planting mix in identical one-liter containers. Plants received normal care for three days, then unhealthy plants were discarded. The remaining 14 plants were divided into two groups. The experimental group received fertilizer (amount stated on label) in its water. Otherwise, all care was identical. Height of all plants was measured three days a week for one month. Average height for each group was graphed.

**RESULTS**

Data recorded in tables and graphs.

**CONCLUSIONS**

Added fertilizer appears to have no effect on the growth of corn plants. The hypothesis was not supported.

---

**FIGURE 3.13   An Example Report**

An experiment that gives negative results provides just as much opportunity to think and learn as when the results are positive. When the results are unexpected (as in this case), it is a good idea to verify that the procedure was carried out as originally stated and then to check for any possible measurement errors. If no such problems occurred, you must examine whether the question or procedure needs rethinking. All these steps are a part of real science and are valuable in practicing critical thinking. In this experiment, you might consider two alternatives:

1. Fertilizer X is worthless, and people who buy it are being cheated.
2. Some important factor in our experiment was overlooked.

Consider the second possibility. What was different in the experimental procedure from conditions in real gardens? One obvious difference was the soil: commercial potting mix rather than ordinary garden soil. What if the potting mix contained added fertilizer? If so, the control plants might have had enough nutrients to grow as fast as the plants grown with added fertilizer. In that case, you would modify the hypothesis to:

> When grown in common garden soil, corn plants treated with fertilizer will grow taller than untreated corn plants during the same length of time.

A new experiment based on the modified hypothesis might result in a graph like that shown in Figure 3.14.

## ASSESSMENT

Write a report similar to the example shown in Figure 3.13, using the new hypothesis and the results shown in Figure 3.14.

## ADAPTING THIS ACTIVITY

As mentioned at the beginning of this investigation, this experiment was presented as a model of how to think about, plan, and conduct a scientific investigation. The steps in it involved defining variables, asking a question, planning an experiment, interpreting results, and deciding what to do if the results weren't what you expected. You can follow these steps in planning investigations, even very simple ones, with your pupils.

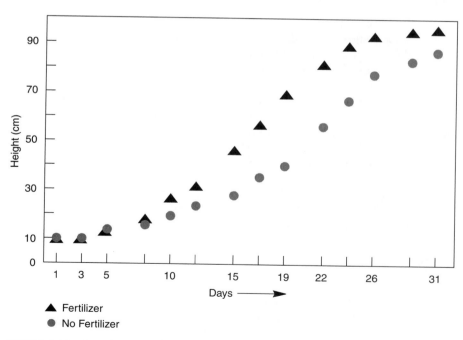

**FIGURE 3.14    Growth of Corn Plants in Garden Soil**

# EXERCISES IN METRIC MEASURING

The following activities are presented as exercises rather than an investigation. They were written for those who may need practice in using metric units, but they can also be adapted for use with children. They may be done at home or in class. Metric units are used in all scientific work and in the science activities of the elementary school. These exercises will refresh your memory if you have not had recent experience with metric units.

Measuring, like classifying, is both a concept and a process. It was invented to bring some order to people's experiencing of the world and to facilitate communication. Of course, measuring is also a process, and that is how we usually think of it.

## Measuring Activity 1: Length

Cut a strip from an index card or similar material to match the length of the rectangle shown in Figure 3.15.

Then make a list of things in your home that are the same length or close to the same length. For example, you may notice that an electrical switch plate is very close to that length. Find other objects to bring your list to about 10 items. Share your list in class. Which things named by your classmates did you also have on your list?

## Measuring Activity 2: Area

Because of the way area is sometimes taught in school, it is often thought of as something calculated by multiplying linear measurements. This multiplying procedure is a shortcut for finding area, but it does not help in understanding the meaning of area or the meaning of measurement. This activity is designed to make these meanings clearer. Area is the extent of a surface. Choose a surface whose area you will measure, such as a table or small "area" rug. Next, choose a convenient area unit, using something that possesses area itself. Also, you will want multiple copies of the unit. A string or a pipe cleaner will not do as an area unit because each only has length. You could use playing cards, small index cards, little self-adhesive notes, or pages from a small tablet. First, look at the surface to be measured—say, a card table. Just by looking, estimate how many of your units—say, playing cards—you will need to cover the table. Write down this estimate. Then check your estimate by actually covering the table with cards. Finally, count the cards. How close did you come to your estimate?

**FIGURE 3.15    A Rectangle of a Certain Length**

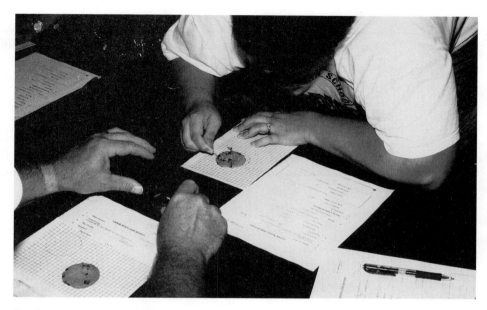

*Teachers use a 1-cm grid to measure area.*

## Measuring Activity 3: Liquid Volume

Select a group of containers in your kitchen. They might be a sauce pan, drinking glass, coffee mug, pie pan, mixing bowl, or cereal bowl.

You will also need a measuring cup. It can be one-, two-, or four-cup capacity. Turn the cup around and look at the markings on the side opposite the fractional-cup markings. Unless your measuring cup is an antique, you will find milliliter markings. Now follow these steps:

1. Look at the containers you've gathered. Which do you think will hold the most? Which will hold second most? Arrange your containers in the order you think will be from least to most volume. This task may not be as easy as you think. Containers of different shapes may be hard to compare without pouring, but for now do not do any pouring. List your containers on a sheet of paper in the order you estimated.

2. Check your estimated volume sequence by first filling with water the container you think is the smallest. Then pour it into the next largest container. Did the second container still have room for more water? If not, rearrange the order. Continue in this way until you have checked all the containers and are sure that they are correctly ordered by volume.

3. Find another container that is smaller than the smallest container you listed. It might be a small paper cup, a spray can lid, or a demitasse. Make your list into a worksheet, as shown in Table 3.1. If your small additional container is not a lid, substitute its name in your worksheet.

**TABLE 3.1  Metric Worksheet**

| Container | Lids | | Milliliters | |
|---|---|---|---|---|
| | Estimate | Measure | Estimate | Measure |
| Drinking glass | | | | |
| Coffee mug | | | | |
| Cereal bowl | | | | |
| Pie pan | | | | |
| Sauce pan | | | | |
| Mixing bowl | | | | |

4. In the estimate column under the heading "Lids," write the number of lids you think each container will hold.

5. After you have entered all your lid estimates on the worksheet, use the lid to measure each container. Pour and count the number of lidfuls necessary to fill each container to the brim. Enter your results in the worksheet.

6. Fill the measuring cup to the one-cup mark. Turn the cup around and note the milliliter equivalent. If you have a larger measuring cup, fill it to two cups and four cups, noting the milliliter equivalents.

7. Without pouring, look at the drinking glass (or whatever is first on your list) and estimate the number of milliliters needed to fill it to the brim. You may look at your milliliter measuring cup as a reference but don't touch it. Enter your estimated milliliters on the worksheet. Continue for each of the items on your list.

8. Now, measure the volume in milliliters of each container, using your cup. Write your results in the far-right column. Are you getting better?

You may not realize it, but by virtue of having done Measuring Activity 1, you now have a mental picture of a decimeter. The strip of tag board you made to match Figure 3.15 is exactly 10 centimeters, or 1 decimeter, long. The purpose of the activity was to establish the beginning of confidence in you as a measurement teacher and a user of the metric system. Try to avoid translating metric units into units in the U.S. customary system (i.e., the foot–pound system). Because Americans grow up with the customary system, most already have mental images of many of its units. The way to feel comfortable with the metric system is to experience its units and build up mental pictures. It is much like learning a foreign language. If you have to translate word-for-word into and out of English, you will never approach fluency. Just live with the new language through firsthand experiences, and you will pick it up before you realize it.

You did so in Measuring Activity 2, which involved covering a table with cards. It would have been more efficient to use a ruler and measure the length and width of the table and then multiply, but the objective was to learn, so you did it the hard way.

## ■ SUMMARY

Science content and process are two sides of a coin; sometimes you look at one and sometimes at the other, but the two sides are tightly bound together. The content of science includes concepts, understandings, and theories, along with established factual knowledge. Science processes are the methods scientists use as they go about the systematic investigation of the natural world. The *National Science Education Standards* provide guides for planning and carrying out a science program that integrates science content and process in activities that capture children's interest and imagination. To interpret the processes or standards as individual packets of knowledge that must be transmitted to learners would be to misunderstand their purpose. They are not the goals of science teaching but a means of reaching those goals.

A series of investigations to be carried out in class form the bulk of this chapter. Topics include the pendulum, classification, electric circuits, and the effect of fertilizer on plant growth. All investigations except the final one involve the learner in hands-on experiences, manipulation of equipment, communication of results, and discussion. The chapter ends with a series of exercises on metric measurement.

## ■ QUESTIONS FOR DISCUSSION

1. Refer to the list of processes at the beginning of the chapter and explain how each is used in the investigations that you carried out.

2. How would a science program guided by processes of science differ from a program guided by the NSE Standards?

3. Read and discuss the Borges and Gilbert article on children's mental models of electricity.

4. What was the most important thing you learned from the investigations in this chapter?

5. How are the investigations in this chapter different from the "labs" you have had in science courses?

## ■ REFERENCES

American Association for Advancement of Science. (1967). *Science—A process approach*. Washington, DC: AAAS/Xerox.

Borges, A., & Gilbert, J. (1999). Mental models of electricity. *International Journal of Science Education, 21*(1), 95–117.

National Research Council. (1996). *National science education standards*. Washington, DC: National Academy Press.

Shepardson, D., & Moje, E. (1999). The role of anomalous data in restructuring fourth graders' frameworks for understanding electric circuits. *International Journal of Science Education, 21*(1), 77–94.

# PART III

# Focusing on Instruction

# Teaching Basic Science Skills

The term *hands-on* means that children have their hands on science equipment and materials. Inquiry science activities involve the use of a wide variety of interesting apparatus, including simple instruments such as meter sticks, thermometers, and balances. Children can focus on the real purposes of science lessons only after they have acquired skill and confidence in using whatever equipment and instruments are required. The need for these skills is recognized in the *National Science Education Standards*. One of the Content Standards for pupils in Grades K–4 is that students should

> learn to use rulers to measure the length, height and depth of objects; thermometers to measure temperature; watches to measure time; beam balances and spring scales to measure weight and force; magnifiers to observe objects and organisms; and microscopes to observe the finer detail of plants, animals, rocks and other materials. (NRC, p. 122)

For students in Grades 5–8 the NSE Standards include this statement: "Writing, labeling drawings, completing concept maps, developing spreadsheets, and designing computer graphics should be a part of science education (NRC, p. 144). These are not skills that children should be left to discover on their own.

The method of planning and presenting lessons described in this chapter is teacher-centered rather than pupil-centered or activity-centered. It is appropriate for teaching skills of the kinds just listed, but it is not appropriate for teaching higher level science processes or concepts. The method described is one example of what is called *direct instruction*.

## DIRECT INSTRUCTION

A direct instruction lesson comprises specific types of activity that are carried out in a specific sequence. Using this structure ensures inclusion of many important elements of lesson presentation. It is relatively easy to learn and can be used effectively by beginning teachers. One reason for its ease of use is that decisions about structure are made during the planning stage, thus reducing the number of instructional decisions the teacher must make during the progress of the lesson. Direct instruction is favored by many administrators because it is relatively easy to observe and evaluate.

Direct instruction is the use of the traditional methods of lecture, demonstration, seat work, recitation, and feedback. The method is teacher-centered because virtually all the instructional decisions are made by the teacher. The level of pupil self-direction is low. Pupils are generally not free to pace their own learning, to move about the room, to discuss their work with other pupils, or to follow up interesting ideas they come across in the course of the lesson. In all these ways direct instruction is the opposite of inquiry-based instruction. When this kind of lesson is operating as planned, the pupils' attention is focused on the lesson objective as determined by the teacher. Thus direct instruction constitutes a series of actions taken by the teacher to bring about a predetermined learning outcome. This method is not to be confused with simply talking to pupils or what may be called "discussing a topic" when all the discussion is actually teacher talk. In direct instruction as defined in this book the pupils are not self-directed but are, nevertheless, engaged much of the time.

## Research on Effective Teaching

Researchers have attempted to discover relationships between what teachers do and how well students learn. Many studies have used achievement (gains made by students on tests of content) as the indicator of learning; these studies are called *teacher-effectiveness research*. From this work, a consensus has emerged about the most effective behaviors for teachers to use in teaching basic skills in the early grades. In a comprehensive review of more than 200 such studies, Brophy and Good (1987) summarized the findings. They found that two common themes cut across the findings. One is that academic learning is influenced by the amount of time students spend in appropriate academic tasks. The other is that students learn more effectively when their teachers first structure new information for them and help them relate it to what they already know, and then monitor their performance and provide corrective feedback during recitation, drill, practice, or application activities (p. 366).

The second theme implies the following steps in a direct instruction lesson: (a) review of previous related material, (b) presentation of new skill or content, (c) guided practice, (d) independent practice, and (e) closure. The specific sequence of these steps (described more fully later in this chapter) is called the *direct instruction model*. Researchers generally agree that using this model is more effective than using individualized or discovery methods for teaching basic skills in fourth grade and below (Rosenshine & Stevens, 1987). Thus explicit teaching is clearly appropriate when the objective is learning a straightforward skill and the pupil is young. A straightforward skill is one that can be taught in a step-by-step manner and reinforced by practice and application. In reading and mathematics, the subjects in which most of the teacher-effectiveness research has been carried out, basic skills are easy to identify. In mathematics, basic skills include multiplication facts (such as 5 times 5) and the use of a multiplication method, or algorithm, for computation involving numbers larger than 10. Some mathematics skills that are beyond the basics include estimating and problem solving. In reading, basic skills include word attack, as compared to comprehension, which is a higher level skill. In science, identifying basic skills proves more difficult because science is less hierarchical and sequential than either reading or mathematics. Many science educators would agree, however, on two areas of science instruction that could be called basic skills and thus can be taught effectively by the direct instruction model: (a) learning to use tools and equipment and (b) learning processes such as making measurements or writing reports. Both are needed for later application in science activities.

## Effective Teachers

Research shows that well-organized teachers are more effective than others, no matter what instructional method they use. One of the most interesting and important studies of the relation of teacher behavior to pupil achievement was carried out in

Texas in the early 1970s (Brophy & Evertson, 1976). Pupil achievement data for three consecutive years were obtained for a large sample of second- and third-grade teachers. Teachers whose pupils consistently showed gains in achievement were studied through many hours of careful classroom observation and through individual interviews. Researchers found that these effective teachers were businesslike and task-oriented and that they demanded that their pupils spend their class time engaged in learning activities. They tended to maintain well-organized classrooms and to plan activities on a daily basis. Because their activities were well prepared, the class ran smoothly with few interruptions and little time lost in confusion or aimless activity. When some pupils found the activities too difficult or could not keep up, these teachers often prepared special materials for them. Likewise, the teachers provided additional activities for pupils who finished early. These teachers spent a minimum of time getting the class started, making transitions, and bringing closure at the end of the lesson. To sum up, these teachers were prepared to start on time, to move right into the lesson, to provide materials needed for pupils to engage in the learning activities, and to take care of special needs of individuals.

Time spent in preparation allows a teacher to spend class time in effective and productive teaching. Although this kind of preparation takes considerable time and energy, a well-prepared teacher is not as tired at the end of the day as one who is poorly prepared. Consider two teachers: one who is well prepared and one who is not. The poorly prepared teacher has to rush around at the last minute gathering materials and making copies of worksheets while pupils are left with nothing to do. The class is off to a poor start, nothing seems to work right, and many behavior problems arise. This teacher goes home exhausted, but the teacher who was prepared goes home tired but satisfied that the class is doing well.

## PLANNING AND PRESENTING A DIRECT INSTRUCTION LESSON

As mentioned earlier, the usefulness of this method for science is limited—mostly to teaching specific, stepwise procedures for pupils to learn how to use equipment and showing how to construct and use graphs, for example. Also, at times specific procedures for an activity or specific behaviors, such as how to clean an animal cage, call for direct instruction. Procedural learning of this type constitutes only a small percentage of instruction in any science program. Additionally, some science procedures may be less clear-cut, and they could be presented either directly or indirectly. Most science instruction should be more interactive and inquiry-based, but the direct instruction model has its uses. It is an excellent device for beginning teachers to learn how to plan a well-structured lesson. An understanding of this model and the interrelation of its elements provides the beginning teacher with a reasonable basis from which to understand other more complex models to be described later.

Several main parts make up the lesson plan. Each will be briefly described. Then a structured lesson plan for the balance lesson will be described. Finally, the idea of each component will be explained in more detail. First, though, read a general description of one of Ms. Oldhand's lessons.

## ■ MS. OLDHAND'S BALANCE LESSON

In this lesson, Ms. Oldhand's second graders learned to use an equal-arm balance, also called a beam balance. Although the balance is an interesting example of a lever, in this lesson, Ms. Oldhand mainly wanted her pupils to learn to use the balance as a tool. Later, the pupils will need to use the balance to compare and measure weights of objects.

To save space, the balances were stored disassembled in boxes. In this lesson, Ms. Oldhand wanted each pupil to learn to put a balance together, learn the names of the parts, and get the general idea of how the balance works when objects are placed in the pans.

First, she showed the class how to put a balance together, explaining each step and naming the parts as she did so. Next, she showed them what happens when objects are placed in the pans. Then, she asked individual pupils to come to the front of the class to try doing these things themselves, which they did one at a time. Each pupil's work was watched by the others and closely monitored by Ms. Oldhand. When a problem arose, the pupils were helped in some way so that each mistake was gently corrected before the next step was taken. Then all the children had a chance to practice the new skills at their desks. Today, Ms. Oldhand decided to have them work in pairs. As they worked, she circulated to help as needed to encourage, to acknowledge accomplishments, and to provide special advanced tasks for those who finished early.

## Lesson Plan Parts

A direct instruction lesson plan has eight parts. As you read the description of each part, think about Ms. Oldhand's balance lesson. Can you decide what would be written for each of these parts?

1. *Objective(s)*. Statement of what the pupils will know or be able to do after the lesson that they did not know or could not do before.
2. *Materials*. List of materials that must be prepared or assembled for the lesson.
3. *Motivation*. What the teacher does to create interest or focus attention at the beginning of the lesson.
4. *Learning activities*.
   a. *Presentation*. What the teacher does to give information on how to meet the lesson objectives. Presentation is usually accomplished by showing, telling, or both.
   b. *Guided practice*. What the teacher does to provide closely supervised practice on the lesson objectives with immediate feedback on correctness. Guided practice is normally done one pupil at a time, with the others observing both the practice and the teacher feedback.

*Independent practice on balances engage children's full attention.*

    c. *Independent practice.* What the teacher does to provide independent practice for all the pupils at once. Teacher supervision is individualized.

    d. *Closure.* What the teacher does to close the lesson. For closure, a teacher may decide to review, summarize, relate to previous lessons, or otherwise pull the lesson together.

5. *Assessment.* What the teacher does to evaluate whether the lesson was a success.

In addition to these eight main parts for the direct instruction lesson plan, additional parts may be added for clarity. In Lesson Plan 1, given next as an example, the grade level, a descriptive topic title, and a materials preparation statement are examples of optional lesson-plan parts. Also useful for inclusion is a statement of the NSE Standard that the lesson will meet.

LESSON PLAN 4.1

## LEARNING TO USE THE BEAM BALANCE

### NSE STANDARD

Employ simple equipment and tools to gather data and extend the senses. Includes using beam balance (NRC, 1996, p. 122).

## GRADE LEVEL: 2

### OBJECTIVES

By the end of these activities, the pupil will be able to

1. assemble a pan balance from provided components;
2. identify and name the parts of the balance—base, support, fulcrum, beam, and pans; and
3. describe the general behavior of the pan balance when objects are put into and taken out of the pans, such as "When one pan goes up, the other goes down" or "You can make the beam even by adding to the high pan or taking away from the low pan."

### MATERIALS

*For the teacher:*

    Parts for one pan balance
    Several one-inch cube blocks

*For each pair of pupils:*

    Parts for one balance
    Ten one-inch blocks
    Two balance worksheets (see Figure 4.1)

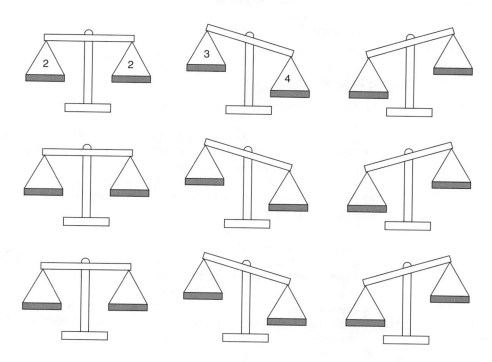

**FIGURE 4.1
A Balance
Worksheet**

## MATERIALS PREPARATION

Place materials at each double desk during lunch or recess. When pupils return, have them sit on the front rug.

## MOTIVATION

Ask whether pupils have ever played on a seesaw or teeter-totter. Ask what happened if a heavy child and a light child tried to seesaw together. "If you didn't know who was heavier, how could you find out with a seesaw? Today you will learn about a pan balance, a science tool something like a seesaw. You can use it to find out which things are lighter and which are heavier."

## LEARNING ACTIVITIES

## PRESENTATION

1. Teacher demonstration: "Watch very closely while I show you how to put your pan balance together." Name the parts as you put the balance together (base, support, fulcrum, beam, and pans).
2. When assembly is complete, hold a block over one pan. Ask, "What do you think will happen to the beam?" Take a few responses without comment and then place the block in the pan. Continue adding blocks to alternate pans. Ask, "Who wants to predict what will happen when I put this on the pan?" Then, without comment, do it.
3. Write the names of the balance parts on the board and go over them with the class.

## GUIDED PRACTICE

1. Take the demonstration balance apart. Hold up the parts one at a time and ask for their names. Then ask a pupil to come up, do a step of the assembly job, and describe the assembly activity, using the correct names of parts. Continue by asking, "Who can show us the next step?" If someone has trouble, ask another pupil to help. As a last resort, do the assembly yourself, using the names of parts in clear, direct sentences.
2. Ask questions about the behavior of the balance, such as, "Who can tell how to make the balance go down on this side?" (Up on this side, down on the other side, etc.) Regardless of the answer, have that child come up and do what he or she suggested.

    The balance will provide feedback. "Who can make the balance beam even? Is there another way to make the beam even?" Ask pupils to use the names of the balance parts as they demonstrate. Correct any incorrect naming of parts.
3. During part 2 of the guided practice, begin drawing sketches of balances on the board to illustrate the actions demonstrated.

## INDEPENDENT PRACTICE

1. Prepare the pupils to return to their desks by giving directions for the seat work. Hand a worksheet to each pupil and explain how it corresponds to the diagrams drawn on the board. The worksheet consists of diagrams of balances in left-pan-up, right-pan-up, and even-beam positions (several of each). Explain that each student will work with a partner to put the balance together and then to make the balance look like the pictures by adding or removing blocks. They should record their work by writing a number in the pan of each diagram to show how many blocks were required to make the balance look that way.
2. Give a prearranged signal for the pupils to return to their seats. As they work, circulate to help as needed.

## CLOSURE

Give the signal for attention. Announce that time is up for the lesson and that more balance work will continue later in the week. Ask the pupils to take the balances apart and put the parts in the box. When this task has been done, the table monitors should collect the boxes.

## ASSESSMENT

Informal observation during the independent practice and responses on the worksheets will provide information for deciding whether the objectives have been met.

# EXPLANATION OF LESSON PLAN

In this section, the parts of the lesson plan are explained in some detail, each part supported by research and expert opinion. The lesson-plan parts fall into two categories: sequences and organizers. *Sequences* include motivation, presentation, guided practice, independent practice, and closure. All are bound together in a time sequence and occur one after another. Sequences may also be called *learning activities*. By contrast, *organizers*—performance objectives, materials, and assessment—are not sequential; rather, they help the teacher organize thoughts about the total lesson. The performance objective and materials parts generally are not things the teacher "does." The assessment is something the teacher does, but the time in which assessment happens is not fixed. It may occur simultaneously with other lesson parts, afterward, or both. All the parts have a strong and necessary relationship to one another.

## Objective(s)

The point of stating the objectives as pupil performance or behavior is to make them observable and therefore easier to appraise. Not all pupil behaviors during a lesson, though, need to be significant new abilities. Many desirable pupil behaviors are simply procedural; that is, the behaviors do not indicate new abilities but are simply "housekeeping" actions necessary to the progress of the lesson. Examples of procedural (or nonsubstantive) behaviors in the balance lesson are

> sitting on the front rug,
>
> discussing the activity with a partner,
>
> taking the balance apart, and
>
> passing the boxes to the end of the table.

These behaviors are important to the lesson's progress but are not in themselves new abilities acquired as a result of the lesson activities.

## Materials

What materials would be most effective for your objectives? What quantities would be optimal? The ideal should be considered first. Then, if there are constraints, you can make adjustments, consciously recognizing the compromises being made. In the balance lesson, Ms. Oldhand decided to have her pupils work in pairs because she wanted to encourage pupil-to-pupil interactions, not because there was a shortage of balances. Suppose that she had decided that it was important for every pupil to work alone with a balance, but she had only 10 balances. She could have chosen to do the lesson with successive groups of 10 while the other pupils did something else. After you have decided what and how many materials you will use, list them in a way that helps you organize for teaching. You will find that designating the number of each material needed is a helpful way to plan. Note how that was done in the balance plan.

The one-inch blocks used in the balance lesson were selected because they were simple, uniform, and available. Many primary-school classrooms have such blocks. If they had not been available, Ms. Oldhand could have used any uniform objects, such as washers, nails, or checkers.

## Motivation

Some educators call this part motivation/review. Review is an important way to focus pupils at the beginning of a lesson that is one of a continuing series of lessons. The balance lesson example was the first lesson on that topic, so there was no preceding lesson to review. Instead, the teacher used two other techniques to focus attention and set a meaningful context for what was to follow. First, she asked the children to recall a previous experience. She figured there was a good chance that most of the children had played on a seesaw because their small town had seesaws in the public park. An assumption of this sort is becoming less and less certain, however. As the United States becomes more urbanized and the school population becomes more diverse socioeconomically and ethnically, it becomes harder for the teacher to be sure that all pupils share any particular experience from outside school.

Ms. Oldhand used another technique, just in case. She used an actual balance to show, as well as tell.

In the example lesson, the use of a real balance for demonstration does not seem remarkable. Especially with young children, teachers often use real objects. In fact, in almost every lesson with learners of any age, real materials are highly effective as a motivational or focusing device. Many adults have a hard time remembering what it was like not to know about some common object or experience. For any new information to be meaningful, it must be "hooked on to" an older understanding. The same is true for adults, but they have a rich store of previous experiences to form a context for understanding new information. The more removed from a person's past experience a bit of new information is, the harder it will be for that person to understand that information. Imagine how relatively poor a child's experience base is—compared to an adult's. The child simply hasn't had time to build up many experiences. Because of a child's inexperience, a lesson is more effective if real things are used to provide a firsthand experience.

Once teachers know that all the children in their classes have had a certain experience, they can call up the pupils' memory with less tangible stimuli, perhaps even with words alone. In any case, the motivation part of the lesson should be short, and the pacing should be fast.

## Learning Activities

### Presentation

There are three characteristics of effective presentation: clarity, focus on the objective, and brevity (Smith & Land, 1981). The teacher must be clear in explaining what pupils are to do and how to do it. It is helpful to write out directions ahead of time so that you will have them clear in your own mind before you begin.

Pupils cannot accomplish the lesson objective unless the teacher can create and maintain their focus on that objective. To do so, the teacher must focus on the new skill or concept that constitutes the objective. Digressions (jumping ahead and backing up) and ambiguous phrases distract pupils from the main point and confuse them.

Brevity is especially important. If the teacher remembers while planning the lesson to keep the presentation as short as possible, clarity and focus will probably be maintained. Attention span is almost always shorter than you might think. Underestimating it is better than overestimating it.

With primary-school pupils, brevity and clarity are even more important than with older pupils. The teacher should directly tell and show with a minimum of asking. The pupils do not know how to achieve the objective; time and clarity should not be compromised on trying to elicit answers during the presentation. (If pupils can already accomplish the objective, it needs to be revised.) Instead, show and tell directly and briefly; then move into the guided practice. The following guidelines, partly developed from a summary of research (Rosenshine & Stevens, 1987), may be helpful:

- Start with an example or a demonstration, not with a definition. A definition is meaningless until some understanding of the skill or concept has been attained.

- Use examples or demonstrations that are simple. Above all, they should not be harder to understand than the skill or concept you're trying to teach. Examples must be concrete and must already be familiar and well understood.

- Present material in small steps. Stop frequently to check for understanding.

- Model the objective whenever possible. Show your pupils what you want them to learn. Showing is always better than telling, though the combination of showing and telling makes things easier to remember than either showing or telling alone.

### Guided Practice

The main purpose of this part of the lesson is to provide an opportunity for pupils to practice a new skill in a controlled environment where mistakes can be corrected and gaps in understanding can be identified. Consider guided practice in a piano lesson: The piano teacher shows the pupil how a passage should be played, the pupil tries it out while the teacher watches, the teacher gives feedback and corrects any mistakes, the pupil goes home to practice, and the pupil finally comes back to the teacher to demonstrate that he or she has learned how to play the piece. Guided practice in science in a classroom may not seem the same, but there are a number of similarities. In one class, the teacher asks questions, gives cues or help as needed, and gently corrects errors. In another class, pupils work problems at the board under the teacher's guidance or come to the front of the room to try a new skill while the teacher gives help and feedback.

A secondary purpose of guided practice is to provide the teacher with feedback on how the presentation was understood, or rather, how it was misunderstood. By sampling the class for misunderstandings, the teacher can refine and modify the presentation to correct those misunderstandings. Identifying incomplete or otherwise faulty comprehension of the presented content is a positive and desirable part of the lesson—as much a part of learning as any other component of the lesson.

One of the finer points of teaching is learning to judge the most effective way to give feedback and correct errors. On the one hand, the teacher must provide clear, unmistakable guidance; a pupil must not be permitted to leave this part of the lesson with an uncorrected error. On the other hand, the teacher must be sure that the pupils are not embarrassed to make mistakes and be corrected. They must be guided toward the objective skill or concept in a manner that will ensure a high success rate. The objective is practiced until the teacher is satisfied that most of the pupils can do the work on their own with a reasonable expectation of success. Only then does the teacher move on to independent practice. Guided practice should not be as brief as the preceding parts but should not be any longer than absolutely necessary because pupil involvement in this part is relatively low.

Although the guided practice part is described separately from the presentation part, in actual practice, there may be some overlap between the two. Most lessons have more than one important point. The lesson should be organized so that one point is practiced and understood before the teacher moves on to the next. That is, there may be several periods of guided practice, questions, and discussion within one lesson. Note how guided practice was used in the balance lesson. Also, when pupil responses show misunderstandings, the teacher often chooses to repeat the presentation in a shortened and modified form to clarify particular points needing more emphasis.

## Independent Practice

Up to this point in the lesson, pupil involvement has been relatively low. The teacher has been showing and telling, asking questions of the whole class (but questions answered by only one child at a time), and having one pupil at a time perform guided practice. Independent practice provides a time for every child in the class to be involved to a much greater extent. To be effective, independent practice must provide each child an opportunity to think about, try, rehearse, apply, or otherwise internalize the new skill or concept set out in the lesson objective. An independent practice that lets pupils practice a skill 10 times is more effective than one that lets them practice it 5 times. Practice means multiple applications or trials.

Before setting the class to work on this part of the lesson, the teacher must give clear directions and be sure that everyone understands what is to be done and what kind of general behavior is expected. At all times during a lesson, all pupils should understand what they are supposed to be doing, especially during independent practice. Depending on the complexity of the task and on the maturity of the pupils, procedural directions for going about the task may be presented as a series of steps during the guided practice part of the lesson. The teacher who doesn't think through the planning of this part will have to interrupt the pupils after they have started in order to clarify the procedure and give further directions. This type of distraction diverts pupils from the main objective and should be avoided if at all possible.

An example from the balance lesson may clarify the difference between the substantive learning tasks and the procedural tasks of independent practice. The substantive task (in every lesson) is to practice the new skills or ideas; in this case, it is to put the balance together, learn the names of the parts, and recognize how to produce certain positions by placing objects in the pans (see the lesson objectives). The procedural task is how to practice the task. Directions given by the teacher might include the following:

**Listen carefully so you will know what to do. Stay on the rug until I give the signal. First, you will return to your seats. Then you will work with your partner to put your balance together. Look at my balance to see how it goes together. [Give each child a worksheet.] Look at the pictures. Your job is to find how many blocks it takes in each pan to make the balance look like each picture. When you find out, write the number on your paper to show how many blocks you used. Let's do the first one together. [Teacher shows with demonstration balance.] Now, how many blocks are in this pan? [One.] Fine. Now write a "one" there on your paper. How many blocks in the other pan? [None.] OK. Then write a zero**

on that pan. You may talk quietly with your partner, but please do not leave your seat. If you need help, raise your hand. Who remembers the first thing you will do? [And so on.]

In this example, the independent practice involved working with a partner and using real objects. Sometimes the work will be only paperwork; sometimes the work will be done alone, with a partner, or in a group. In every case, the level of engagement will be high. Each pupil will be doing things directly and actively, more so than at any other time in the lesson. For this reason, independent practice should get the lion's share of the lesson time.

The teacher is also active during this part of the lesson, walking around, noticing who is having trouble, giving advice as needed, providing a word of praise here or there, and speaking to any pupil who is not being productive. Comments are made quietly to individuals and only as needed, without interrupting the whole class. The effective teacher knows when to be quiet and let the pupils work.

### Closure

To bring closure means to end the lesson in an orderly way, usually with a short summary or reminder of what the lesson was about. You should allow time for materials to be put away by the children, for things to be turned in if necessary, and possibly for questions and comments from the pupils about the lesson. If there is to be a related lesson at a later time, you may choose to mention it briefly. Closure functions to "clear the decks" for the next lesson or activity in a logical and orderly fashion.

## Assessment

How do you recognize a successful lesson? If, on the whole, the pupils can do the objective behaviors, the lesson is a success. The importance of clearly stating worthwhile objectives becomes more apparent in this context. The clearer the statement of the objective, the easier assessment is. It is often not possible to make a thorough and systematic evaluation of each student during the course of a lesson. The main need at this time is to determine whether enough of the pupils "got it" to continue with the next lesson of the unit or sequence or whether the lesson "bombed" and needs rethinking, replanning, and reteaching.

Lesson assessment is not so much evaluation of the pupils as evaluation of yourself as a teacher. If the lesson failed, what was the reason? Was it too hard for the pupils? Maybe it was too easy. Boredom with overly easy tasks can result in misbehavior. Was something overlooked? Were behavior standards appropriate for the type of activity? When a lesson fails, you must take the responsibility to decide what went wrong and to correct the problem in the next lesson.

In the sample lesson, pupil achievement was assessed by informal observation and checking worksheets. Informal observation is not difficult when the pupils are working with concrete materials. Ms. Oldhand notices which pairs are having trouble putting their balances together as she circulates during the independent practice.

It is seldom necessary to have an activity separate from the learning activities to decide whether a lesson was successful. In the balance lesson, Ms. Oldhand is appraising at the same time that the pupils are learning. In this case, her informal observations are augmented by checking the worksheets. The pupils' responses there will tell her who understands how to get the balance to do various things.

## ■ TALKING IT OVER

Mr. Newman observed the balance lesson in Ms. Oldhand's classroom, and the two discussed it after the pupils left for the day.

MR. NEWMAN: I noticed that you laid out the balances on the desks before the children came back from lunch. Why didn't you just let them pick them up after the guided practice?

MS. OLDHAND: Well, I do want them to learn to manage their materials eventually. I just thought it would be too much for them to handle this first time. I did have them take care of cleanup. Next time we use the balances, I'll let them do the whole thing. Today, the length of the lesson was just about right. Any more would have taken too long, and they might not have had time to finish.

MR. NEWMAN: Why did you have them come up to the front rug? Couldn't you show them just as well if they were in their seats?

MS. OLDHAND: Not really. These children are only seven years old, remember. They wouldn't have the maturity to ignore the materials on their desks while we did the first parts of the lesson. Something I learned the hard way was never to expect children to pay attention or listen when interesting materials are within reach. Come to think of it, that's pretty hard even for grownups.

# A POSTSCRIPT ON PREPARATION

When a beginning teacher observes an experienced teacher conduct a lesson that flows smoothly with few interruptions and little off-task behavior, the novice is often unaware of the amount of planning and preparation that have gone into the lesson. Although experienced teachers seldom need the detailed lesson plans that student teachers are required to make, inquiry will reveal that the experienced teacher is clear about what to do, how to do it, and what the expectations for the pupils are. The student teacher, because of inexperience, needs to think specifically about all these details in advance in order to minimize the number of unpleasant surprises during the lesson. The lesson plan helps to structure this specific thinking. A well-designed lesson plan, backed by well-prepared materials, gives the inexperienced teacher a feeling of confidence and being in control that is communicated to pupils and prevents many of the behavior problems that new teachers dread.

# ■ MS. OLDHAND'S LESSON ON LINE GRAPHING

Ms. Oldhand was planning a lesson for her sixth graders to introduce them to line graphing. Line graphs are a powerful means of displaying information. Patterns and trends that are difficult to discern by looking at raw data become immediately apparent when presented in graphic form. Learning to construct and interpret graphs is an essential element of scientific literacy, as graphs appear frequently in newspapers, magazines, television programs, and other means of mass communication.

The pupils in Ms. Oldhand's class had done many bar graphs and recently learned about circle graphs. Ms. Oldhand carefully developed the pupils' understanding of how to make and use these types of graphs, and when to select one over the other for a particular purpose. They knew, for example, that bar graphs are useful for showing distributions of things or events (e.g., how many of their birthdays fall in each month of the year) or for indicating which kinds of animals are most popular as pets. They also understood that circle, or "pie," graphs are useful to show the percentages of different parts that go together to make up a whole object, class, or situation. For example, one of the circle graphs they constructed showed the different percentages of pupils in the class who walk to school, who ride bikes, who come by private car, by school bus, and by city bus.

In this lesson, Ms. Oldhand helped the pupils learn to make line graphs. Because this lesson is the first on line graphs, she didn't try to teach them everything there is to know about the topic. She simplified many of the technical details by the way she presented the task. Ms. Oldhand didn't expect the pupils to learn how to create a scale (how many units of measure to represent by one square on the grid). She didn't expect them to understand or remember the names for the kinds of variables (independent and dependent). And she didn't expect them to use the terms $x$ axis and $y$ axis at this time. Ms. Oldhand simply provided other details of this kind during this first lesson on line graphing so that the amount of new material to master was not overwhelming. As sixth graders, Ms. Oldhand's pupils already knew a great many prerequisites for this lesson. In addition to knowing about other kinds of graphs, they were familiar with ordered pairs of numbers, number lines, and counting by 2s, 5s, 10s, and 100s. They also knew how to use the metric system for simple measurements.

In a recent science activity, the pupils collected data on how high balls bounce when dropped from certain heights. Ms. Oldhand used that experience to make the introduction to line graphing more concrete. Her main goal for the lesson was for the pupils to see and appreciate the line graph as a powerful tool for communicating information and predicting what would be shown if additional data were available.

Ms. Oldhand used three different situations for graphing in this lesson. First, during the presentation, she showed the class how to make a line graph, using data the pupils had collected earlier on the bounciness of a table-tennis ball. Then for guided practice, she showed them a setup for testing how much a rubber band is stretched when weights are added. With data previously collected on the stretching setup, Ms. Oldhand guided the pupils to make a class graph using the overhead projector. Finally, she distributed a worksheet for independent practice. It consisted of a labeled grid, a set of data for graphing, and some questions. The pupils were to graph the data on the grid and then use the graph to answer the questions. The subject of the graph, the growth of a plant, was new to the pupils.

LESSON PLAN 4.2

**Note to Instructor.**
This lesson plan can be adapted as an in-class activity for professional development of preservice and in-service teachers.

# COMMUNICATING AND PREDICTING WITH LINE GRAPHS

## NSE STANDARDS

(5–8) Use mathematics to present, organize, and interpret data (NRC, 1996, p. 148).

## GRADE LEVEL: 6

## GOAL: LEARN TO CONSTRUCT AND INTERPRET LINE GRAPHS

## OBJECTIVES

At the end of this lesson, the pupil will be able to

1. locate points on a grid to represent pairs of observations,
2. connect the located points with a smooth line,
3. describe an unfamiliar system from a graph of that system, and
4. make predictions using a line graph.

## MATERIALS

*For the teacher:*

Overhead projector
Grid transparencies (labeled but not plotted)

    a. Bounciness (see Figure 4.2)
    b. Stretchiness of rubber band (see Figure 4.4)

Transparency marker
Two meter sticks
One table-tennis ball
A rubber band stretcher (see Figure 4.3)
Bounciness data (see Table 4.1)
Rubber band data (see Table 4.2)

*For each pupil:*

One plant-growth worksheet (see Figure 4.5)
One worksheet with questions (see Figure 4.6)

## MATERIALS PREPARATION

1. Tape two meter sticks to the wall vertically, one above the other, to measure distances from the floor. Both sticks should have the low numbers below the high numbers. (Add 100 to readings of the upper stick.)
2. Set up a rubber band stretcher (as shown in Figure 4.3). Add weights and record data for the guided practice activity. Short rubber bands approach the limit of their elasticity sooner than long rubber bands and are thus better for this lesson. This apparatus must be set up well ahead of time because it provides the data for making the transparency (see Figure 4.4). Use the same setup and the same rubber band for the class activity.

## MOTIVATION

Remind the pupils that yesterday they collected data on how high different balls bounce when you drop them from certain heights, "Do you remember that I asked you to use only those heights on the chart and not to do any extras? Well, today you will find out why. I will show you how scientists are able to make predictions. Then you should be able to do it yourselves! You will check out your new powers by predicting how high a ball will bounce from some of those drop heights you didn't try yesterday, and then we will test your predictions."

## LEARNING ACTIVITIES

*Presentation*

1. Demonstrate the bouncing of the table-tennis ball as a reminder to those who did that activity or as an introduction to others.
2. Turn on the overhead projector to show the grid labeled "Bounciness" [Figure 4.2]. "I will show you how it works." Point to locations on the projection as they are mentioned. "A line graph has two number lines. The number line across the bottom includes all the values for the drop heights we want to consider. The other number line is vertical, going up the left side. It includes all the bounce heights we are interested in, not only what we observed but also a range where our predictions will fall. Now take a look at this data table for the table-tennis ball. See how the observations go in pairs? For every drop height we observed, we also observed a bounce height. The line graph lets you show a pair of observations as a single point. To locate the point for this first number pair, we go across on the drop height number line until we come to 40 centimeters. Then we go straight up until we come to the line extending from the second number of the number pair, 27, on the bounce height number line. Where these two lines intersect is our point." Make a fat dot to mark the point. Continue in this manner for the other number pairs.
3. "When you find and mark a point like this, it's called plotting the point." Continue to show and tell until you've plotted all the points. "The points are sometimes called 'plots.' Let's look at the points we've plotted. Do they seem to have any pattern or regularity?" Pause. "Let's connect them and see." Draw

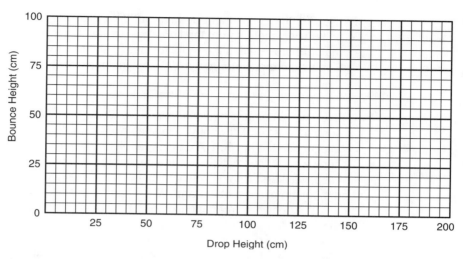

**FIGURE 4.2 Bounciness of Ball**

**TABLE 4.1 Bounciness Data**

| Drop Height (cm) | Bounce Height (cm) |
| --- | --- |
| 40 | 27 |
| 60 | 40 |
| 100 | 54 |
| 120 | 63 |
| 140 | 72 |
| 200 | 85 |

a smooth curve through the dots. "You know about the bouncing ball system because you collected the data. But just looking at the data, can you describe the system?" Take a few comments but move on rather quickly because now isn't the time for a real discussion. Mention the following generalizations if the pupils aren't forthcoming:

a. The greater the drop height, the greater is the bounce height.

b. The line looks straight at the beginning, but it begins to level off at the end. In other words, the bounciness of the table-tennis ball stays steady for a while and then begins to decrease.

4. Show pupils how to predict the bounce height for drop heights of 80 centimeters and 170 centimeters. "Find 80 on the drop height number line, from there go straight up until you reach the line we drew to connect points, and then go directly left to the bounce height number line. The reading there should be the bounce height. Enter the drop heights in the blank spaces of the table of bounciness data [Table 4.1]. Then enter in the table the values predicted from the graph, but put parentheses around them."

5. "Now for the moment of truth! Will our prediction work?" Hold the table-tennis ball 80 centimeters from the floor (next to the 80-centimeter mark of the meter rulers taped to the wall), release it, and observe the bounce height. Repeat the procedure at the 170-centimeter mark.

*Guided Practice*

1. "Now we're going to try something new." Show the rubber band stretching setup [Figure 4.3]. "I want you to see how this works. A rubber band is attached to the support. A bent paper clip is on the other end, so we can hook a paper cup onto it. Into the paper cup we'll put equal weights—in this case, washers. With no washers in the cup, I'll set the ruler so that zero is at the bottom of the rubber band. When I add a washer, the rubber band stretches down to [read measurement on the ruler]. I think you can guess that, if I add more washers, the rubber band will tend to stretch more and more. But I'm not going to show you all the data-collecting procedure just now. Instead, I'm going to put up a chart [Table 4.2] with the results I got when I did it last night. Then we'll make a graph together, using the data."
2. Project the transparency of the labeled grid [Figure 4.4] on the chalkboard. Lines and labels will be pale but visible. Ask a pupil to come up and plot the first ordered pair of observations on the projected grid by drawing on the chalkboard. Continue with other pupils for the remaining points. Be sure that the pupils remember to move "over and up" and to locate points on lines rather than between them.
3. When all the measurements have been plotted, have the next pupil draw a smooth line to connect the points.
4. Get predictions from the pupils for several intermediate points on the graph. Get a prediction for one point beyond the observations.

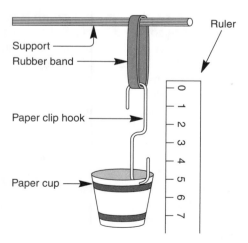

**FIGURE 4.3   A Rubber Band Stretcher**

**TABLE 4.2   Rubber Band Stretch Data**

| Number of Washers | Rubber Band Length (cm) |
|---|---|
| 0 | 0.0 |
| 5 | 2.0 |
| 10 | 6.0 |
| 15 | 10.0 |
| 20 | 13.5 |
| 25 | 15.5 |
| 30 | 17.5 |
| 35 | 18.5 |
| 40 | 19.0 |

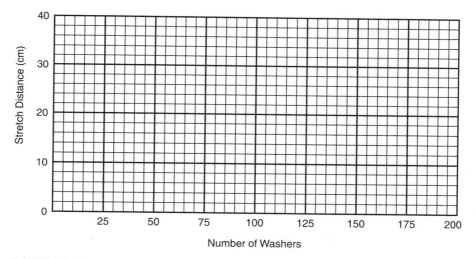

**FIGURE 4.4   Stretchiness of Rubber Band**

5. Discuss their predictions and then check the predictions by demonstrating with the rubber band setup.

*Independent Practice*

1. Distribute the plant growth worksheet labeled Growth of Mystery Plant [Figure 4.5] and give directions. Point out the Days number line across the bottom and the Height number line up the left side of the grid. Also distribute the worksheet with questions [Figure 4.6]. "Your job is to plot the points, draw a smooth line to connect points, and answer questions. You will have 15 min to do the worksheet. At 1:45 we'll stop to discuss your results and ideas."
2. Circulate and help as needed.

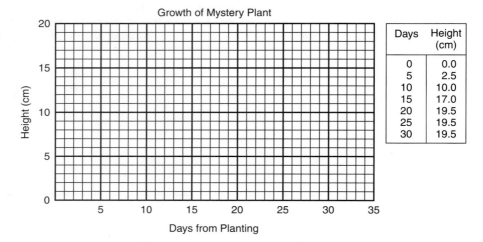

FIGURE 4.5   **Worksheet Grid and Data**

1. A seed was planted on Day 0. What day did the plant come up? _____
2. How tall was the plant on Day 10? _____
3. How tall was the plant on Day 15? _____
4. Plot the points on your grid. Then use your graph to find how tall the plant was on these days:
   • Day 8 _____
   • Day 12 _____
   • Day 14 _____
   • Day 18 _____
5. Predict how tall the plant will be on Day 35. _____
6. Write a sentence to tell what happens to the plant's growth during the last two weeks shown on the graph.

FIGURE 4.6   **Worksheet Questions**

*Closure*

1. Compare a few answers to the prediction questions. Emphasize a range of acceptable prediction values rather than a precise result, but try to identify the cause of any "wild" results.
2. Compare the pupils' speculations about possible reasons for the shape of the curve.
3. "Next time you will learn how to choose useful number line values for the two variables."

### ASSESSMENT

Observe informally during the discussions and check the pupils' worksheets.

■ **TALKING IT OVER**

Ms. Oldhand asked Mr. Newman to study the preceding lesson plan and decide whether he would like to teach it. After reading the plan, Mr. Newman had several questions.

MR. NEWMAN:     I have studied your plan, and I understand most of it. I wanted to ask about the length, first of all. It seems kind of long. I'm afraid I won't be able to keep them interested that long.

MS. OLDHAND:     Quite right. It is too long for one period. When I've taught it before, I have taken two or three 40-minute periods to do it all. And that's not counting the data collection. You look surprised.

MR. NEWMAN:     I just never thought about a lesson being longer than a period. I guess I just thought lesson and period were synonyms!

MS. OLDHAND:     Well, often they are, but they don't have to be. I find that it makes more sense to keep all the learning activities with the set of objectives they go with and call the whole thing a lesson. I expect some people do it differently. There is no shortage of ideas on how to format a lesson plan.

# THE TEACHER'S ROLE AND THE PUPILS' ROLE

When teaching a lesson, the teacher's role is far different from the teacher's role when performing other duties (e.g., lunch monitor or playground supervision). Moreover, the teacher's role is different for different types of teaching. It consists of one set of responsibilities when teaching a direct instruction lesson and another set when teaching an inquiry lesson. The nature of the pupil's responsibility also differs according to type of instruction.

When considering the roles of both teacher and pupil in direct instruction, try to keep in mind that some responsibilities will be different when other instructional methods are used. In a direct instruction lesson, the decisions for the nature, direction, and pacing of the lesson are determined by the teacher. The pupils not only have little to say about lesson decisions but also have little latitude for movement or talking. Pupil and teacher roles will be explained further in later chapters. Comparisons of the differences and similarities—along with the advantages and disadvantages of different ways of teaching—will be drawn. The following are the roles of teacher and pupil in a direct instruction lesson.

*The teacher goes from group to group during independent practice.*

## Teacher's Role in Direct Instruction

- Set and enforce behavior standards and sanctions.
- Provide direct information by telling, showing, or by other means.
- Speak clearly and as briefly as possible.
- Listen carefully and check for understanding.
- Provide hands-on experiences whenever possible during independent practice.
- Estimate beforehand a time allocation for each part of the lesson.
- Plan carefully for smooth and efficient distribution and picking up of materials, involving children when possible.

## Pupils' Role in Direct Instruction

- Follow standards at all times during a lesson.
- Pay attention when others are speaking or demonstrating.
- Follow directions.
- Ask for help if anything isn't clear.
- Answer questions when called on.

## Behavior Management

Special attention to pupil behavior may be needed when pupils are working with materials, especially if they have not had opportunities to work with interesting objects in other classes. If you have ever seen children given the opportunity to work with concrete materials, you know how keenly interested they become. This natural motivation can be harnessed to the benefit of both the lesson and the children's growth in responsibility. Simply explain, before the materials are distributed, how the materials are to be used—and perhaps give a few examples of inappropriate use. Explain that children who cannot manage their behavior while working with the materials will be separated from the materials until they are in better control. Then enforce the rule strictly, or all is lost.

## Materials Management

Using concrete materials adds some logistical concerns that must be carefully planned, like any other aspect of a lesson. It is an absolute must for you to try out ahead of time the demonstrations and activities with the actual materials to be used. Attempting to "wing it" with untried materials or with last-minute changes is one of the most frequent causes of lesson failure among beginning science teachers. The method of distribution and cleanup must also be carefully planned.

## Verbal Techniques

Giving information and giving directions are important techniques in every teacher's repertoire. Although the two tasks may seem different, they have many similarities. Listening is hard work for children. The teacher should not rely on a child's being able to understand from the spoken word alone. Here is a short list of tips for giving information and directions:

- Keep comments brief. Attention span for spoken language is very short.
- Be clear. Think and plan ahead for clarity.
- Ask children to repeat instructions or information back to you. This is feasible when the comments are as brief as they should be.
- Model both procedural information and lesson content. Use props and body actions to help children understand.
- For all but the youngest children list key words of the directions or information for them to read and refer to later.
- Establish an atmosphere in which the children feel safe in asking questions. Then be sure to solicit questions before assuming that everyone understands.

In other words, directions as well as lesson content should be taught rather than simply told. In summarizing a large body of teacher effectiveness research, Brophy and Good (1987) described the actions of good classroom managers: Effective managers not only told their students what they expected but also modeled correct procedures for them, took time to answer questions, and, if necessary, arranged for the students to practice the procedures and get feedback. In short, key procedures were formally taught to students, just as academic content was taught.

In the context of this chapter, note that giving directions for a new procedure should be taught directly, using elements of the direct instruction model. For very young children, it may be necessary to prepare an entire lesson on the new procedure, applying all the lesson parts. Older children may be able to understand with just a few of the lesson parts. As a beginning teacher, you will need to decide how much teaching is needed in order for your pupils to learn a new procedure. Assuming that children will be able to carry out new procedures without special instruction is risky.

## MODIFYING THE DIRECT INSTRUCTION FORMAT

Up to this point, only the standard model for direct instruction has been described and illustrated. This model is a useful starting point for beginning teachers. Once you get a feel for the function of each part, you can begin to consider modifications in certain situations.

An experienced teacher can usually make effective judgments about when and when not to modify the way direct presentation is made. A beginning teacher may not be able to do so. A common difficulty that beginning teachers have is in trying to get pupils to "figure out" or discover names or procedures. Examples of procedural objectives are how to line up for cafeteria, how to draw a graph, and how to focus a microscope. Although the intention to have a discovery lesson is commendable, asking pupils to guess names or procedures ("It starts with a B") simply slows down a lesson and wastes time without providing any benefits. Furthermore, having to guess names of things can be confusing to pupils because it emphasizes the name rather than the idea. It is better to be straightforward and supply the name and spend instructional time on helping the children understand the idea.

## ■ SUMMARY

Research has shown that psychomotor skills, factual knowledge, and procedures not requiring deep understanding can be taught effectively by direct instruction. The research results are best established for teaching in the lower grades; continuing research may show a similar relationship for teaching in the higher grades. Some educators are reluctant to use the term teacher effectiveness for this body of research because it looks only at pupil achievement and says nothing about affective and personal development—areas that are often included as educational goals.

The main strength of the direct instruction model is its systematic treatment of elements known to be important in basic skill learning. Inexperienced teachers increase their success rate by using this model because it reduces the number of judgments and complex teacher behaviors required. Teaching is a complex business under any conditions; the direct instruction model simplifies it a bit, with the result that new teachers have fewer lesson failures. With success comes confidence and the beginning of insight into the effects of particular teacher behaviors. With insight comes the beginning of conscious self-control of teacher behaviors to produce the pupil effects desired in a given situation. At that point, the teacher can begin to recognize some of the limitations of the direct instruction model and to consider alternatives.

# ■ ACTIVITIES FOR THE READER

Some ideas for lessons are given here. Select one or more to develop, using the direct instruction model described in this chapter. Then form a discussion group in class with others who considered the same idea. Finally, present to the whole class your group's pros and cons of various ways to present the lesson idea.

> **Note to Instructor.**
> In many schools the phrase "The pupil will be able to. . . ." following the word "Objective:" is standard usage and is required of teachers in their lesson plans.

1. *Planet names.* Objective: Name the planets in the order of their distance from the sun (Mercury, Venus, Earth, Mars, Jupiter, Saturn, Uranus, Neptune, and Pluto). Use the mnemonic "My very educated mouse jumped suddenly under Nathan's pizza" (or make up your own). Include instruction to aid in remembering the order of the planets whose names have the same initial letter.

2. *Learning to read a thermometer and relate the reading to temperature as sensed by touch.* Objectives: (a) describe in words (cold/colder, hot/hotter, or cold/hot) the temperature of two objects of very different temperatures by touch alone and (b) describe the effect of change in temperature on a thermometer as movement up or down (e.g., when it gets hot, the mercury in the thermometer goes up). Materials could be chilled water from a drinking fountain, warm water from the hot-water tap, and a thermometer with label tape over the numbers. The label could be marked to show change.

3. *Classifying.* Objectives: (a) learn to pick a characteristic by which a set of objects can be sorted into two groups—those that have the characteristic and those that do not; and (b) reclassify the same objects by a different characteristic and tell what the characteristic is. Materials could be unshelled peanuts, flowers, leaves, sea shells, or buttons—any set of things that has sufficient variety to permit multiple classifications. Pupils should be encouraged to use their own ideas for sorting but must be able to defend their categories without switching them during a sort. For example, a first sort of buttons could be into groups of two holes and more than two holes. A second sort of the same set could be into blue buttons and nonblue buttons.

# ■ QUESTIONS FOR DISCUSSION

1. What are the differences between teaching by telling and direct instruction?

2. How can the degree of pupil engagement in a particular instructional activity guide the teacher's decision about pacing and time spent on the activity?

3. Explain differences between individual pupil evaluation and lesson assessment. Why not do a thorough pupil evaluation for every lesson?

4. What are (a) some signs and (b) possible causes of lesson failure?

# ■ REFERENCES

Brophy, J., & Evertson, C. (1976). *Learning from teaching: A developmental perspective*. Boston: Allyn & Bacon.

Brophy, J., & Good, T. (1987). Teacher behavior and student achievement. In M. C. Wittrock (Ed.), *Handbook of research on teaching* (3rd ed., pp. 328–375). Upper Saddle River, NJ: Merrill/Prentice Hall.

National Research Council. (1996). *National science education standards*. Washington, DC: National Academy Press.

Rosenshine, B., & Stevens, R. (1987). Teaching functions. In M. C. Wittrock (Ed.), *Handbook of research on teaching* (3rd ed., pp. 376–391). Upper Saddle River, NJ: Merrill/Prentice Hall.

Smith, L., & Land, M. (1981). Low-inference verbal behaviors related to teacher clarity. *Journal of Classroom Interaction, 17,* 37–42.

# Teaching Science as Inquiry

■  MS. OLDHAND:    Last week you observed the class while I conducted a direct instruction lesson. Today you will be able to observe a guided inquiry lesson.

MR. NEWMAN:    Would you explain just what *inquiry* means and whatever happened to the processes of science that used to be the basis for science lessons?

MS. OLDHAND:    You sound like my sixth graders, who always seem to ask me more than one question at a time! To answer your first question, *inquiry* is the process of asking a question, designing and carrying out an investigation, interpreting the results, and presenting the results to others. It includes all the science processes, but the processes themselves are not the focus of the lesson.

MR. NEWMAN:    How do children carry out inquiry if they don't know the basic science processes of observing, communicating, measuring, and so on?

MS. OLDHAND:    As much as possible, we teach those processes in the context of learning science concepts, but we also teach skills separately, as you saw in the lesson on the balance [see Chapter 4]. In the lessons on mealworms you'll see how science processes are integrated into an inquiry lesson, and afterward we can talk about it.

Y ou have already learned about a teaching method called *direct instruction*. The rationale for direct instruction is that it is efficient and has been shown to achieve the stated objectives. The method introduced in this chapter is called *inquiry-based instruction,* or, simply, *inquiry.* In Chapter 1 you saw that, in the NSE Standards, the National Research Council (NRS, 1996) recommends this method for teaching science at all levels. The rationale for inquiry is that learning is more meaningful and lasting if children are given opportunities to ask questions, explore materials, gather data, come to conclusions, and discuss results. It is not as efficient as direct instruction, but it leads to deeper understanding. This method does not follow exact procedures and requires more skill in classroom management and assessment of learning than does direct instruction, but there are special reasons for choosing such a method that more than compensate for the difficulties. Inquiry-based science capitalizes on children's natural curiosity about interesting objects. It results in a type of knowing that is not memory of disembodied words from a book but a fully integrated part of the learner. The difference between knowledge derived from active learning and knowledge derived passively is the difference between *knowing something* as opposed to *knowing about something.*

**TABLE 5.1   Changing Emphases to Promote Inquiry**

| Less Emphasis On . . . | More Emphasis On . . . |
| --- | --- |
| Knowing scientific facts and information | Understanding scientific concepts and developing abilities of inquiry |
| Studying subject matter disciplines (physical, life, earth sciences) for their own sake | Learning subject matter disciplines in the context of inquiry, technology, science in personal and social perspectives, and history and nature of science |
| Separating science knowledge and science process | Integrating all aspects of science content |
| Covering many science topics | Studying a few fundamental science concepts |
| Implementing inquiry as a set of processes | Implementing inquiry as instructional strategies, abilities, and ideas to be learned |

*Source:* Reprinted with permission from NATIONAL SCIENCE EDUCATION STANDARDS. Copyright 1996 by the National Academy of Sciences. Courtesy of the National Academy Press, Washington, D.C.

Hands-on experiences are part of inquiry teaching in the elementary school, but inquiry is much more than just hands-on experiences. Other essential steps, even for children in the early grades, are asking questions and reflecting on the hands-on activity by comparing, looking for patterns, predicting, and making trial explanations. The knowledge acquired from working with and acting on objects becomes the building blocks with which children construct knowledge that truly belongs to them. Duckworth, Easley, Hawkins, and Henriques (1990) give an eloquent and practical description of this kind of teaching with many examples taken from their work in classrooms. Their book contains suggestions for a broad range of topics that interest children and lead to the development of knowledge. The concept of inquiry-based teaching may become clearer to you as you study the two lists in Table 5.1, showing the changes in emphasis recommended in the NSE Standards (NRC, 1996). The shift in focus is from other methods of science teaching toward inquiry-based instruction.

# Guiding Children into Inquiry

Many attempts at using inquiry methods have failed because children did not receive the initial guidance they needed. In reaction to the excesses of traditional instruction in which children were passive receivers of information, enthusiastic teachers sometimes overcompensate by giving children more freedom than they can handle. *Guided inquiry* avoids both of these extremes and helps children acquire the habits and ways of thinking that they can use later in independent investigations. Guidance is accomplished through the initial selection of materials, the type of data children will collect, and, especially, through skillful use of discussion techniques. By using indirect guidance and suggestions, the teacher increases the likelihood of outcomes that are both interesting and worthwhile.

An aspect of guidance that is essential to the success of inquiry teaching involves helping children become more responsible for their behaviors and their own learning. Children who are accustomed to listening to the teacher, to reading from science textbooks, and to filling in worksheets as the main or only classroom science activities will not automatically function well at this higher level of independence and responsibility; they must be taught how. Behavior standards provide children a way to decide for themselves whether a behavior is acceptable. Most children are not mature enough to judge without a standard; having a standard allows them to practice regulating their own behavior. Teaching new behavior standards can be done in a direct instruction format. Once the standards have been learned, children practice applying them to their behavior in the limited freedom of the guided inquiry lesson and gradually become able to regulate their own behavior, with occasional reminders, with less and less guidance.

## PLANNING AND PRESENTING A GUIDED INQUIRY LESSON

Guided inquiry lessons, like direct instruction lessons, can be structured as lesson plan parts, each with its specific function. Some of the parts are the same in both methods, but the learning activities are different.

### Comparison of Direct Instruction and Guided Inquiry Lesson Plans

In Chapter 4 you learned to structure a lesson for direct instruction. Guided inquiry lessons also need to be structured, but there are more options to choose from, based on the particular goals of the lesson. Consider a generic lesson-plan format:

**All-Purpose Lesson Plan Format**
1. Learning Objectives
2. Materials
3. Motivation
4. Learning Activities
5. Assessment

Every lesson plan needs objectives, a list of materials, something to interest and motivate pupils, and a way to assess learning and evaluate the lesson. Every lesson plan also needs learning activities, but their type and sequence depend on the method to be used and the nature of the lesson goals. Now examine the differences in the type and sequence of learning activities in direct instruction and guided inquiry.

| **Direct Instruction** | **Guided Inquiry** |
|---|---|
| 1. Student objectives | 1. Student objectives |
| 2. Materials | 2. Materials |
| 3. Motivation | 3. Motivation |
| 4. Learning activities | 4. Learning activities |
|    a. Presentation |    a. Questions |
|    b. Guided practice |    b. Data collection |
|    c. Independent practice |    c. Data processing, checking, and interpreting |
|    d. Closure |    d. Closure |
| 5. Assessment | 5. Assessment |

Note that everything in the two outlines is the same except for the central section of the learning activities. The new parts that make guided discovery possible are described in the next section.

# Parts of Guided Inquiry Lesson Plans

## Question(s)

Inquiry lessons start with a question. It may be one that the teacher suggests or one that the pupils themselves ask. In the example beginning on p. 114, Ms. Oldhand asks the children to observe and then tell what they have noticed. She asks the question herself because she is just getting the children started on a new unit. As she later said to Mr. Newman, she wanted to demonstrate that there are degrees of freedom for the children; a new teacher—such as Mr. Newman—may have to ease into this way of teaching.

## Data Collection

*Data collection* simply means gathering information needed to answer the question. The information may be recorded as a list of words describing an object or event or as numbers representing measurements. Data (the plural of the Latin word *datum*) may be recorded in many different ways, not only as words or numbers. Data can be collected as sound recordings, pictures, impressions in stone, or in countless other ways. In any case, data collecting involves making and usually recording observations. Data are records of observations involving the senses: sounds, touches, tastes, smells, and visual observations. In some situations, especially with younger children, data may not be physically recorded but simply reported during discussion. Guesses, predictions, speculations, inferences, conclusions, and other mental constructions go beyond observation and are, therefore, not examples of data.

### Data Processing

Now that the data have been collected (i.e., the observations have been made), what happens to the data? First, the data should be checked to see that children in the same group agree on the information they have collected and that discrepancies or differences are acknowledged as something to consider. Data should be displayed or reported orally to be available for discussion and interpretation.

Once their observations have been made and recorded, pupils need guidance in thinking about those observations. Teachers must guide children in using their observations to arrive at inferences, speculations, and generalizations and otherwise engage in higher level thinking. Guided inquiry stimulates thinking that goes beyond reporting observations. With younger children, the discussion may be limited mostly to describing and comparing the objects observed. Older children can begin to do more powerful thinking. Leading a discussion indirectly to help children think about observations and connect these observations logically with prior knowledge is itself a higher level skill. The idea, after all, is for the children to reflect on their recent experience, not to read the teacher's face. Another way to think about this part of the lesson is in terms of the type of knowledge for which it is designed. In Chapter 1 you were introduced to four kinds of knowledge: arbitrary, physical, logical, and social interactive. Data collecting involves acquiring physical knowledge; data processing should lead toward understanding and the construction of logical knowledge.

### Closure

Leaving time to bring the discussion to a close is important. Several children may be asked to summarize what they have learned. Remaining questions may be called for and written on the chalkboard, to be saved for the next lesson. The point is to take a few minutes to help the pupils consolidate what they have learned and think ahead a bit to the next lesson in the unit.

### Assessment

Assessment is not described here because it is the subject of Chapter 6.

# APPLICATION OF INQUIRY

The following investigation is for you to carry out in class. It is similar to those in Chapter 3, but now you have learned more about inquiry and can think about what you will be doing in a more knowledgeable way. After you have carried out this investigation you will learn how Ms. Oldhand guided her third graders in a two-part unit as they investigated mealworms.

## Observing a Mealworm

### Objectives

1. Gain confidence in handling a mealworm.
2. Describe the general appearance and behavior of a mealworm.

### Materials

*For each student:*

Mealworm in a paper cup
One magnifier
Drawing paper

> **Resource Materials Note.** Mealworms can be obtained for a few cents each at pet stores, where you can also obtain advice on their care and handling.

### Materials

*For the teacher:*

Enlarged photo of a mealworm

### Question to Investigate

What can you find out about the appearance and behavior of a mealworm?

### The Investigation

Step 1. Use a magnifier to examine details of the mealworm's anatomy.
Step 2. Describe in writing specific details of the mealworm's anatomy, such as number of legs, number of segments, and appearance of mouth parts.
Step 3. Describe the way a mealworm walks.
Step 4. Make a large drawing of a mealworm.
Step 5. Post drawings and compare with those of classmates.
Step 6. Participate in class discussion of what has been learned.

### Assessment

Compare each drawing with an enlarged photograph of a mealworm.

---

Now that you have carried out this investigation yourself look at Ms. Oldhand's first lesson plan (Lesson Plan 5.1) for the unit. Then consider how she implemented it.

*These boys are getting a closer look at their mealworm.*

## GETTING TO KNOW YOUR MEALWORM

### NSE STANDARD

Characteristics of organisms (NRC, 1996, p. 127).

### GRADE LEVEL: 3

### OBJECTIVES

1. Gain confidence in handling a mealworm (affective objective).
2. Describe the general appearance and behavior of a mealworm (cognitive objective).

### MATERIALS

*For each pupil:*

One mealworm in a paper cup

### MOTIVATION

"Look at what I have in my hand."

### LEARNING ACTIVITIES

*Data Collection:*

Give directions such as "See what you can notice."
Allow 15 minutes.
Collect materials.

*Data Processing:*

Ask questions such as
"What did you notice about your mealworm?"
"Did anyone notice something different?"
"What else would you like to find out about your mealworm?"
Write several of the ideas on chart paper.

### CLOSURE

"Tomorrow we will take a closer look at our mealworms."

### ASSESSMENT

Informal observation.

---

# IMPLEMENTING LESSON PLAN 5.1

Introducing a guided inquiry lesson requires an explanation of some science activity standards because this kind of work will be new to the pupils. In addition, the pupils need to be familiarized generally with what the unit will cover and what they will be doing.

## ■ MS. OLDHAND'S INTRODUCTION OF THE UNIT

"Today we will begin a new science unit," Ms. Oldhand told her pupils, "but first we must discuss behavior standards for science." She brought out a chart on which she had written the following standards.

---

**Science Activity Standards**

1. You may talk quietly.
2. Stay in your seat.
3. Raise your hand if you need help.
4. Stop, look, and listen at the signal.

---

Ms. Oldhand explained the standards to her third graders and checked to be sure that each pupil understood them. For standard 4, she said that when she needed to speak to them she would sound the chime. The class already knew this signal because she had used it previously in similar circumstances. "Working directly with the materials is a privilege for those who are grown up enough to remember the standards," she said. "If you forget, I will have to take away your materials until you are ready to be more responsible."

Ms. Oldhand also explained that she would need some help in distributing and collecting materials and that she would appoint a helper, or monitor, at each table. "You will take turns being monitors," she said. "Each week, I will appoint a new monitor for each table, so everyone will have a chance to be a helper."

Ms. Oldhand took a mealworm from the container on her desk. "Look at what I have in my hand. It isn't harmful in any way, but it is a living creature with feelings, so we must be careful not to hurt it. It is called a mealworm, and each of you will have one to observe. See what you can notice. After a while, I will give the signal, and then we'll discuss what everyone noticed about their mealworms."

She passed among the children, placing a paper cup containing a mealworm on each pupil's desk. There was a great deal of interest, but some of the children seemed reluctant to touch their specimens. Ms. Oldhand did not insist that they do so, and after a few minutes of poking their worms with pencils, the reluctant children gradually became confident enough to touch and handle them directly. Ms. Oldhand walked among the pupils, sharing their excitement and listening to their comments.

The room was arranged in groups of four double desks, with eight pupils to a "table." After about 15 minutes, she sounded the chime. Most of the class remembered to look up from their mealworms; the others did so as soon as they heard her begin to speak. "Thank you for remembering the special science standards so well! Please take a minute to place all your mealworms in the paper cup and then put the cup back in the center of your table." Ms. Oldhand then asked the table monitors to collect the cups and place them on her desk.

"What were some things you noticed?" Ms. Oldhand called on several pupils to share their observations. "Did anyone notice how many legs there were?" Some thought there were one number, some another. "Well! Do you suppose that all mealworms have the same number of legs or that maybe some are different? Let's think about how we could find out. Did anyone notice other things?" Discussion revealed that most of the children did not notice fine details, being more interested in how the mealworms moved and how they reacted to pokes and other stimuli. "What are some things you'd like to investigate with your mealworms next time?" Ms. Oldhand asked. Several ideas were offered, and Ms. Oldhand listed them on chart paper. "Fine," she said. "Let's be thinking about how we might find out some of these things. Tomorrow we will decide what to do next."

## ■ TALKING IT OVER

MS. OLDHAND:    Mr. Newman, I wanted you to know that I included the strict behavior standards for your benefit. When I am just teaching my pupils without your being here, I can be a bit more relaxed. I even let them move around the room. Student teachers usually need more structure, though.

MR. NEWMAN:    Thanks. I appreciate seeing how you did it. I feel really insecure trying to think about how to present this method and how to prevent behavior problems at the same time.

MS. OLDHAND:    [Smiling] You will soon internalize how to do that and forget that you ever needed this technique.

MR. NEWMAN:    When I looked at what was happening as a pupil, it was fun, but when I think about teaching it, I get nervous because I don't understand how it works. Like the questions about the number of legs. If it's important for them to know, why didn't you just tell them, or settle it in some way? It seemed like a lot of questions came up that didn't get settled.

MS. OLDHAND:    The main goal of this lesson was just to get started—to get the "new" off the mealworms. In particular, I wanted everyone to get comfortable with handling the mealworms. Now they all know that the worms don't bite and that they don't move suddenly. In fact, mealworms don't do much of anything very startling. Because the students know that from their own experience, they now will be able to turn their attention to more specific observations and tasks. Later in the unit, we will decide together how to answer some of the questions. What they find out by observing, like the number of legs, is less important than the act of finding out for themselves.

MR. NEWMAN:    I'm not sure I know how to decide what's more and less important.

*Getting to know his mealworm.*

MS. OLDHAND:     This lesson was more process than content. I wanted them to work on the skills of observing and communicating. You may understand better if you study my lesson plan for this lesson.

The next morning, Mr. Newman spoke to Ms. Oldhand before class began.

MR. NEWMAN:     I have thought about the lesson I observed yesterday and how processes and content were integrated. Although I studied your lesson plan, I still don't understand exactly how to do this in a lesson.

MS. OLDHAND:     Here is the beginning of my plan for the second lesson. I have the topic and a set of objectives. Why don't you try writing the rest of the plan? You'd better take a couple of mealworms and a magnifier with you tonight, too.

MR. NEWMAN:     Really? Do I need to do that?

MS. OLDHAND:     How much do you know about mealworms? You have about a 200 percent better chance of planning a successful lesson if you have thoroughly experienced what you want the pupils to do and have tried out everything with the specific materials you plan to use.

# Thinking about What Comes Next

The lesson you have just studied is the beginning of a unit that Ms. Oldhand planned. She wanted the lessons to relate to one another in a logical way, with the skills and concepts developed in the earlier lessons to be used and further developed in the later lessons. To begin thinking about lesson sequence and learning activities to provide instruction for given objectives, you are invited to try your hand at lesson planning. Figure 5.1 shows the beginning of Ms. Oldhand's plan for the second lesson of the unit. How would you complete it?

Ms. Oldhand's second lesson plan (Lesson Plan 5.2) for the unit follows. Compare it with the plan you developed for this lesson. Note that it contains all the elements of an inquiry lesson plan as outlined previously.

Topic: A closer look at mealworms
(Lesson 2 of unit)

Student Objectives

By the end of these activities, the learner should be able to

1. Use a magnifier to examine details of mealworm anatomy.

2. Describe specific details of mealworm anatomy, such as number of legs, number of segments and appearance of mouth parts.

3. Describe or enact the way a mealworm walks.

4. Construct an enlarged drawing of a mealworm.

5. Compare his/her own drawing with an enlarged photograph of a mealworm and explain how to resolve disagreements between the two (by rechecking the real mealworm).

**FIGURE 5.1   Beginning of Ms. Oldhand's Plan for the Second Lesson of the Mealworm Unit**

## A CLOSER LOOK AT MEALWORMS

### NSE STANDARD

Characteristics of organisms (NRC, 1996, p. 127).

### GRADE LEVEL: 3

### OBJECTIVES

1. Use a magnifier to examine details of the mealworm's anatomy.
2. Describe specific details of the mealworm's anatomy, such as number of legs, number of segments, and appearance of mouth parts.
3. Describe or act out the way a mealworm walks.
4. Make a large drawing of a mealworm.
5. Compare their drawings with an enlarged photograph of a mealworm and explain how to resolve disagreements between the two (by rechecking the real mealworm).
6. Cooperate with partners and monitors.

(Note that these objectives are from the cognitive process, cognitive content, social, and psychomotor domains.)

### MATERIALS

*For each pupil:*

One mealworm in a paper cup
One magnifier
One sheet of drawing paper

*For each four pupils:*

One set of crayons

*For the teacher:*

Enlarged photo of a mealworm

### MOTIVATION

"Today we will be observing our mealworms with magnifiers."

### LEARNING ACTIVITIES

Recall questions from previous lesson.

"Here is the list of questions you had at the end of our last lesson. Does anyone want to add any other questions to this list?"

*Data Collection:*

1. Give directions such as: "Look for answers to your questions and see what new details you can notice."
2. Distribute mealworms and magnifiers by monitors.
3. Allow 15 minutes.
4. Monitors collect mealworms, magnifiers, and crayons.

*Data Processing:*

1. Have pupils describe findings by asking them questions such as "What new details did you notice?" "How many legs?" "How many segments?"
2. Ask volunteers to act out how a mealworm walks. Discuss their demonstrations.
3. Have pupils compare drawings with the photo and ask for comments on discrepancies between their drawings and the photo. List these on chart paper to refer to at the next lesson.

## CLOSURE

"We will use this list next time as a guide to find out more. How do you think we will do it? Look at our real mealworms to decide."

## ASSESSMENT

Apply behavior checklist, review written observations and drawings in workbooks (note careful and accurate versus fanciful entries), and describe pupil answers and comments during discussion.

# IMPLEMENTING THE SECOND LESSON PLAN

Implementing the second lesson plan of the mealworms unit involves a brief review of the behavior standards and of the first lesson. It also involves motivating the pupils to build on what they learned in further discovery.

## ■ MS. OLDHAND'S MOTIVATION OF THE PUPILS

Ms. Oldhand picked up a magnifier and a mealworm from her desk. "Today we will look at our mealworms with magnifiers." She held the mealworm in the palm of one hand and used the magnifier to peer at it. The pupils watched with interest. Ms. Oldhand congratulated the pupils on what good scientists they had been.

She thanked them for making science period pleasant by remembering the special behavior standards. She then reviewed the standards with the class and asked them if they remembered what would happen if they forgot to stay seated. "You have to lose your mealworm for a while," replied one child. "And what happens if you forget to keep your talking quiet?" she asked. In this way, she went through the standards with the children to help them remember. Then she went on to give directions for the day's activity.

"The next thing we will do with our mealworms is something very interesting. Yesterday you noticed certain things about your mealworms, and you had some questions about other things that you would like to know. I saved your questions and have put them on the chalkboard to help you remember what they were. Today we will use magnifiers to help you notice new things. In a few minutes, I will also give you some drawing materials so that you can record your observations by making a picture of your mealworm. Make your drawing big enough to cover most of the page. Your picture should be much bigger than the actual mealworm. Notice every detail you can and show it in your picture. How many legs? How many segments? How does the mouth look? Look very carefully at your mealworm and then draw what you notice. Then look again and draw what you notice. Keep looking back at your real mealworm and then use what you see to make your picture more realistic. Compare your picture with your partner's picture. If they are different, look back at your mealworm to see if you can tell how.

"Now, before we begin, who can remember today's procedure?" Ms. Oldhand made sure that they remembered to make their drawings large and that they would include details in their pictures.

Before the lesson began, Ms. Oldhand had assigned one monitor from each table to hand out and pick up materials. "Would the materials monitors please come get the things for your tables?" She gave each of the monitors a box-lid tray with mealworms in cups and plastic magnifiers, which they then distributed.

The children went right to work, looking at the mealworms with their magnifiers. Ms. Oldhand then passed out the drawing paper and crayons without interrupting or interfering. As they worked, she walked around and answered questions that some children had.

After about 15 minutes, she rang the chime for attention and asked the monitors to pick up the mealworms, magnifiers, and crayons. There were a few groans from the pupils as the mealworms departed.

"What new details did you notice today?" The discussion first involved comparing observations. "How many legs?" "How many segments?" "Shall we count the head as a segment or not? Let's decide and then all use the same rule." Next, she asked about how the legs moved. This proved hard to describe, so she asked for three volunteers to come forward to act as the three pairs of legs on a mealworm. Several groups of three demonstrated their versions of the gait of their specimens. Afterward, they debated which rendition was the most realistic.

Finally, Ms. Oldhand revealed a large photographic enlargement of a mealworm. She asked them to compare the photo with their own drawings and to notice any differences. Discrepancies that the pupils pointed out were listed on a large chart paper. "Fine," she concluded, "We will use this list next time as a guide to find out more. How do you think we will do it? A look at the real mealworms would help us decide. Thank you for being such good scientists today. Please pass your drawings up, and let's get ready for lunch."

# Working toward Greater Pupil Freedom and Responsibility

In both of the lessons just described, the pupils were given only limited freedom within specific bounds. They weren't permitted to move freely about the room, and the activities were relatively simple without a great many choices for them to make. Ms. Oldhand was demonstrating for Mr. Newman how to begin a unit with third-grade children whose experience with inquiry learning is limited. To demonstrate techniques that could be used by a less experienced teacher such as Mr. Newman, Ms. Oldhand was more conservative in allowing pupils freedom than she might have been otherwise. Nevertheless, she used several techniques intended to help the children increase their learning independence. They were allowed to talk as long as they kept the volume down. In this way, they practiced being responsible by exercising judgment. The distribution and pickup of materials were easy and quick. Children were given the responsibility of being monitors; with monitor duty rotating each week so that everyone had a chance to practice this kind of responsibility. In cases where more or messier materials were involved, every child participated more actively in cleanup.

# Getting Started with Guided Inquiry

Each of the following steps has been or will be described in detail, either in this chapter or in others. You will find it useful to refer to this list from time to time as you gain experience and become more aware of the subtle aspects of guided inquiry.

1. Set or review behavior standards.
2. Do not tell pupils the objective of the lesson or present the concept.
3. Give clear, brief directions for the procedure to be used. Pupils should not be expected to invent their own procedures in this method. Directions for procedures should be made clear before the pupils begin working.
4. Introduce new vocabulary only as needed in context, that is, when it arises naturally in the lesson.

5. When pupils are working productively during the data collection part of the lesson, don't address the class as a whole. Don't interfere when they are doing what they are supposed to be doing.

6. Speak softly to children only as needed to prevent serious boredom or terminal frustration. Mild, occasional frustration and limited boredom are to be expected in any worthwhile endeavor, including guided inquiry lessons.

7. Separate pupils from materials before trying to hold a discussion.

8. During the data processing part of the lesson, first ask pupils to report their data, that is, to describe their observations.

9. When possible, continue the discussion beyond description by asking for higher level thinking such as inference, justification, generalization, and speculation about related systems not yet experienced.

10. Do not summarize the lesson for the pupils. Ask them to do so.

## DATA COLLECTION AND PROCESSING

It is important to give directions for the entire data collection part of the lesson—before data collection begins. Also give reminders about behavior standards and special directions for distribution and cleanup of materials. Otherwise, you will have to interrupt when the children are concentrating on the most interesting part of the lesson. Suggestions for this phase of the lesson include the following:

■ *Keep directions short and clear.* Avoid adding unnecessary details and giving more directions than children can remember. Break lessons into steps, giving directions for each step as the children are ready for it.

■ *Minimize interruptions during data collection.* When pupils are doing what they are supposed to do, try not to interfere!

■ *Plan materials distribution and cleanup carefully.* Making children wait while materials are passed out usually leads to behavior management problems.

■ *Enforce behavior standards strictly.* One child who "gets away" with misbehavior can start a trend.

■ *Limit novelty.* Whenever new elements of learning are to be introduced, limit the amount or number of new things that happen at the same time. New procedures, new locations, new ideas, new tools, or new objects to study should be introduced gradually. The trick is not to avoid novelty but to spread it out over time so that it doesn't all happen at once. Novelty is the essence of learning; to avoid it is to take the interest and life out of learning.

■ *Allow time for exploration.* Exploration is a preliminary examination in which children find out the general nature of the unknown object, place, or situation. Exploration reduces the degree of novelty to the point where children aren't overwhelmed. Whenever a new physical object is present in a lesson, problems in management will be minimized by allowing some time for exploration. Before they are able to work systematically with or on an object, children must be allowed to play with it and "get some of the new off." Exploration also serves as a legitimate first step of investigation used by scientists and other adults in new situations.

## Pupils' and Teacher's Roles during Data Collection

During data collection, the pupil's role is to work with the materials, following the directions given earlier. The teacher's role is to refrain from addressing the whole class and to speak to individual pupils or small groups as little as possible. In other words, during data collection, the teacher is supposed to keep quiet and let the children work. Learning to keep quiet and out of the limelight is one of the hardest things the teacher has to do in inquiry-based teaching. When a teacher speaks loudly to the whole class, pupils experience conflict. They know that they are supposed to be working, but they also know that they are supposed to stop and listen to the teacher. Not only do the children have trouble shifting attention in this situation, but also the authority of the teacher is eroded. The way to avoid or at least minimize the need for interruption during data collection is to give brief, clear, and complete directions before data collection begins.

In addition to keeping quiet, the teacher's role during data collection involves noticing how pupils are doing. If a child is having trouble with equipment or has forgotten the directions, an indirect suggestion that leads the pupil to figure out the problem independently is best. For example, "What does the directions chart say to do next?" "What would happen if you fastened this connector here?" "Do you remember what we did about this problem yesterday?" Occasionally, you will find that a problem stems from faulty equipment or some other difficulty beyond the child's ability to solve alone. Simply replace or fix the problem when possible or arrange for the pupil to work with another team. Sometimes you may find one or more children misusing or playing with the materials in nonproductive ways. If proximity control or other mild management techniques do not work, quietly remind the children involved of the behavior standards.

## Watching and Listening to Pupils

Watching pupils work with materials is like looking through a magic window into the workings of their minds. They act out their thinking in concrete, observable ways. One way to get fully involved with a group's thinking is to sit or bend down with them at eye level and then simply watch and listen without speaking. You may ask questions or make indirect suggestions (quietly) but avoid correcting the children's misconceptions. The feedback coming directly from the materials is much more effective than anything you could say and is emotionally neutral besides. Children revise their thinking when they are cognitively ready to do so.

In a task such as "Can you make the bulb light?" in a lesson on electric circuits, an intervention is necessary in the case of pupils who cannot solve the problem after a reasonable time. You might suggest that they look around for ideas. An even more effective technique is to ask some pupils to draw diagrams on the board of circuits that "do work" and diagrams of circuits that "don't work." That way, everyone can be involved, and interesting arrangements that do not light the bulb can be recognized. There should always be an open atmosphere of thinking and sharing ideas during guided discovery. Children should never feel that they are being tested or that getting ideas from other children is cheating.

Although the situation is rare, you may sometimes find a pupil who is shy or seems uninterested in working with the materials. Often, placement in the right group is helpful in such cases, but occasionally you may want to sit with this child yourself and, in your best nonthreatening manner, try to kindle interest: "I wonder what would happen if I connect the wire here?" "Have you tried this one yourself?" Feigning puzzlement over something you know the child can figure out is often effective: "I could never get circuit number 3 to work. Juan said that he couldn't either, but Emily did!"

There is no magic formula for deciding when to intervene during data collection and when not to. The main guiding principle is that you cannot make a discovery for children; they must discover on their own. You can only facilitate, or arrange the environment to increase the probability of success. Most of the time, especially until you feel more at home with this new teaching method, the most effective intervention is none at all.

## LEADING INTERESTING DISCUSSIONS

The material in this section is often included under the heading Questioning Techniques, as though the main point is the questions teachers ask. That puts the emphasis on what the teacher is saying rather than on what the children are saying. In a discussion, as opposed to a question-and-answer session, everyone involved is getting new ideas, giving their ideas, and constructing new knowledge. The teacher has to be a participant, not just a question-asker.

Rowe, in her classic book, *Teaching Science as Continuous Inquiry* (1978), characterizes the difference between this kind of teaching and more traditional methods as "inquiry versus inquisition." Everyone is familiar with the traditional "discussion," where the main focus is reciting correct answers and getting lots of praise. Learners are often intent on studying the teacher's face for clues to whether answers are acceptable. Thinking has little or no place in this game. An inquiry-style discussion, by contrast, has everything to do with pupils' learning to think and with learning a whole new set of "rules" for doing well. These discussions are more like normal conversations about things that the pupils and teacher alike are really interested in. The teacher's role in inquiry is to stimulate and encourage thinking. But how?

*A teacher gives her full attention to one pupil's answer.*

The first rule is to keep teacher talk to a minimum. Ask questions that elicit longer pupil responses. It is a good idea to begin with a few questions of description, such as "How many legs did you count?" Begin at a fairly low level but move on quickly to questions requiring more thought, such as "What kind of food do you think mealworms like?" Open-ended questions are desirable for eliciting several different hypotheses quickly. Then you can ask the pupils to justify their points of view in terms of their observations: "What evidence do you have to support your idea?" "Have you noticed something that leads you to think that?" Further investigations can be planned together to get more evidence for some of the ideas, such as by asking, "How could we find out about what mealworms eat?"

## ■ TALKING IT OVER

MR. NEWMAN:   I'm beginning to catch on to the way you get them started and then keep quiet while they're working, but I was wondering about the groans I heard when the materials were collected.

MS. OLDHAND:   It's better to stop the activity while interest is still high than to wait until they are starting to get bored. The groans just show that they would rather work with actual things than have a discussion. That's natural; it's why I engineer the transition so carefully. Once they get into a discussion, they like it well enough.

# ESTABLISHING AN ATMOSPHERE FOR DISCUSSION

An important part—maybe the most important part—of an inquiry lesson is discussion of what the data mean. An inquiry lesson is not complete without this phase where "hands-on" becomes "minds-on." The pleasant, mutually respectful, stimulating atmosphere of the inquiry discussion requires the establishment of an atmosphere that is psychologically safe for speculation as well as the sharing of thinking that is not yet finished. This open climate does not simply happen. It is not enough for a teacher to know how to avoid behaviors that reduce trust and how to use behaviors that favor inquiry. There must also be cooperation from the pupils. Because children are usually accustomed to classrooms with fast exchanges, they tend to respond to questions immediately—with short, superficial answers. If you want inquiry to succeed in your classroom, the pupils must be taught (directly) the procedure of the new discussion method.

The first thing to do is to separate pupils from materials before a discussion. If you try to compete for their attention with attractive materials, you will probably lose. There are several ways to separate pupils from materials. Collecting the materials while the pupils remain seated is one way. Moving the children to a discussion area away from their activity tables is another. In extended units when pupils have time to get accustomed to the materials, you may be able to get by with giving each child or team its own container for storing materials. Then, if the container is small enough (and opaque), have them put materials in the container and move it to the center of the table, out of touching range. When pupils are mature enough to manage it, this method has the advantage of reducing the interruption of thinking between activity and discussion.

## Planning a Discussion

As you plan a discussion, consider that you will first want pupils to process their data by reporting and comparing their observations:

> What did you notice about the detailed structure of your mealworm?
>
> How many segments did your mealworm have?
>
> Was it the same for everyone's?
>
> Should we count the tail as a segment? The head?
>
> Which characteristics do you think would be the same for all mealworms, and which might be different?

Later in the discussion, ask for speculation on relationships or generalizations based on the observations:

> Did you notice any patterns in the mealworm's behavior?
>
> How do these behaviors help the mealworm to survive?
>
> Have you seen other living things behave this way?
>
> What are some characteristics (things) that you have in common with mealworms?

## Wait Time

Discussions that are more than rote drill require some silent time for thinking, both by the pupils and by the teacher. Rowe's (1974) research in this area has identified two kinds of wait time: (a) wait time 1 is the time after a teacher asks a question and before anyone speaks again, either teacher or child; and (b) wait time 2 is the time after a pupil speaks before anyone else speaks.

Rowe found that teachers typically wait less than one second for pupils to answer a question. That doesn't give pupils time to form an answer unless it is only something from memory, that is, something that requires no thinking. Many teachers, especially those who ask a series of rapid-fire questions, even interrupt pupils who are trying to respond by praising inappropriately or calling on another child. Some teachers answer their own questions before pupils have time to respond. With training and practice, you can learn to wait a few seconds for an answer after you ask a question. When you learn to extend your wait time to three to five seconds, the following things can happen:

- The average length of pupil responses is longer, indicating more thoughtful answers.
- Pupils initiate more responses.
- There are fewer failures to respond to the teacher's question.
- The quality of pupil responses is better.
- Teachers become more flexible in their questions and reactions to pupil responses.
- Previously silent pupils participate.

## The Learning-to-Discuss Cycle

Labinowicz (1985a) described a way to teach children to function in a discussion in which thinking is valued more than correct answers. Many of the following ideas are taken from his book. Before beginning an inquiry discussion, inform the children of the reason for wait time through these types of comments:

**Waiting time is thinking time. I'll ask a question, and then I'll wait for a while before I call on someone. I won't always call on someone with a raised hand. I'm interested in how you think. It's important not to call out and not to wave hands so that everyone has time to think. Different people will have different ideas, which is good because you'll be learning from each other.**

In later discussions, you will need to remind the children of the wait-time procedures. You can explain that, when someone forgets and calls out an answer, any pupils who are still thinking about it will stop thinking. Pupils should understand that the idea that was interrupted could have been very interesting to everyone. You will need to give additional reminders for a while until waiting and respecting the views of others become second nature. You can encourage pupils to tell whether they agree or disagree with another pupil's comment and to give their reasons. You can establish hand signals to remind the impulsive or overeager child to wait quietly while thinking is going on.

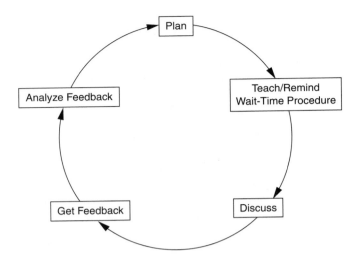

**FIGURE 5.2   Learning-to-Discuss Cycle**

Neither pupils nor teachers learn to function in an inquiry discussion overnight. Leading a good inquiry discussion is a complex skill that requires thought and effort. Figure 5.2 illustrates a cycle of teaching and learning that you may adopt as a plan for your own professional growth.

A good class discussion in an inquiry lesson involves many advanced teaching skills. Good and Brophy (1987) describe six characteristics of good questions: They are clear, purposeful, brief, natural, adapted to the learners' level, and thought provoking. Clear questions are usually brief, and long questions are hard to understand. But not all brief questions are clear. "How about the habitat?" is vague and may be misleading. "What alternative paradigm might be applied?" contains words that might be unknown to children. Questions should have vocabulary and word order that are natural to children. Some beginning teachers plan a discussion by simply thinking up every question possible that has anything to do with the subject. A much more effective practice is to plan a logical sequence of questions, all of which are pertinent to the gradual development of the lesson objectives.

# Praise

No teacher likes to be negative, and, to many teachers, praise sometimes seems the only alternative to negativity. As a result, they may use praise too much, in the wrong way, or inappropriately. Praise is effective when it is genuine, appropriate, not overly dramatic, and directed to specific tasks or skills (Good & Brophy, 1987). Several research studies have revealed that praise is often given for incorrect answers, especially when directed to low achievers. How can that happen? Teachers often use global praise or vaguely worded, random phrases that cannot readily be identified as praise of pupil, effort, or solution. When asked about specific instances of inappropriate praise, teachers report that they were attempting to encourage effort.

Pupils in a classroom in which a great deal of praise is used are discouraged from learning to think for themselves. The primary payoff for the pupils becomes more praise; thus the probability of developing interest in the subject for intrinsic reasons is reduced. Like an addiction, praise tends to prevent normal development toward independent thinking.

Rowe (1974) concluded that overt verbal praise is effective in certain situations, but for establishing an inquiry atmosphere and encouraging higher order, independent thinking, praise is actually counterproductive! In classrooms where praise was frequent, children were less confident, as evidenced by inflected responses and checking the teacher's face. When verbal rewards were high, pupils tended to give short responses and incomplete explanations, wave their hands more ("Call-on-me!"), and listen less to other pupils' ideas. Discussions in classrooms where praise is frequent are more likely to resemble a game of competition for the teacher's attention than an interesting conversation. By contrast, when the frequency of overt verbal praise is decreased, these negative effects tend to diminish or disappear.

## A Framework for Leading Discussions

Another approach to learning to lead good discussions has been explored by Watt (1996), who was interested in the questioning behaviors needed to develop a constructivist teaching philosophy in primary-school science. She proposed a framework, shown in Table 5.2, that recognizes both the social and cognitive attributes of discussions. Social attributes set the tone of the discussion, encourage all children to participate, and allow time for children to respond. Cognitive attributes guide children's thinking, stimulate development of ideas and promote logical thinking. Note that both social and cognitive attributes are described at two levels.

## Practical Suggestions for Leading Discussions

Planning questions is only one part of planning a discussion. You will also want to think about your reactions to possible pupil responses. During reporting of data, very little reaction from you is needed or desirable. Simply accept the responses without judging—instant judgment is not required. Remember the knowledge types described in Chapter 1. Observations are physical knowledge. The best feedback for questions of physical knowledge comes from the objects. If there is a discrepancy between the observations of different children, the children themselves will often raise questions about them. If not, you can suggest that they check again to see whether their observations can be duplicated. During initial reporting, you may jot down the observations on the board, especially if you plan to refer to them later for comparison or analysis. In this way you can accept children's responses without making judgments. When children share their explanations, probing for further thinking is useful, regardless of whether the children are right or wrong. Remember, in inquiry science, thinking is at least as important as a result. By asking for more ideas, you'll not only get additional ideas already in place and ready to be reported, but you'll also stimulate additional thinking.

**TABLE 5.2   A Framework for Teacher Questioning During Class Discussions**

## Social Attributes of Discussion

*Level one: General management of discussion*

Respond verbally to any answer with equal interest.

Use tone of voice in a manner which reinforces the interest in any answer.

Give a child ownership of an answer by using phrase such as, "What do you think. . . ?" to begin a question.

Allow a child sufficient time to formulate a response.

*Level two: Enabling greater participation in discussion*

Cue a child to the cognitive level of response required by using phrases such as, "What do you think. . . .?" to begin a question.

Invite an answer from every child who wishes to contribute.

Encourage children to respond to each other's views.

## Cognitive Attributes of Discussion

*Level one: Maintaining logical continuity in discussion*

Seek clarification of a child's answer by repeating words.

Seek clarification of a child's answer by asking what s/he means.

Extend a child's answer by asking for a hypothesis or for evidence to support one.

Be sure of the area (rather than the specific content) of the discussion.

Ask questions according to a considered sequence.

*Level two: Monitoring the development of ideas in discussion*

Seek clarification of a child's answer by reflectively rewording his/her response.

Extend a child's answer by challenging his/her hypothesis.

Word questions so that the intention behind them is clear.

Listen to a child's answer and use it as the basis for the next question.

*Source:* From "An Analysis of Teacher Questioning Behavior in Constructivist Primary Science Education Using a Modification of a Descriptive System Designed by Barnes & Todd (1997)" by D. Watt, 1996, *International Journal of Science Education, 18* (5), p. 605. Copyright 1996 by Taylor & Francis Ltd. Reprinted by permission.

Children's language is often imprecise; by asking for clarification, you help them develop more careful use of language as well as sharper thinking. Listen for "magic words" that children may use without fully understanding their meaning: *gravity, force, friction, density, photosynthesis, oxygen,* and so on. In addition, children often report inferences or other speculations as if they were observations. When that happens, ask for observations with questions such as:

How do you know?

Did you notice something that supports your idea?

That's an interesting inference. What observations did you base it on?

What do you mean by *friction?*

Can you say that another way?

Please explain for everyone what that word means.

Is that anything like the term used earlier?

That's an interesting theory. Let's see if there are others.

## Encouraging Pupils to Listen and Respond to One Another

Avoid repeating pupil responses. Instead, ask a child to repeat so that everyone can hear or ask another child to paraphrase. When you repeat a pupil's response, you send two undesirable messages: (a) it isn't necessary to listen to other children because the teacher will repeat what was said and (b) a child's comment counts for nothing until it has been "authorized" by coming out of the teacher's mouth. Ask questions such as:

What do you think of Kal's idea? Who would like to agree or disagree and say why?

Can you state Jennifer's idea another way?

How does Jeremy's idea relate to yours?

Tyrone, you also mentioned decomposition. Would you like to react to Felipe's idea?

Sometimes pupils get stuck in a blind alley with untestable explanations. Try to redirect them into a more interesting line of thinking by making indirect suggestions:

Are other interpretations possible?

Are there any other ways to think about this?

Are there any other clues or observations that we haven't thought about? What other factors could be involved?

What would happen if we . . . ?

And if that were changed, what would happen then?

## Handling Incorrect Responses

Learn to handle incorrect responses in a constructive way. Again, remember Piaget's knowledge types (see Chapter 1). Only errors in arbitrary knowledge need correcting by the teacher or some other authority, such as a dictionary. Physical knowledge is best corrected by further observation or experience. Logical knowledge must be constructed in each learner's head; correcting logical knowledge only undermines children's confidence in their own thinking and makes them dependent on the teacher. Children's logical knowledge grows internally and at its own rate. Respect children's misconceptions and prelogical responses as a temporary stopover on the long journey of mental development and the construction of knowledge.

# ■ Summary

Inquiry-based instruction is a method by which children ask questions, explore materials, gather data, come to conclusions, and discuss results. Science content and processes are integrated in lessons based on hands-on activities in which pupils use science processes to learn directly from interaction with materials. Data processing often begins in a class discussion led by the teacher to guide the pupils to reflect on the experience they have just had. Discussions are begun with questions of a relatively low level to elicit description and comparison of the objects and events studied. Gradually, the teacher increases the cognitive level of the questions to help pupils construct higher level ideas and deeper understanding.

Because pupils must function more independently in guided discovery than in direct instruction, special, indirect teaching techniques are needed. These techniques were illustrated and explained in two lessons on mealworms taught by Ms. Oldhand.

In the first lesson the children learned about a mealworm by handling it and observing its actions and reactions to simple stimuli. They also thought of some questions they would like to answer. In the second lesson they were given magnifiers to observe the mealworm in greater detail and to find answers to some of their questions. Then they made drawings to represent their knowledge of a mealworm's structure and displayed their drawings in the classroom.

Ms. Oldhand's teaching methods as she guided the children through the lessons were explained step by step. First she explained behavior standards and ensured that each child understood what was expected. In the first lesson she showed a mealworm to the children and asked them to remember that mealworms are living things and must be handled with care. After the children received their own mealworms, Ms. Oldhand let them work on their own, observing but not disturbing them. After about 15 minutes the children returned their mealworms and Ms. Oldhand led a discussion of what they had observed. The second lesson was a continuation of the study of a mealworm, and Ms. Oldhand's methods were the same as those used in the first lesson. In both of these lessons, the pupils were given only limited freedom, within specific bounds. As the children gain practice and experience in guided inquiry they will be given more responsibility for their own behavior.

The verbal techniques used in inquiry-based instruction differ in important ways from those used in direct instruction. Time spent listening to the teacher is minimized. The teacher provides an appropriate situation and then allows the learners to do their own learning. For physical knowledge, the teacher provides objects and allows pupils to interact with those objects, essentially without interference. For logical knowledge, the teacher asks thought-provoking questions and then listens carefully to the responses, often providing additional thinking on the same idea before leaving it. Both social interactive knowledge and logical knowledge develop in an atmosphere of respectful give and take as ideas are compared and tested during group discussions. Teachers using inquiry-based instruction spend most of a lesson watching and listening, allowing pupils to concentrate on the topic of study.

The chapter ends with a consideration of the factors that make discussions interesting and worthwhile to pupils. Some of the ideas that have been put forth to aid in leading discussions are the importance of giving children time to answer, a learning-to-discuss cycle and the classification of questions into levels and categories.

## ■ ACTIVITIES FOR THE READER

The following activities can best be done in groups and then discussed by the class as a whole.

1. In the body of the chapter, you were asked to complete Ms. Oldhand's second lesson plan for the mealworms unit. Share and discuss your results with your classmates.

2. Examine an elementary-school science textbook on a topic such as insects. Try to list the main objectives of the section. Then classify the objectives according to kind of knowledge (cognitive, psychomotor, social, or affective).

3. Select a topic from an elementary-school science textbook and develop a guided inquiry lesson plan for it. (Be careful to select just enough content for one lesson; don't try to cover too much.)

4. This activity was developed by DeTure and Miller (1984) and used in an unpublished teacher education videotape, *Teaching by Listening*, by Ed Labinowicz (1985b). He reports that almost all teachers were able to achieve an average wait time of three seconds or more after only two practice cycles. For this activity

   a. select about 10 children;

   b. audiotape a discussion of about 10 minutes' length;

   c. choose a 5- to 7-minute portion to transcribe verbatim;

   d. record teacher talk and pupil talk on separate lines with space between;

   e. on blank lines, note wait time as type 1 or type 2;

   f. time the wait time to the nearest second, using a stop watch, but if there is no wait time, record 0; and

   g. calculate averages for wait time 1 and wait time 2 separately.

Tapes and written transcripts should be saved, as transcripts or tapes can also be analyzed for other verbal behaviors such as those suggested in the section on leading discussions.

# ■ QUESTIONS FOR DISCUSSION

1. What processes of science did you use in the mealworm investigation?

2. What is the difference between guided inquiry and guided practice?

3. What are the differences between hands-on science and inquiry science?

4. How would the mealworm lessons be different if all the objectives were to be achieved at the level of arbitrary knowledge?

5. Dinosaurs are a popular topic in first and second grade. Is it possible to have an inquiry lesson about dinosaurs? Explain why it is not possible or outline a lesson plan for this topic.

6. With some children, especially the very young, it may be much easier for the teacher to do the setting up and cleaning of materials. How important is it for children to do these tasks?

7. In Chapter 4 (on direct instruction), you read that during guided practice a pupil should be corrected immediately in case of an error. Why is it different when a pupil demonstrates an erroneous concept during guided inquiry?

8. React to the remark, "Teachers like to praise. Children like it. I don't see the point of reducing or avoiding praise."

9. Teachers need to let pupils know that they are listening to what the pupils say. What are some alternatives to praise and mimicry? What is different about their effects?

10. Is the same amount of wait time needed for responses to all the following questions? Explain. If you think not, which questions require more and which require less wait time?

    a. How many legs did you find on your mealworm?

    b. Do you think that all mealworms have the same number of legs?

    c. Have you noticed any patterns in what they do?

    d. Would any of these behaviors help a mealworm to survive?

# ■ REFERENCES

DeTure, L., & Miller, A. (1984, March). *The effects of a written protocol model on teacher acquisition of extended wait-time.* Paper presented at the annual meeting of the National Association for Research in Science Teaching, New Orleans.

Duckworth, E., Easley, J., Hawkins, D., & Henriques, A. (1990). *Science education: A minds-on approach for the elementary years.* Hillsdale, NJ: Erlbaum.

Good, T., & Brophy, J. (1987). *Looking in classrooms* (4th ed.). New York: Harper & Row.

Labinowicz, E. (1985a). *Learning from children: New beginnings for teaching numerical thinking.* Menlo Park, CA: Addison-Wesley.

Labinowicz, E. (1985b). *Teaching by listening: The time dimension* [Video series]. California State University, Northridge.

National Research Council. (1996). *National science education standards*. Washington, DC: National Academy Press.

Rowe, M. (1974). Relation of wait-time and rewards to the development of language, logic, and fate control: Part II. Rewards. *Journal of Research in Science Teaching, 11*(4), 291–308.

Rowe, M. (1978). *Teaching science as continuous inquiry: A basic* (2nd ed.). New York: McGraw-Hill.

Watt, D. (1996). An analysis of teacher questioning behavior in constructivist primary science education using a modification of a descriptive system designed by Barnes and Todd (1997). *International Journal of Science Education, 18*(5), 601–613.

# Teaching Science to Promote Independent Learning

■ Ms. Sanchez, a beginning teacher, had observed her mentor, Ms. Oldhand, several times during the year. One day she visited Ms. Oldhand's class and was surprised to see that the children, who had been in their seats carrying out directions on her first visit, were now spread out all over the room, some on the floor, some standing together in a corner, some talking excitedly in groups around their desks. The classroom was not quiet, but it wasn't really noisy either. It reminded her of a beehive; there was a low buzz of children talking, but no one voice rose above the others. Ms. Sanchez walked over to Ms. Oldhand, and the following conversation ensued.

Ms. Sanchez:     This certainly looks different from the way it looked the last time I was in this class.

Ms. Oldhand:     Oh, yes. The way I teach depends upon the goals of the lesson. When you visited this class before, I was teaching the children a specific skill that they needed to know in order to do other things later on. They were learning to use the balance, and they needed to practice until they had mastered the skill. Today each group is working on its own, planning how to find out something that the children of a group want to know about trees. Children in each group have thought of a question about trees that interests them, and now they are planning how to collect data to help them answer their questions.

Ms. Sanchez:     This must be an easy way to teach. It looks as if the children are doing all the work.

Ms. Oldhand:     (Laughing) Well it may look easy, but actually, this kind of teaching is a real test of a teacher's skill. In the first place, the pupils have to be taught to conduct themselves appropriately and responsibly when they are working independently. Then an attitude of mutual respect and trust between pupils as well as between pupils and teacher has to be developed. The teacher has to plan very carefully and thoughtfully and then has to monitor the pupils' progress toward the goals of the day's work.

Ms. Sanchez:     I'd like to walk around and observe what the groups are doing to get a better idea of what's going on.

This chapter covers two kinds of investigations that promote independent learning: group investigations and independent projects. In both cases the pupils assume a higher level of responsibility than in the teaching methods previously described. The detailed descriptions in this chapter are intended to encourage you to plan thoroughly and thoughtfully before you begin teaching units that place this degree of responsibility on your pupils. Few elementary-school children are able to organize their work and carry through without careful adult guidance and support.

## GROUP INVESTIGATIONS

In Chapter 1 you read about a class investigation that began when a second grader was puzzled because water was disappearing from a watering can every night. The class planned a series of experiments that included testing the hypothesis that Willie, the hamster, was getting out of his cage and drinking the water. Eventually they learned that the water was evaporating. That investigation is an example of a class investigation of a question raised by one of the children. The children in that class had developed confidence in their own ability to select questions to investigate, to decide how to investigate, and to understand the result of their investigation.

The teaching method described in this chapter is for a class investigation of a topic of interest to the children but with a difference: The class is organized into small groups that investigate different questions about the same topic. Science teaching based on investigations of questions of interest to children has its theoretical basis in the work of the thinkers discussed in Chapter 2. Dewey, Piaget, and Bruner stressed the importance of active participation and exploration in the construction of knowledge and meaning. Vygotsky stressed the importance of social interaction among peers in the process of learning. Kohlberg's ideas of moral development can only be realized in a classroom atmosphere of respect and trust between teacher and pupils and among the pupils themselves. All of these ideas are put into practice in this teaching method.

Although you may never have experienced open investigations of this kind, it is by no means a new method. It was advocated in the United States by Dewey in the early 1900s and has been used successfully in other countries through the years. Group investigations are a part of elementary-school science education in many schools in both Great Britain and Japan.

An American teacher who spent many hours in elementary science classrooms in Tokyo reported that group investigations were used by all the teachers she observed, as well as by all those who answered a questionnaire she distributed (Charron, 1987). In the classrooms she visited, children worked in groups as they planned investigations, obtained teacher approval for their plans, found the necessary materials and equipment, and spent their period interacting with each other and asking questions focused on their own ideas, predictions, findings, and conclusions rather than on facts and memorization of information. Her findings should reassure teachers who hesitate to try independent investigations because of a concern that pupils will not attend to their work or that they will even become loud and unruly. This chapter includes a section on cooperative learning that will show you how to set up productive groups.

### Practical Considerations

You shouldn't attempt a group investigation until you have been with your pupils long enough to have worked out basic rules of classroom behavior and for the pupils to understand what is expected of them. Some important things for pupils to remember (or be reminded of) are to

interact courteously with one another,

stay on task without constant reminders from the teacher,

use simple equipment correctly, and

persist in a task until a "stopping point" is reached.

This teaching method makes high demands on both teacher and pupils. This chapter and the two preceding chapters have been arranged so that each higher level allows new instructional methods but doesn't rule out the use of methods previously described. The decision about whether to use group investigations depends on the goals of instruction, the teacher's experience in guiding instruction, and the pupils' ability to assume responsibility for their own behavior and learning.

## Choosing a Topic

The main topic may be suggested by the teacher or arise from the pupils' interests. Topics suitable for this style of teaching are those that can be studied through first-hand exploration of objects and materials that are readily available. An important consideration in choosing the topic is the potential of the topic for further learning. The topic should be broad enough and important enough to help form the foundation for your pupils' further learning later on.

Remember that most of these children still think predominantly in what Piaget referred to as the concrete mode; that is, their thinking is still based on their own experiences with objects and events. Investigations should always be based on children's own experiences, although that doesn't mean that they can never use books or other sources of information to answer questions that their own investigations have raised. When the needed knowledge is arbitrary knowledge, such as the names of different kinds of trees, the use of books or other sources of information will be necessary. Such information will be more meaningful for children who have already had firsthand experience with the topic.

Questions to ask yourself when choosing a topic include the following:

- Is the topic broad enough to allow for many kinds of investigations at different levels of ability?
- Are materials available in this locality at this time of year?
- Are the materials safe for children to gather and handle?
- Can children find out interesting things through activities they can do on their own?
- Will there be opportunities to use a variety of science processes in their investigations?

# GROUPING FOR INSTRUCTION: COOPERATIVE LEARNING

If you have decided to use group investigations and have chosen a topic, you will then need to consider how to organize the pupils to ensure a successful learning experience. As the children will be working on their own much of the time and will have a great deal of responsibility to monitor their own behaviors and progress toward task completion, it is important that the groups work cooperatively. Cooperative learning is a structured way to set up groups to work together on learning tasks. Although the method seems to be highly structured and detailed, many teachers have found that children catch on quickly and like the security of knowing what is expected of themselves and other group members. Johnson and Johnson's (1987) work is a good source for those who want to know more about cooperative learning; this chapter provides only enough information to get you started.

> **Note to Instructor.**
> Setting up your class in cooperative learning groups for at least one class period will help students get a feel for this method.

## Setting Up Groups

Groups of four or five pupils seem to work best. The groups should be as heterogeneous as possible, which means a mix of (a) boys and girls; (b) pupils with special problems, low ability, and high ability; and (c) the various racial and ethnic groups in your class. Research on the effects of using cooperative learning has shown that this strategy effectively promotes better working relationships in the classroom

*These children are working independently and cooperatively.*

**TABLE 6.1   Formation of Cooperative Learning Groups**

| Ranking | Quartiles | Groups |
|---|---|---|
| 1. Judy | 1. Judy | Group I |
| 2. Bill | Bill | Judy, Luis, Liam, Sam |
| 3. Joseph | Joseph | |
| 4. Luis | 2. Luis | Group II |
| 5. Marta | Marta | Bill, Marta, Dolores, Amos |
| 6. Takeisha | Takeisha | |
| 7. Dolores | 3. Dolores | Group III |
| 8. Nabeel | Nabeel | Joseph, Takeisha, Nabeel, Rita |
| 9. Liam | Liam | |
| 10. Amos | 4. Amos | |
| 11. Rita | Rita | |
| 12. Sam | Sam | |

between boys and girls, children with and without disabilities, and children from minority and nonminority groups (Slavin, 1980).

The first thing to do in setting up groups is to make a list of your pupils, ranking them from high to low ability. Use whatever information you have in ranking them and don't spend time worrying about fine distinctions; approximations are all you need. Next, divide this list into four sublists of equal or nearly equal size: the top fourth, the second fourth, and so on. These sublists are called *quartiles*. Now choose one pupil from each sublist (quartile) to form learning groups of four pupils each. As you choose from the sublists to form the groups, balance the groups as well as you can by gender, race, and other individual characteristics.

To see how this works in practice, consider a sample class of 12 pupils. Ranking them in ability from 1 to 12, will give you a list like the one shown in the first column of Table 6.1.

After you have made that list, go back and divide it into quartiles (fourths), as shown in the second column of the table. You will have as many groups as there are names in each quartile; in this case, you will have three groups.

Now, distribute the names in quartile 1 (the top-achieving fourth of the class) among the three groups:

Group I Judy

Group II Bill

Group III Joseph

Now distribute the names in quartile 2 (the next fourth) among the three groups, trying to balance the groups by ethnicity and gender as best you can. For example, you could make a group based on ability alone that would be composed of

Judy, Takeisha, Dolores, and Rita. However, that wouldn't be a good combination because it would contain only girls. A better distribution would be:

Group I Luis
Group II Marta
Group III Takeisha

Continue the process of group formation by distributing the names in quartiles 3 and 4 among the groups. Finally, you will have three groups similar to those shown in the last column of Table 6.1. These will be heterogeneous groups because of the way you put them together.

The same groups shouldn't stay together for longer than about six weeks. If you continue to use groups for guided discovery, group investigations, or other kinds of lessons, the memberships of the groups should be changed by repeating the process described.

## Teaching Cooperative Group Skills

Groups have two basic objectives: to complete a task and to maintain good working relationships among the members. To complete a task successfully, group members must obtain, organize, exchange, and use information. Members have to contribute, ask for help when needed, accept help when offered, and keep the objective of task completion in mind.

For the group to function well, members must encourage each other to participate actively and learn to manage differences of opinion, ideas, and interpretations constructively. Such differences often cause people to reassess their assumptions and give up misconceptions or deepen their understanding of important concepts. Part of your responsibility as a teacher will be to help your pupils develop these skills as they work together in groups. The groundwork has to be done before you start the unit. Here are some steps that you can take:

- Explain to the pupils that they will be working in cooperative learning groups. These groups will not be exactly like groups they have worked in before (unless they have already experienced cooperative learning groups).

- Explain that they will be assigned to groups and will be expected to work productively with everyone in the group.

- Ask for their ideas about the behaviors that will be needed for groups to be successful. Suggestions may include acceptance of others' ideas, sharing materials, showing trust for each other, trying to communicate clearly, listening to each other, and trying to see another's viewpoint. Take time to discuss each of these ideas.

Make it clear that you expect each child to work within the assigned group and that you will be available to help them work through any problems that arise. You cannot expect the groups to function flawlessly, but group skills are needed everywhere in life and can be developed through patience and firmness. You will probably find that you have to call the class together from time to time to review the basic principles of cooperative learning and to remind them of some of the things they may have forgotten.

# DEVELOPING A PLAN FOR A GROUP INVESTIGATION

Lesson plans in previous Chapters 1–4 were designed to be used for one class period. Daily planning is always necessary, but day-by-day planning isn't adequate for the instructional method described here. To accomplish its desired goals, a group investigation must be planned as a unit comprising a series of integrated lessons taking place over a longer period of time. As you learn to use teaching methods that give more freedom and responsibility to children, you will see the advantages of unit planning.

You are already familiar with most of the parts of a unit plan. The main difference is that in developing lesson plans for other instructional methods the teacher does the planning, but in developing a plan for a group investigation, pupils are also involved in the planning. Because it is a plan for a series of lessons over a period of two weeks rather than a single lesson, it may seem complicated. However, examination of Ms. Oldhand's unit plan, which begins on page 147, illustrates how the familiar parts of a lesson plan can be adapted to a group investigation. An integral aspect of planning a group investigation is to develop goals for it.

## Goals for a Group Investigation

The following cognitive, affective, psychomotor, and social goals are generally applicable to group investigations. These goals should be discussed with pupils during planning of the group investigation.

### Knowledge of Subject

Children are expected to learn many things about trees that they did not know before, but what they learn and how much they learn will depend on their own interests and activities. This kind of goal is very different from the goals of a lesson, in which pupils are expected to have acquired specific knowledge that has been determined by the teacher ahead of time. When you think about it, there is very little essential knowledge about trees that every sixth grader needs to know. It is more important at this age for children to become interested in the subject and to develop the motivation, the confidence, and the skill to find answers on their own to questions that interest them.

### Skill in Use of Science Processes

Most group investigations will require children to use the processes of (a) making, recording, and organizing observations; (b) recognizing patterns and relationships;

(c) making inferences or drawing conclusions; and (d) representing and reporting results. In some cases, pupils will also carry out experiments to test their inferences and may seek information from other sources.

### Build Self-Reliance and Self-Confidence in Their Own Ability to Think

Children learn to believe that their ideas are valuable when adults value those ideas. Self-confidence grows when children are encouraged to plan and carry out a task by using their own ideas and initiative. But when science is taught as facts, formulas, and theories to be memorized or "experiments" to be performed by carefully following directions, pupils need make no decisions and need not even think about what they are doing. A teacher who uses group investigations believes that pupils have their own ideas and interests that will be motivating and sustaining.

### Increase Awareness of and Interest in Subject

Children learn to look at things more closely, to understand them better, and to value them more highly. Think about something you have studied or observed in detail—whether football or birds or automobiles—and you will realize that you have a greater appreciation for that subject than someone who knows little about it.

### Learn to Work Cooperatively with Others

This social skill is probably as important as any single skill a child can learn in school. The unit style of teaching gives children the opportunity to develop and practice the skills of cooperative group work under adult guidance.

### Care in Handling Materials

Many things of interest to children are fragile and must be handled with care. This is particularly true of things that are alive or come from living materials, such as flowers, insects, moss, and small plants. Telling children to be careful is not as helpful as showing them how to exercise care and patience, recognizing that there are large differences in children's physical coordination. The use of dangerous materials or equipment should not be allowed. The close supervision needed to handle even minimally dangerous materials is not advisable in this method of teaching.

### Skill in Handling Equipment

Every effort should be made to provide children with sturdy equipment, but some items require care and skill in handling. As in the handling of materials, pupils cannot be expected to know how to handle equipment without instruction. Even when reasonable care is exercised, some breakage is inevitable.

### Learn to Work in Proximity to Others

Everyone has seen children who can't move around a room without bumping into other people, stepping on someone's materials, and knocking something over. These children will need help and patient guidance in developing spatial awareness and in learning how to exercise more control over their bodies.

## ■ MS. OLDHAND'S GROUP INVESTIGATIONS OF TREES

In introducing her sixth-grade class to group investigation, Ms. Oldhand applied the NSE Standard for Life Science. Populations and ecosystems (NRC, 1996, p. 157). She began by listing the scientific processes that would serve as the objectives of the group investigations: observe, organize, record, infer, and experiment.

### Motivation

Before the pupils began the work projects that Ms. Sanchez had seen when she entered the classroom, they had already spent several class periods on the investigation of trees. A week or so before this investigation began one of the children had brought in an article about a group of local people who were trying to save a large, old tree from being cut down to make way for a shopping mall. The issue had become controversial in the town, and several children had heard it discussed at home. Their interest in the topic prompted Ms. Oldhand to ask whether the class would like to investigate some questions about trees. When the children agreed that they would like to do so, Ms. Oldhand developed an initial plan to get the class started (which she would later build on by involving the pupils).

On the day the investigation began, Ms. Oldhand brought in branches with leaves from five or six different kinds of trees. She had selected them to show contrasts in leaf size, shape, color, and type—as well as contrasts in color and texture of tree bark. Some of the leaves Ms. Oldhand brought in are pictured in Figure 6.1.

She assigned pupils to groups, gave a branch and a short list of questions to each group, and allowed a few minutes for groups to decide on answers before she called on each group in turn. Ms. Oldhand had made the questions simple so that at least one person in each group would probably be able to answer. Her questions included: What is the name of the tree that this branch came from? Where does it grow? What color do the leaves turn in the fall? and Do they fall off in the winter? After each group had been given a turn to answer its questions, she called attention to the articles on the bulletin board. Then she asked for a few volunteers to tell why they thought that trees are important or to tell about their experiences with trees. Ms. Oldhand allowed the children a few minutes to talk and then brought the lesson to a close.

**FIGURE 6.1**   **Samples of Branches with Leaves**

## Planning Activities

On the following day Ms. Oldhand moved into the next phase of planning by asking the pupils to think of some things they would like to find out about trees. Calling on one pupil at a time, she wrote questions on a transparency on the overhead projector. When she had written six questions, she asked the children who had not spoken to write their questions on pieces of paper and to save them for later. The questions she wrote on the transparency were:

1.  What kinds of trees grow in our town?
2.  What kinds of fruit grow on trees? Do all trees have fruit? What is inside the fruit?
3.  What happens when a tree dies?
4.  What is the difference between an evergreen tree and a tree that loses its leaves?

5. What is a tree like on the inside?
6. How is wood from one kind of tree different from wood from another kind of tree?

By then it was time to move on to another subject, so the questions were saved for the next day's lesson.

When Ms. Oldhand returned to the children's questions the next day, she said, "Now we will decide how we might find the answers to these questions. What data would we need? How could we collect them? Let's start with the first question and see what we can do with it." After 15 minutes of skillful questioning and a few suggestions from Ms. Oldhand, the children read the following list displayed by the overhead projector:

1. What kinds of trees grow in our town? How will we answer this question?
    a. Look around the area where we live and identify all the different kinds of trees.
    b. Find out the names of the trees.
2. What happens when a tree dies? How will we answer this question?
    a. Bring a rotting log to school and find out all we can about it.

At this point Ms. Oldhand said, "Now that you have seen how we tackle these questions, it's time for you to do some of this on your own." She assigned children to groups of four or five and wrote these instructions on the board:

1. Decide on a question for your group. It may be one of the questions already identified, or it may be another question that your group likes.
2. Record the question.
3. Decide what you need to know or do in order to answer the question.
4. Write that decision down.
5. What materials or resources will you need? Which can you get yourselves and which will require some help?

After writing these directions on the board, Ms. Oldhand said, "I will come around to each group to hear your plans and to answer your questions. I'm really looking forward to hearing all your ideas because I know they will be good ones. At the end of the period, I'll collect your plans."

## Group Plans
By the end of the class period, each group had a plan. The following is what each group wrote.

### Group 1
"Our question is, What kinds of trees grow in our town?

"We will each take an area close to our homes and make a survey. First, we will look for as many different kinds of trees as we can find. Each person will bring in a few leaves from each different kind of tree. If we can't reach the leaves, we will draw a picture. We will bring all those in to class and see which are the same and which are different. Then we will have samples of all the different trees that we found.

"We will identify the leaves by looking them up in a book from the library.

"If we have time, we will go back and look at the shapes of the trees and try to draw them, because the shape of the tree may tell what kind of tree it is."

### Group 2

"Our question is, What happens when a tree dies?

"We will bring two pieces of wood to class. One will be a log that is solid and strong, and the other will be an old rotting log. We can get a good piece of wood from a parent who bought wood for the family's fireplace. For the rotting log, one of us will have to find a log in the woods or get one from someone who sells firewood and has an old piece that has been lying on the ground and has become rotten. A parent may have to help on this.

"We will compare the bark and the inside of the logs."

At this point, Ms. Oldhand came over to the group and heard its plan. She asked whether the pupils thought anything might be living in the old log. With this suggestion, they added the following to the plan:

"We will put the log down on a big piece of white paper and watch to see whether anything crawls out. If it does, we will save it. Then we will dig into the log to look for insect eggs, cocoons, and other signs of life.

"We will need something to gently dig into the rotten log, a big piece of paper, and a container for insects (if we find any)."

### Group 3

"Our questions are, What kinds of fruit grow on trees? Do all trees have fruit? What is inside the fruit?

"We will collect nuts and other kinds of things that grow on trees in the neighborhood. First, we will make a chart to compare them for size, shape, color, and so on. Then, we will find out what is inside the nuts and fruits and seeds and compare them."

### Group 4

"Our question is, Do all trees float in water after they have been cut down?

"We will get samples of wood from different trees and see whether they all float."

When Ms. Oldhand came over to this group, she suggested that it could expand the question. She thought that the group needed to dig deeper into the subject of floating than just determining that wood floats—which most of them knew already. They could ask whether all kinds of wood float the same way. Do some kinds of wood sink farther into the water than others? What else happens when wood is put in water? How could you make an experiment that would be a fair test of this? Her questions prompted the group to expand its investigation.

"We will get blocks of the same size of different kinds of wood, put them in water, and mark the level of the water on each one. Then we will compare them.

Next, we will weigh them, put them in water, leave them there for three days, and then weigh each block to see if it changed weight. We will see if woods from different trees absorb different amounts of water."

### Group 5
"Our question is, How are evergreen trees different from leafy trees?

"We will get branches from evergreen trees and from broad-leafed trees and compare them. Some of the things we will observe and record are

bark,
shape of leaves or needles,
how leaves or needles are attached,
smell,
the kind of seeds on the tree or lying on the ground under the tree,
shape of the tree (we will have to go after school, observe the trees, and draw them if we can), and
anything else that comes to our attention"

### Group 6
"Our question is, What is on the inside of a tree?

"We will get four different logs, if we can. Each one of us will observe and draw the cut surface of a log and then cut away the bark and observe what is underneath. We will also count the rings, because that tells how old a tree is."

### Preparing for the next stage
At the end of the period, Ms. Oldhand collected the papers so that she could read them over and see whether she needed to make any further suggestions. She told the children that they would have several days to collect their materials in order to be ready to begin their investigations on Monday. Thus they would have a reasonable amount of time to enlist the help of their parents and find all the materials that they would need.

## Materials
Ms. Oldhand looked over the papers the pupils had handed in and noticed that there were very few things that she would have to provide for the investigations. She was pleased to see that the children were planning to find most of the things themselves. She made a note of the materials that she would have to assemble and planned to have most of them ready by Monday.

## Group Activities
On Monday the groups went to work, collecting data, making observations, and carrying out the tasks that they had assigned themselves. Each pupil kept a workbook to record what was done each day. Sometimes pupils recorded their observations by drawing a picture or making a chart.

Although the children were interested and busy, Ms. Oldhand did not relax. She moved about from one group to another, asking questions, answering questions, and keeping an eye on everything that was happening in the room. She was particularly watchful of whether the children were using science processes appropriately. For example, she noted whether children took variables into account when they made comparisons so that a test of an idea was a fair test. As she moved around from group to group, she asked questions such as the following.

"Group 1, how can you find out which kind of tree is more abundant? Would you have to count all the trees in town? When you have thought of a way it might be done, let me know your idea so we can discuss it."

"Group 3, have you decided on categories for size, shape, and color? How will you agree on what category a seed belongs in?"

Ms. Oldhand also checked frequently to see that all the children were keeping up their workbooks. She had them turn in their workbooks each Friday so that she could take a look during the weekend. Sometimes a question from her helped children think again about how best to make an observation or test an idea.

During this time, Ms. Oldhand kept in mind the objectives of group investigations. She had made a notebook that contained the class list, with spaces beside each child's name for recording a bit of information each day. This notebook wasn't the formal grade book that every teacher must keep but her own way of appraising and recording performance. She had a line in her book for each pupil. As she moved about the room, she noted whether each child was on task and contributing to the group. At the end of the period, she put a plus, minus, or check by each pupil's name (see Figure 6.2).

She used the plus to indicate extra effort, the minus to indicate too much time off task, and the check to show what she considered appropriate effort and behavior. At the end of the group investigations, Ms. Oldhand used this record as part of the assessment. This record also helped her give feedback to parents about their children's participation and effort in science.

Ms. Oldhand was also interested in the science processes that the children were using. In the same notebook that contained the children's names, she used other pages to record the use of science processes, one page for each group. She set up columns for each day and each process previously listed as an objective in the unit plan. As Ms. Oldhand moved about the room, she watched for indications that the groups were making observations, recording data, and using the other processes. She recorded her observations by making check marks in her notebook. The record for Group 1 is shown in Figure 6.3, which illustrates the record that she kept for each group.

Note that Ms. Oldhand was actually using the science processes that she was teaching her pupils. She had made observations of pupil behavior (gathering data about their activities), recorded data, and eventually drew inferences. She was modeling for her pupils the behaviors and thinking processes that she was teaching. When she had an opportunity, she pointed this out to them to show that what they were learning in science class has many useful applications.

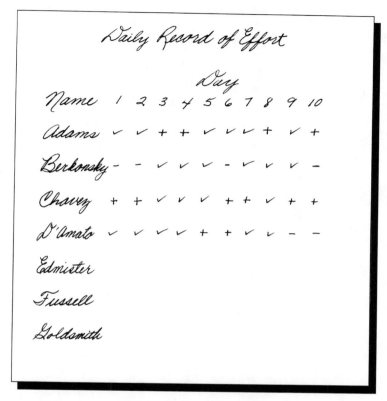

**FIGURE 6.2   A Page from Ms. Oldhand's Notebook**

The pupils and teacher continued to work in this way for the remainder of the week. When a group became satisfied with the answers to its questions, the children began to plan how they would present their results to the class by means of charts, graphs, and illustrations.

## Closure

Ms. Oldhand reminded the class on Wednesday that they would have to bring their investigations to a close in time to present their results to the class on Monday. There was a great scurrying about to finish up. Some groups planned to meet on Saturday to complete their displays. On the following Monday, each group was given time to explain what the members had done and display their results for the class. Two of the presentations are described here.

### Group 1

Group 1 displayed a poster with labeled drawings of the kinds of trees found. Under each drawing of a tree was a drawing of the corresponding leaf. Figure 6.4 shows some of the drawings the pupils had made to use on their poster.

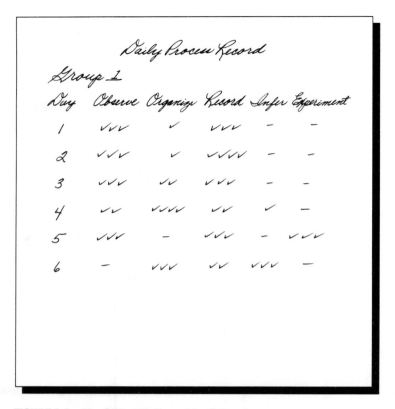

**FIGURE 6.3   Ms. Oldhand's Record for Group 1**

The pupils had also made a map of the town, with their neighborhoods outlined and indications of the kinds of trees found in each area. Finally, they had made a bar graph to show and compare the number of trees of each kind. The group explained the posters and graphs and answered questions.

### Group 2

This group had found some interesting signs of insect life in a dead log. The pupils drew pictures of what they had found and identified as many things as they could. They also had found moss and lichen, which they put into plastic bags and displayed on a poster. Another item of interest was some of the dead and rotted wood—also in a plastic bag—displayed beside a small piece of wood from a tree that had just been cut. The members of this group, like those in Group 1, explained what they had found and answered questions.

### Assessment and Feedback

Now it was time for the teacher to decide whether the objectives of the lesson had been met. As Ms. Oldhand had kept the investigations' objectives in mind all

Oak          Maple          Alder

**FIGURE 6.4  Drawings for Poster on Local Tree Population**

along and had made notes of her observations, she had several things that could help her make an assessment.

The reports that the children gave were one indication of whether cognitive goals had been met. Did the children learn anything about trees in their groups? And did they present what they learned in such a way that other children learned something, too? Because this style of teaching allows children to make many decisions about their own learning and because there was no predetermined information that all children were required to learn, Ms. Oldhand did not give a multiple-choice or fill-in-the-blanks test. Instead, she asked pupils to write answers in their own words to two questions.

"I'm going to give you two questions," she said, "and I want you to close your eyes and think about what you have been doing for the past two weeks. After you have thought about it, write the answers as clearly as you can. It is important to express your thoughts clearly. I want everyone's best answers." Her questions were:

1. List three important things about trees that you learned by working in your group.
2. List two things you learned about trees from other people's reports.

*Children plan how they will present the results of their investigation.*

Ms. Oldhand did not expect everyone to have learned the same things. She wanted to know what the children would take with them for the future, not what they had memorized and would forget quickly.

The answers to her questions gave Ms. Oldhand some data about what the children had learned. Did they consider trivial facts to be most important, or did they learn something that they would take with them as the basis for further learning? Did the groups present their reports in such a way that other children understood what they had done?

Ms. Oldhand also had her record of the children's use of science processes and she had her records of daily performance to help her make judgments about an individual child's progress in becoming an autonomous learner. She would also use this information when she talked to parents about individual children.

Ms. Oldhand gave feedback to each group in the form of written comments, indicating the objectives that had been met and suggesting areas that remained to be worked on. She emphasized the positive outcomes because her pupils were still learning to work in this way and she did not wish to discourage them.

### Reflection

Now it was time for Ms. Oldhand to reflect on the investigations. She had to use her intuition and common sense to decide whether the topic and the activities captured and maintained the children's interest. She asked herself some other questions: Did she allow enough time? Too much time? What would she do differently? and Would she select this topic again? Ms. Oldhand reflected on these questions and then wrote her own assessment in her journal for her future use.

# INDEPENDENT PROJECTS

Independent student projects require some of the same teacher skills that are required by group investigations. In both cases pupils are acting as independent learners, responsible for their own behavior and task accomplishment. And in both cases they require a great deal of guidance, monitoring, and reminding—as well as frequent feedback, support, and reassurance. The demands on the teacher are very different from the demands of direct instruction and even of guided inquiry, but the reward is seeing children become independent learners.

A recent study on out-of-school science activities of third and fourth graders found that many children were carrying on little projects of their own without the help or even the knowledge of parents or teachers (Charron, 1987). For instance one fourth-grade girl said, "Sometimes I do stuff, but I don't really know that I'm doing science then. Sometimes I'll just follow an animal around and see what it does, like a worm" (p. 10). The wide variety of science activities of the children in this study makes it plain that children are interested in science and that they have ideas that they would like to try. Individual projects give them that opportunity and also stimulate other children to think of things that they might like to do.

As in group investigations, the particular knowledge to be gained by each pupil is not specified in advance by the teacher but is left to the interests of the individual pupils. By allowing pupils to choose projects that interest them, the teacher is demonstrating that the pupils' ideas and interests are important and worthy of consideration. When pupils see that the teacher values their ideas and believes that they can learn on their own, they begin to believe it themselves. That is one of the most important goals of science teaching: for children to believe that they can learn on their own and become autonomous learners. By working on projects of real interest to them, children are stimulated to make the mental connections that result in new knowledge and understanding; that is, they construct their own knowledge.

## Science Fair

Not everyone agrees that science fairs are appropriate for elementary-school children, but they are popular with parents and administrators and participation in a fair can be a positive experience. Remember that projects do not have to be used as entries in a science fair. Shorter, simpler projects can be prepared for parents' nights, for a school fair, or for display one at a time on a science table. Requirements for planning and monitoring are the same, though simpler projects take less time. For example, one teacher assigned pairs of pupils to prepare projects for display in class throughout the year. The teacher did the first one; then twice each month thereafter, a pair of pupils

*These children have worked hard on their Science Fair project.*

prepared a new display or experiment. The children kept their projects a surprise until the day a project was unveiled and explained to the class.

If you plan for your class to participate in a science fair, you have the responsibility to make it a learning experience for all your pupils. Here are some guidelines that may help you achieve that goal:

- Emphasize the learning experience rather than competition.
- Do not use participation as a basis for the course grade.
- Activities supplement rather than replace science classes.
- Insist that the children do the work themselves.

Children younger than fourth graders do not usually participate in science fairs because of the difficulty that young children have in sustaining interest and motivation over a long period of time. For younger children, shorter term projects without competition are more appropriate. In the project plan that follows, the assumption is that all pupils will participate in the fair. The argument against having all pupils participate holds that some children have to undertake a project in which they have no real interest. The argument for total participation holds that children who are not interested in science may become interested if allowed to choose a topic on their own. And because the project objectives are broader than learning about a specific science topic, those who do not participate will lose important learning opportunities. Different viewpoints on participation and many useful suggestions and ideas for projects are presented in a useful booklet published by the National Science Teachers Association ([NSTA], 1985).

## Three Types of Projects

Most projects for science fairs can be divided into three categories: (a) collections, (b) demonstrations, and (c) experiments. All three can be planned to include the use of science processes and should be expected to increase knowledge and understanding. These categories are described later in this chapter along with suggestions of some things to keep in mind for each type of project.

As you study the following plan for projects for a science fair, note how the parts of a lesson plan that are now familiar to you have been adapted for this purpose. You will see that the plan includes objectives, motivation, materials, learning activities, and assessment and feedback.

## PROJECTS FOR A SCIENCE FAIR

### GRADE LEVEL: 5

### OBJECTIVES

1. Plan and carry out a project.
2. Communicate the results.
3. Develop habits of independent work.

### MATERIALS

Materials will be gathered as needed, depending on projects.

### SCHEDULE OF ACTIVITIES

This schedule is for a five-week period preceding the science fair, which takes place on a Saturday. Other science lessons continue, but time is set aside every Monday, Wednesday, and Friday for planning and discussing the pupils' projects.

*First Week*

*Objectives:* By the end of the week pupils will have decided whom they will work with and selected a project.

MONDAY (1)

*Motivation:* The teacher explains that there will be a science fair right in their school and that they can all participate. The teacher adds that there will be three categories—experiments, collections, and models—and gives a short description of each category.

*Experiments:* Each experiment starts with a question that can be answered by collecting data and putting the information together in a meaningful way. The questions chosen have to be answerable by the pupils themselves from the data they collect. To do so successfully, pupils should plan to control as many factors as possible and then vary only one thing (or one thing at a time) and measure the result. One way to help pupils plan their experiments is to give them a checklist to be filled in before the experiment is approved. An example of an experiments checklist is shown in Figure 6.5.

**Birds' Feeding Habits**

The question we want to answer:

Will more birds come to a feeder hanging from a tree or to a feeder placed on the ground?

What we will do:

Get two similar bird feeders. Place one feeder on a wire and hang it from a tree limb and place the other on the ground. Observe both feeders for one hour each morning and evening and count the number of birds that come to each feeder.

The variable we will change:

Placement of the bird feeders.

The variables we will keep constant (unchanged):

1) Bird feeders are the same type
2) Time of observation
3) Length of time of observation
4) Kind of bird food

The variable we will measure:

How many birds will come to each feeder

How we will measure it:

Counting the number of birds

How we will report our results:

A bar graph that shows the number of birds that came to each feeder. We will also show how many came in the morning and how many came in the evening. (We may be able to keep a record of the number of each kind of bird, such as sparrows, blue jays, etc, but if there are too many kinds we will not be able to do this.)

**FIGURE 6.5   Example of a Checklist for Experiments**

**Microorganisms in a pond**

**What we will collect:**
Samples of water from different places in a pond, then we will look at tiny drops under a microscope.

**Where we will find them:**
In a pond near one of our homes

**How we will identify them**
Using books in the school library (we have found the books we need)

**How we will classify them**
We will decide after they are collected

**How we will display them**
For each organism we will display a drawing, give the name, tell where it was found, and any other interesting information.

FIGURE 6.6 **Example of a Checklist for Collections**

**Note to Instructor.**
An example of an overused model is a plaster cone shaped to resemble a volcano. The center is filled with a chemical that burns and gives off smoke and sparks. This model can be dangerous and should not be allowed.

_Collections:_ Almost any natural materials that can be found locally and in some variety are suitable, including shells, leaves, rocks or minerals, nuts and acorns, insects, and flowers. Finding, identifying, classifying, and arranging for display are important processes for children at this age (Howe, 1987). Observations may also fall into this category, such as a record of sighting of birds or observations of the night sky over several weeks. Such observations would be interesting to some children and would provide data for conclusions about patterns. An example of a collections checklist is shown in Figure 6.6.

_Models:_ Some teachers have justifiably criticized the use of models, because so many of the same models have appeared over and over at science fairs. The models that are most interesting and teach the most are those that demonstrate a scientific principle or show a cause-and-effect relationship. Children design and make these models themselves to illustrate a principle or to show how something works. Simple models with working parts can be fun to build, but they must be kept simple. If complicated pieces of apparatus are attempted, the children will become frustrated and either abandon the project or get their parents to step in. Anything that incorporates gears, pulleys, switches, or similar mechanisms is interesting and motivating. The construction of an object or a model that illustrates a principle or relationship requires knowledge of the principle or relationship and, in addition, psychomotor skills and imagination. An example of a models checklist is shown in Figure 6.7.

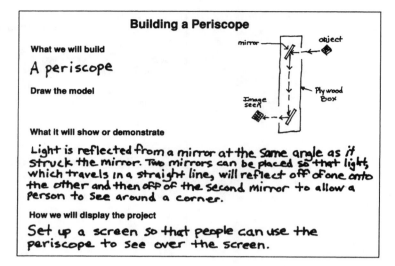

**FIGURE 6.7    Example of a Check-list for Models**

After a 10- to 15-minute discussion in which pupils are asked for ideas and the teacher mentions some possible projects, the teacher asks them to think about some things they might like to do and be prepared to talk about them on Wednesday.

WEDNESDAY (1)

*Discussion:* Discussion continues, with the teacher asking for ideas, reacting to suggestions, and guiding the discussion toward projects that are suitable and appropriate for the children in the class. Projects should be simple.

*Assignment:* On Friday, each group, pair, or individual will turn in a paper giving a brief, general idea of what they want to do. Questions about these ideas are answered. Any pupils who haven't been able to think of a project that they really want to do can talk to the teacher. The teacher makes suggestions and also helps those who are ready to come to closure.

FRIDAY (1)

Pupils turn in papers.

*Second Week*

*Objectives:* By the end of the week, each pupil or group will have

- developed a plan for a project, and
- made a list of materials and identified sources.

MONDAY (2)

The teacher approves and returns the plans or works with pupils to improve plans if necessary. The teacher has prepared a checklist for each category of project: experiment, collection, or model, similar to the checklists in Figures 6.5, 6.6 and 6.7.

The teacher hands out these checklists and explains how they should be used. Pupils respond to the items in the checklist with specifics about their projects. They will hand in their responses and a list of materials on Friday. (A strict limit should be placed on the cost of the materials. Pupils who need help in obtaining materials are advised to speak to the teacher. The teacher may need help from the PTA, a mothers' club, or some other source for children who need assistance.)

WEDNESDAY (2)

Teacher holds question and answer session.

FRIDAY (2)

Pupils turn in workbooks.

*Third Week*

*Objectives:* By the end of the week, the pupils will have completed their models, experiments, or collections.

MONDAY (3)

Teacher returns workbooks; pupils discuss plans.

WEDNESDAY (3)

Teacher monitors progress.

FRIDAY (3)

Teacher continues to monitor progress.

*Fourth Week*

*Objectives:* By the end of the week, pupils will have

- turned in their notebooks and given quick, informal oral reports;
- learned methods of reporting results; and
- produced a plan for reporting results.

MONDAY (4)

Teacher continues to monitor with pupils reporting informally.

WEDNESDAY (4)

Teacher gives a direct instruction lesson on reporting results; a one-period lesson. The lesson plan includes objectives, guided practice, and the other parts of a direct instruction lesson. Ways to report results, including bar graphs, line graphs, drawings, and written accounts, are demonstrated.

*Assignment for Friday:* Bring in a plan for reporting your results.

FRIDAY (4)

Teacher and pupils discuss ways to report results.

*Fifth Week*

*Objectives:* By the end of the week, the pupils will have

- completed a poster or other means of presenting results, and
- practiced explaining their projects to their classmates.

MONDAY (5)

Teacher returns reporting plans to pupils.

WEDNESDAY (5)

Pupils continue work on reports.

FRIDAY (5)

Pupils put finishing touches on reports, form groups of four, and take turns explaining their projects to each other.

## ASSESSMENT AND FEEDBACK

Informal methods of assessment, similar to those suggested for group investigations are appropriate. Questions that could be asked of pupils include:

What science process or principle does your project demonstrate?
How is that process or principle demonstrated in your project?
What is the most important thing you learned from your project?
What would you do differently if you could do it again?

The teacher gives feedback to each child, the method depending on the kind of project. When independent projects are undertaken for a science fair (as in the example plan), the winners receive feedback from judges, and all other participants receive a certificate. The teacher praises all who participated and perhaps points out to the class some aspects of the winning entries that were particularly good.

All pupils who completed their projects should receive positive feedback and encouragement. This kind of teaching is developmental and requires sensitivity, patience, and persistence on the part of the teacher.

## ■ SUMMARY

This is the third chapter on science teaching strategies. Chapter 4 described *direct instruction,* a method appropriate for teaching basic skills and knowledge that cannot be obtained by direct experience. The objectives are clear, and the outcomes are predictable if a lesson is successful. Chapter 5 focused on guided *inquiry,* a method of teaching based on direct experience followed by discussion and reflection. In this method the teacher plans activities but the pupils have more freedom of thought and action than in direct instruction learning tasks are the same for all children, but they can approach the tasks in their own ways. This chapter covered teaching strategies designed to promote independent learning. The learning outcomes cannot be predicted except in a general way and won't be the same for all pupils. This method of teaching may look easy to an observer, or to a student intern, but it requires careful planning, constant monitoring, and continuing support.

*Cooperative learning* is a structured way to set up groups to work together on learning tasks. Although the method is highly structured and detailed, many teachers have found that children catch on quickly and like the security of knowing what is expected of themselves and other group members. Because the success of *group investigations* depends on groups working together to achieve the group's goals, the formation and support of groups is an important aspect of this teaching method.

In group investigations the teacher and pupils decide on an overall topic that pupils pursue in various ways. Details are given of Ms. Oldhand's planning, the pupils' plans for their group investigations, Ms. Oldhand's monitoring of their work, and their planning and implementation of ways to communicate results to their classmates.

In the section on *independent projects* the teacher guides and helps pupils plan and bring various projects to conclusion. In this case the projects are intended for exhibit in a science fair, but projects of this kind may also be exhibited at parents' nights or other special occasions. The projects may be displayed briefly in the school's hallways or throughout the year as a continually changing interactive science center in the classroom.

## ■ ACTIVITIES FOR THE READER

1. Choose a grade level and outline a plan for a group investigation. Select a topic, list objectives, and describe motivational activities for five possible group investigations. Then describe your method of assessment.

2. As a class project, divide yourselves into groups of five. Each group should choose a grade or several grades, depending on the number in your class. Each group will develop an annotated list of books and articles that could be used at the chosen grade level(s) as sources of ideas for investigations. Share these lists by distributing copies to all class members.

3. Working with a group of four or five students from your methods class, plan, carry out, record, and display the results of an investigation that would be suitable for a grade of your choice. Report to the class what you learned that will be valuable to you as a teacher.

4. Make a list of five topics that are suitable for group investigations. Using the criteria in this chapter, explain why each topic is suitable.

# ■ QUESTIONS FOR DISCUSSION

1. Choose a grade level and list three problems you foresee in using the method of group investigation with that age group. What might you do to prevent each of the problems?

2. Describe in your own words the activities probably carried out by Group 1, as represented in Figure 6.3.

3. Compare methods of pupil assessment in group or independent investigations, guided inquiry, and direct instruction.

# ■ REFERENCES

Charron, E. (1987). *Teacher behavior in Japanese elementary science classrooms.* Paper presented at the annual meeting of the National Association for Research in Science Teaching, Washington, DC.

Howe, A. (1987). Collecting as a science activity. *Science Activities, 24*(3), 17–19.

Johnson, D. W., & Johnson, R. T. (1987). *Learning together and alone: Cooperative, competitive and individualistic learning* (2nd ed.). Upper Saddle River, NJ: Prentice Hall.

National Research Council. (1996). *National science education standards.* Washington, DC: National Academy Press.

National Science Teachers Association. (1985). *Science fairs and projects: Grades K–8 (2nd ed.).* Washington, DC: Author.

Slavin, R. (1980). Cooperative learning. *Review of Educational Research, 50,* 315–342.

# Enhancing Instruction through Assessment

■    MR. NEWMAN:    I'm trying to write some test questions for the unit I'm going to teach, but I'm having a really hard time.

MS. OLDHAND:    Maybe I can help. I'm glad that you're speaking to me about it now rather than after you've finished the unit. The time to think about testing is before you begin rather than after the unit's almost over. Actually, most teachers don't think of it as "testing" like we used to do. What we want to do is find out whether students are making progress toward learning goals, and there are many ways to do that.

MR. NEWMAN:    I think one reason I'm having trouble is that I always got very nervous when I had a big test coming up. I never felt that I could do my best or show what I really knew about the subject.

MS. OLDHAND:    That's one of the main reasons for changing our ways of measuring student progress. There are other reasons, too. Besides the anxiety that paper-and-pencil tests cause, there are so many important things that they can't measure that they give a very limited view of student progress and achievement. Come to my room after the last class today, and I'll show you some of the ways that I assess student learning.

Have you ever taken a course in which you felt that you learned a lot but didn't get the grade you thought you deserved? There are many reasons why that might have happened. Maybe your disappointment was due to tests and possibly a final exam that didn't tap into what you had learned. Or perhaps you weren't meeting the instructor's objectives all along, but you didn't get feedback to let you know that you weren't doing so well. Or there may be any number of other possible reasons. Whatever the reason may have been, you likely have negative feelings about that course and/or the instructor.

The purpose of this chapter is to help you think about assessment in a different way and to learn a variety of balanced and fair ways to assess student learning. You will also learn how to provide constructive feedback to pupils, parents, and others. The traditional view is that assessment is a linear process of teaching and testing. The teacher teaches and then gives a test—over and over, throughout the year. The view presented here is one of an interactive process in which teaching, learning, and assessment are simultaneous and integrated. In this chapter you will find many specific examples of ways to make assessment an integral part of your teaching.

# FORMAL AND INFORMAL ASSESSMENT

Teachers who use activity-centered teaching methods are constantly making informal judgments about pupils' learning as they move about the classroom from pupil to pupil or one group to another. Informal observation of this kind is not casual, and it is important. However, it may not allow the teacher to be equally discerning about the growth of each individual pupil and usually does not involve record keeping. We refer to it as *informal assessment*, a sort of careful looking around, with special questions asked when problems arise.

By contrast, *formal assessment* involves continuous, systematic data gathering and record keeping. It may include paper-and-pencil tests, but it doesn't rely solely on them. It may include observation of pupil behaviors in much the same way as in informal assessment. The difference is that the teacher records observations of each pupil systematically rather than randomly. Systematic collection of many kinds of data will not relieve the teacher of having to make professional judgments about pupil progress or grades, but it will provide the necessary information on which to base a judgment. It will also provide understandable information about pupil achievement that the teacher can communicate to the pupils and their parents. The information that the teacher gathers about children's progress will also indicate whether the goals of the lesson or unit have been achieved, and where any trouble spots are. So, while assessing pupils' learning, the teacher is also conducting a self-assessment.

# PURPOSES OF ASSESSMENT

Assessment should be closely tied to instruction and be an ongoing part of classroom life. Its purpose is to assess pupils' achievement and/or behaviors, not the pupils themselves as people. Teacher assessment has a profound effect on pupils' growth, achievement, and self-esteem. Psychologists who have developed measures to indicate the factors to which children attribute their success or failure in school have found that they attribute success or failure primarily to ability, effort, luck, or task difficulty. Your challenge is to develop and use assessment methods that will lead pupils to attribute their achievements in school to ability and effort rather than luck or task difficulty. Differences in ability are real and are recognized by the children themselves, but those who make a reasonable effort should be able to accomplish school tasks and know that they are succeeding.

The purpose of assessment is not to sort pupils as "A students" or "B students," or as overachievers or underachievers, or into any other categories. Nor is its purpose to teach pupils to compete for grades. Everything you do, including assessment, should be directed toward helping pupils achieve the cognitive, affective, psychomotor, and social goals of instruction mentioned briefly here in relation to assessment and discussed further in Chapter 8. Assessment and instruction are related to each other as two sides of the same coin.

## Traditional Methods of Assessment

The primary purpose of traditional methods of assessment has been to assess the attainment of cognitive goals. Teachers have relied on paper-and-pencil tests made up of multiple-choice, true–false, and completion items combined with problems and a few essay or free-response questions. Progress toward achieving affective goals has most often been measured, if at all, by statements to which pupils indicate levels of agreement or disagreement. These methods are limited in that they do not provide information about the attainment of many of the important objectives of science teaching and are more appropriate for older pupils than for those in the elementary grades.

Quizzes and tests are sometimes treated as if they were accurate, objective measuring instruments—in the same class with thermometers or speedometers—but a moment's reflection will tell you that that isn't so. Subjective judgment is used in choosing the questions to ask, in assigning weight to each item, and in evaluating answers. However hard you may try to be objective, there is an unavoidable element of subjectivity in the test itself. Have you ever studied for a test and been disappointed that a question you were well prepared for was not on the test? Your instructor was not singling you out but just didn't include every question that could legitimately be on the test. That is another reason not to rely solely on this method of assessment.

## Authentic Assessment

Alternative assessment methods are needed when the purpose of assessment is to measure understanding and reasoning rather than information retained by pupils. Much of the information asked for in traditional tests is not connected to the real lives or interests of children and we, as teachers, all know that much of what is learned for tests is soon forgotten. *Authentic assessment* measures accomplishment of tasks that have significance beyond the classroom—tasks that connect what pupils have learned in school to their lives and interests. This kind of learning goes beyond a collection of facts and is built into pupils' understanding of a subject.

The *National Science Education Standards* (NRC, 1996, p. 5) include the recommended shifts in emphasis and approach to assessment shown in Table 7.1.

**TABLE 7.1   Recommended Changes in Assessment Practices**

| From | To |
| --- | --- |
| What is easily measured | What is highly valued |
| Assessing knowledge | Assessing understanding and reasoning |
| Finding out what pupils *do not* know | Finding out what pupils *do* know |
| End-of-term assessment | Ongoing assessment |

You may have heard someone say that what is not tested will not be taught. That isn't completely true, but it has enough relation to reality to give us pause. In the complex world of the elementary-school classroom, there isn't enough time to do everything that a teacher would like to do; priorities are set consciously or unconsciously. When the main mode of assessment is paper-and-pencil tests that measure a narrow range of outcomes, teachers tend to focus on those outcomes to the exclusion of others that are equally, or more, important, including noncognitive objectives.

# RUBRICS

The questions and tasks that are used for authentic assessment cannot be judged in the same way that traditional quizzes, multiple-choice questions, and true–false statements are judged. The need for different ways of judging and grading brought forth the idea of rubrics. *Rubrics* is a new word for an old idea. You are familiar with getting "partial credit" on a problem in math or science if you set the problem up correctly but make a mistake in calculations. Your teacher had decided on certain criteria that had to be met in order to assign full credit. This decision was probably made informally, but the idea is similar to having a rubric for grading answers to problems. Rubrics are criteria for evaluating any pupil product that allows for free expression of ideas or that does not have one, and one only, correct answer. In the context of elementary-school science such criteria may apply to notebooks, posters, projects, and answers to questions that require writing or drawing. Rubrics define what is to be assessed and may define the levels of performance. They serve several purposes, one of which is to make grading fair by using the same criteria for all students. If you have ever graded essays, for example, you know how hard it is to be certain that you have graded the last papers by exactly the same standards as the first papers. Another purpose is to let pupils know what is expected of them. Will neatness or only ideas count? What kind of evidence is needed to support each statement? Pupils know what the teacher's expectations are before they begin a task or assignment.

The following sections contain descriptions and examples of several alternative or authentic assessment strategies. You can choose those that are appropriate to the grade level, age, and developmental level of your pupils and your own preferences.

# WORKBOOKS

As soon as children learn to write with some ease they should keep a *science workbook* in which they record their activities in science class. This workbook can be a primary source of information about student progress. It is far preferable to a loose collection of papers and lab reports that get mislaid, mangled, and lost. At the beginning of the year, explain that each pupil is to bring a small notebook to be used as a workbook, that it is to be used only in science class, and that it is to be left at school. Workbooks should be handed out to pupils at the beginning of science class and returned to a special place at the end of class. You may assign this responsibility to one of the pupils at the beginning and end of each science class period.

Workbooks are where pupils write their interpretations, inferences, and plans for further experiments. They provide ongoing records of pupils' actions and thoughts about the unit topic and let children see how their thinking has grown. When pupils need to remember what happened in a previous activity, the workbooks provide that information. They also give children a way to develop and apply writing skills. As children engage in a real application of skills that both makes sense and is useful, they learn to value their own writing and their own ideas.

For each activity pupils may write answers to the following.

- What I did:
- What I found out:
- Ideas for next time:

The open-ended form of responses allows pupils to express themselves freely and thus reveals more than you may have asked for directly. For example, misconceptions are sometimes apparent in children's responses: "I think the black stuff [in the aquarium] may be from the sand when they ground it up." Did you know that many children think that naturally occurring sand is created by human beings grinding up rocks? Length and style of children's responses can be indicators of interest and enthusiasm. You don't have to rely completely on reading between the lines, though. You can ask pupils to respond in their workbooks to specific questions and directives related to whatever activity is being performed. Here are some examples from the unit on mealworms:

1. Draw a picture of your mealworm and label the parts.
2. Did your mealworm seem to like one color more than others? What is your evidence?
3. Write a paragraph on
   a. what you learned from today's discussion;
   b. what you liked or disliked most about today's activity and why; and
   c. how your group is working out. Does everyone get along? Are you doing your part? What could be done to make things work more smoothly?
4. In what ways are you taking good care of the materials?
5. Write your suggestions for improving our cleanup system.

## Evaluating Workbooks

Workbooks are more useful to pupils and to you if they are collected weekly and returned promptly. If you have 25 pupils and take up five workbooks each day, you can review them and write appropriate comments rather quickly. Or you may find that taking them all at the same time works better for you.

Rubrics for evaluating workbooks should be developed with pupil involvement at the beginning of the year. Start with simple criteria, use them for a month or two, and reopen the discussion with the pupils. Do they think that the criteria are fair? Are there other things they would like to have assessed? Important criteria are completeness of information and observations, organization, and evidence of thinking. Because children's writing skills are in various stages of development, spelling and writing are best assessed in some other way; let the children freely explain what they did and express their ideas without fear of losing points because of poor spelling. To serve as a basis for evaluation, the information that you select should be summarized and recorded in some way. It could take the form of a checklist combined with anecdotal records. Examples of such checklists for the first two questions in the preceding list for the unit on mealworms are shown in Figures 7.1 and 7.2.

As children become more experienced, you may decide to use rubrics that define levels of responses, but complex rubrics and grading systems are not appropriate at this level; keep it simple, ongoing, and understandable. To become independent learners, children have to be able to work on their own without constant

| | A | B | Comments |
|---|---|---|---|
| Susan | | | |
| Andy | | | |
| José | | | |
| Jared | | | |
| Kelly | | | |

**FIGURE 7.1**
**Journal Summary for Question 1**

A: Drawing is realistic rather than fanciful.
B: Labels are complete and accurate.

| | A | B | Comments |
|---|---|---|---|
| Susan | | | |
| Andy | | | |
| José | | | |
| Jared | | | |
| Kelly | | | |

**FIGURE 7.2**
**Journal Summary for Question 2**

A: Shows understanding of the experiment.
B: States observations supporting conclusions.

adult guidance. For that to happen, they have to have science lessons based on activities, including writing, that they can manage mostly on their own. When science lessons become too abstract or too complicated—or the necessary record keeping and drawing conclusions are too difficult—little meaningful learning can occur.

## CONCEPT MAPS

A *concept map* is a diagram that represents knowledge of a concept. It is an attempt to show, on paper, how the pieces of knowledge and the ideas that make up a concept interconnect with and relate to each other (Novak, 1990). Concept maps have been used as a way to find out what children know before and after instruction; that is, whether instruction increased their understanding of a concept. These maps also are a way to track changes in cognitive structure over time (Stoddart, Abrams, Gasper, & Canaday, 2000).

Figures 7.3 and 7.4 and present concept maps drawn by two children after a unit on vertebrates in fourth grade. The teacher showed his pupils how to make a concept map and drew an example on the board. Next he put the word *water* on the board, asked what they knew about water, and drew a concept map. Then he told them to put the word *mammals* in the center of a page and to make a concept map to show what they knew about mammals. Frieda drew a map that connected names of various mammals to the central concept, showing that she thought of individual examples as the way to represent the concept. Maria's map showed a much broader understanding of the concept by connecting it into the overall concept of *animals with backbones* and by identifying the defining characteristics of mammals. She also represented her knowledge that two vastly different animals (bats and whales) are mammals.

The difference in knowledge represented in these two concept maps would probably not be shown in a paper-and-pencil test where typical test items might include the following:

■   List two ways that mammals are different from other animals.

■   Which of the following are mammals? Monkey, frog, chipmunk, whale, shark.

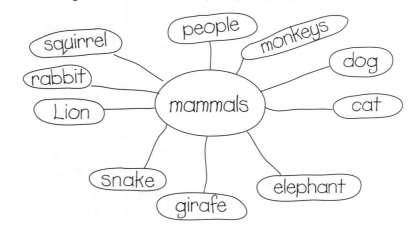

**FIGURE 7.3**
**Frieda's**
**Concept Map**

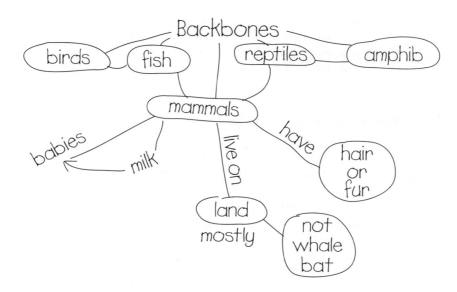

**FIGURE 7.4    Maria's Concept Map**

Elaborate methods of scoring concept maps have been devised (Stoddart, Abrams, Gasper, & Canaday, 2000), but are not necessary when the aim is to get a general idea of children's understanding.

The two concept maps shown in Figures 7.3 and 7.4, taken alone, could not serve as a basis for making a firm judgment about a child's knowledge or understanding but, they can be very useful when combined with other means of assessment.

## ESSAY AND OPEN-ENDED QUESTIONS

Essay and open-ended questions ask pupils to write responses in their own words from their own knowledge without the prompts provided by multiple-choice, true–false, or completion items. They require organization of information followed by reasoning or critical thinking that goes beyond information. In science, workbooks fulfill many of the functions of essay questions in other subject areas, but items of this kind can also be useful both as informal and formal means of assessment. Open-ended questions give pupils a chance to demonstrate what they know and offer opportunities for relating experiences and knowledge from other contexts to science. Children too young to write responses can make drawings, which often reveal a great deal about their ideas and may give clues to their misconceptions and misunderstandings.

Assessment of responses to open-ended questions, like assessment of performance tasks and workbooks, is based on previously developed rubrics. The emphasis in developing rubrics for these questions should be on the level of understanding and use of knowledge, and the items should be such that they can be answered in one paragraph. Questions of this type may also be used to help the teacher determine what understandings pupils have gained from a lesson or set of lessons. In that case, answers would not be scored but would be used as a guide in planning future instruction or to identify pupils who are falling behind.

## PERFORMANCE ASSESSMENT

Watching pupils work with materials is like looking through a magic window into the workings of their minds. They act out their thinking in concrete, observable ways. Performance assessment in its purest form evaluates what a child can *do* as opposed to what a child *knows*. This difference has been explained as the difference between the written test and the road test that are required to obtain a driver's license. The written test shows what applicants know about rules and regulations, and the road test shows what they can do behind the wheel of an automobile.

Science is one area of the elementary-school curriculum where performance assessment is a natural part of the learning process. This type of assessment can be made in several ways. One way is a behavior checklist, in which you record observations of pupil performance and focus on whatever seems most important at any given time—for example, how carefully a pupil or group follows directions, sets up apparatus, makes observations, and records them. If you notice that many pupils

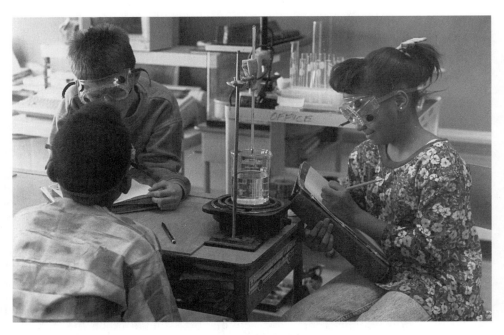

*What questions are we supposed to answer at this station?*

are not setting up equipment as they are supposed to, you can call for quiet and explain the setup again. You can then walk around the room to check each setup. Such an informal performance assessment of a specific task is intended to improve learning rather than to assign a grade. If a formal assessment is needed, performance tasks can be used as a means of assessment at the end of a unit. How this might be done is explained next. Note that, although this approach is a form of performance assessment, it also depends on pupils' abilities to read directions and write or draw answers.

## An Example

Suppose that the two investigations of electric current presented in Chapter 3 were the beginning of a unit on electricity. At the end of the unit you might decide that the best way to find out what pupils had learned would be to have them demonstrate what they could do. Designing a performance assessment for such a unit or series of lessons includes the following steps:

- Review the objectives for each lesson and select those to be tested.
- Decide what you will accept as evidence of acceptable performance.
- Design simple sets of apparatus to test each objective and the means for pupils to communicate their responses.
- Set up stations around the room.
- Work out a system for pupils to rotate among the stations.

One of the first things that you'll notice when you start planning for a performance assessment is that it will not be feasible to test for all the unit objectives. Therefore, as in all assessment procedures, you will have to choose what to test for. There are only three objectives in this example, but you might choose four to six if you were conducting this assessment in a classroom. The objectives that you will assess are these:

1. Pupil can use a bulb, a battery, and a wire to make an electric circuit.
2. Pupil can use a circuit tester to identify conductors and nonconductors.
3. Pupil can draw standard diagram elements to represent a given circuit.

Next you have to decide how pupils will communicate their responses and how you will evaluate them. Because you can't possibly observe each pupil—unless you have an assistant to work with the other children—the pupils will have to write or draw their responses, and you will have to develop rubrics for evaluating their responses. Again, rubrics are developed in advance to ensure that partially correct pupil responses are treated the same and that you know what you will accept as a correct answer. You will also have to have a classroom management plan for this assessment, as some children will be working through the tasks while others are engaged in other learning activities.

## Setting Up Tasks

**Resource Materials Note.**
If nothing else is available, you can make a cubicle by setting a large box, with its top cut off and open toward the pupil, on a table.

After working through all the steps just described, you will set up the tasks, each in its own cubicle. The tasks could be set up to assess attainment of the three objectives listed previously.

### Station 1

A battery, a bulb, and a length of wire are placed on the table along with directions to use the materials to make a complete circuit, to explain how the pupil knows that the circuit was complete, and to draw a diagram of it.

### Station 2

A circuit tester, two conductors, and two nonconductors that were not used in the activity in class. The directions are to test each material, identify each as a conductor or nonconductor, and explain how that was determined.

### Station 3

A complete circuit is set up with a lighted bulb and perhaps a switch. The directions are to draw a diagram of the circuit, using the standard method of representing electrical elements. A rubric to assess these tasks is shown in Table 7.2.

These rubrics are simple and easy for you and your pupils to understand. Rubrics can be much more complex and are often tested ahead of time and revised before use. However, that isn't necessary in assessing children's performance on tasks of this kind. Assessment should be kept as simple as possible and viewed by children as a normal part of their classroom activities. When assessments become elaborate and time-consuming, the process fosters anxiety and competition for grades, both of which should be guarded against and, if possible, avoided.

**TABLE 7.2    Rubric for Performance Assessment of Electricity Tasks**

| | | |
|---|---|---|
| Task 1 | Correct explanation (bulb is lit) and accurate diagram | 2 points |
| | Either correct explanation or diagram | 1 point |
| | Neither correct explanation nor diagram | 0 points |
| Task 2 | Correct identification of all materials and clear explanation | 2 points |
| | Correct identification or clear explanation | 1 point |
| | Neither of above | 0 points |
| Task 3 | Correct diagram | 2 points |
| | Partially correct diagram | 1 point |
| | No diagram or use of pictures instead of standard representation | 0 points |

## BEHAVIOR CHECKLISTS

You can use checklists to make your observations of pupil behaviors during learning activities more systematic. Deciding ahead of time which behaviors to note, communicating this decision to pupils, and then listing the behaviors on a check sheet serve two functions: (a) to focus your observations and (b) to provide a convenient way to record them. The behaviors that you choose to observe will depend on your unit goals. Because goals are normally stated rather broadly, they are not good as checklist items by themselves. You will need to generate some behavioral indicators that could serve as evidence that the goal is being met. Although behavior checklists can be used in any of the goal domains, they are especially useful in the noncognitive domains, partly because such goals are difficult to assess directly. For example, if one of your affective goals is for pupils to develop persistence, you might have a behavior checklist like the one shown in Figure 7.5.

This method can also be used to assess progress in the psychomotor goal mentioned previously—that is, handle circuit elements and connectors safely. What would you use as indicators for this psychomotor goal?

Checklists should be designed so that difficult judgment calls are not required. Rather than use a rating scale from 1 to 10, for example, simply use a check mark for satisfactory, a plus sign for especially noteworthy, or a minus sign for not observed. A checklist must be easy to use so that you can do so without drawing attention to it and so that a record is feasible on each behavior for each child.

## PRODUCTS

The circuits constructed in a unit on electricity and other products that result from science activities give quick and reliable information about a child's understanding

**FIGURE 7.5**
**Behavior Checklist for Persistence**

|  | A | B | C | D | Comments |
|---|---|---|---|---|---|
| Susan |  |  |  |  |  |
| Andy |  |  |  |  |  |
| José |  |  |  |  |  |
| Jared |  |  |  |  |  |
| Kelly |  |  |  |  |  |

A: Continues after novelty wears off.
B: Completes task that others did not.
C: Records data spontaneously.
D: Repeats experiment despite apparent failure.

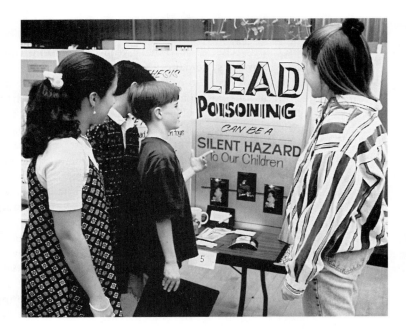

*Authentic
assessment
includes evaluating
student projects.*

of involved concepts. They also provide affective information, such as neatness, creativity, care taken, and so on. Always be sure that the product is judged in accordance with the unit goals. The same child's electric project could show an excellent conceptual understanding and yet be messy and unappealing visually. Giving an overall rating somewhere in the middle isn't useful when both concept and appearance are original goals. Rate achievement for each goal separately.

## PORTFOLIOS

A portfolio is a collection of student work, assembled over weeks or months, that gives an in-depth picture of achievement or progress. You may think of a portfolio as a collection of paintings or drawings that aspiring artists carry around to show prospective employers or gallery owners; a science student's portfolio is similar to that in some ways. A portfolio should allow pupils to display their best work and contain a variety of materials. Pupils should be allowed to choose at least some of the work to include. It is a "collection of evidence with a purpose" (Collins, 1992).

The development and assessment of portfolios require much time and thought on the part of both pupil and teacher and should be undertaken with a clear purpose in mind. Questions that should be answered before deciding to use portfolios as an assessment method include the following:

- What is the purpose of portfolios? Will they be used to motivate pupils, to help them learn to organize their work, to assess their achievements, or to demonstrate their progress?

- Will portfolios be assessed as part of the grading system or will they be used to showcase pupils' work? Will each portfolio be assessed as a whole, or will each entry be evaluated separately? In either case, if portfolios are to be formally assessed, clear criteria must be established at the outset.

- What will be included in portfolios? Responsibility for this decision should be shared with pupils, but without clear guidelines portfolios can become messy collections of miscellaneous papers.

One purpose of building portfolios is to enable pupils to look back on what they have accomplished and reflect on their work. Fourth- or fifth-grade children can write brief statements, and younger children can express their thoughts orally. Some children are very perceptive about their own work if they are encouraged to share their thoughts to a nonjudgmental audience—but only if their reflections are not to be assessed.

# SHORT-ANSWER TESTS

Paper-and-pencil tests that require short answers, such as multiple-choice, true–false, and completion items, may not be necessary. Generally, you can get the sort of information needed to assess learning in the various domains from other assessment methods. The main advantage of these tests is that they gather specific information from every child in a relatively short time. The quality of the information gathered may be rather low, however, especially if the questions are unclear or misleading to pupils. It takes some experience and perceptiveness regarding children's misconceptions to write really good tests. Objective tests that are both fair to the pupil and useful in picking out those who are not "getting it" are especially hard to write. Probably the best use for tests of this kind, if they are used at all, is to check understanding of concepts and ideas as you go along. In that case, the tests are not a means of assessment but a way to let you and the pupils know whether they are meeting instruction goals.

# ADAPTING ASSESSMENT METHODS

There are no assessment formulas that will work in all situations, and there is no substitute for your good judgment. Some of the methods just described should be modified as needed for young children and for those with disabilities.

## Assessment in the Primary Grades

Many of the assessment methods and ideas described involve reading and writing. They can't be used with children who haven't mastered these skills well enough to apply them without undue difficulty in forming and communicating answers. The focus in the early grades should be on observation and simple classification of objects and phenomena, experiences with plants and animals in the classroom, and learning to work with other children in groups to carry out learning activities. Assessments can be carried out by giving oral directions and asking children to make drawings of their observations rather than written records or explanations. Behavior checklists are a useful and appropriate means of collecting data with the emphasis shifted toward affective, social, and psychomotor rather than cognitive objectives. It is more important to provide learning tasks, experiences, and an environment that foster growth in these areas and interest in science than to try to teach science concepts that are beyond the mental reach of the children. Children who have learned to work in groups, who know how to use such simple equipment as magnets and magnifying glasses, who can classify and observe with care, and who are enthusiastic about science are prepared to undertake the more demanding tasks of the upper elementary grades. Assessment should focus on these objectives.

## Assessing Achievement of Students with Disabilities

Assessment tasks can be modified as needed to be appropriate for children with physical disabilities, learning disabilities, or limited English proficiency. Individual interviews may be the most appropriate method of assessment for those who have a physical disability that limits the ability to write or who have limited vision. Assessment tasks that depend on oral communication must be modified for those who are hearing impaired. Let common sense and fairness guide you as you devise assessment tasks and methods that are appropriate for children who have special needs.

## DEVELOPING AN ASSESSMENT PLAN

The first thing to remember is the importance of planning for assessment when you plan the other parts of your science program. The second thing to remember is the importance of using methods that tell you what the pupils have learned and whether they have achieved the goals that you set. Many teachers have found that the most practical and realistic way to plan instruction is by units.

### Guidelines for Unit Assessment

1. Review the objectives for each lesson and your overall goals for the unit.
2. Think about content, process, psychomotor, affective, and social goals and decide what methods you can use to assess attainment of goals in each category. Use a variety of methods. Assessment should be interesting and challenging to pupils rather than boring and frightening.
3. Assessment plans, like all others, are subject to change. If you find that something isn't working, don't feel bound to an unworkable plan. If journals or

behavior checklists don't work well, the opportunity to do them over may be lost when the unit ends, so you will need to devise a written or performance test to salvage needed information.

4. Get ready for the next time that you will use the unit. After taking the time to develop a science unit, you probably will use it with more than one group of children. If possible, revise faulty assessment methods as soon as you recognize a problem. If you can't manage an immediate revision, at least make notes on what worked well and what needs rethinking and modifying. If you are as specific as possible, your job will be easier when you come back to the lesson or unit. If results show that a test is too hard, either fix the test or modify your instruction.

## PUPILS AS PARTNERS IN ASSESSMENT

It may seem contradictory to consider pupils as partners in assessment because assessment is usually thought of as something in which teachers are active and pupils are passive. It is true that teachers are responsible for assigning or "giving" grades at the end of each marking period. However, there are ways that pupils can participate without taking away the teacher's ultimate responsibility and authority. In the process, pupils will move a step closer to assuming responsibility for their own learning.

Some of the ways that you can provide for pupils to participate in assessment are these:

- Allow pupils to give input in the development of rubrics for workbooks and lab reports.
- Help pupils learn to give constructive feedback.
- Allow pupils in cooperative groups to assess each others' work—to be reviewed by you.
- Have pupils, in their teams or groups, give feedback on project presentations of other groups.

When children understand the criteria for assessment, how the criteria are arrived at, and what is expected of them, assessment is no longer a mysterious process over which they have no control.

## Communicating the Results of Assessment

The final step in assessment is communicating the results to those who will use the data you have gathered. The primary users of assessment information are the pupils themselves, but parents have a vital interest in the assessment of their children. School administrators and other officials also have an interest in the overall assessment of your pupils.

## Ongoing Feedback to Pupils

It is essential for pupils to have a clear understanding about what is to be assessed and how it will be assessed. They should know what is expected of them and how they can meet the standards that you have set. Equally important is knowing to what extent they have met the expectations and how they can continue to improve performance. When a teacher gives ongoing feedback, with explanations, on quality of work, pupils can readily understand how they are evaluated, what the criteria are, and what growth is occurring. Informal opportunities for feedback occur almost constantly as the teacher listens and responds to pupils' explanations during classroom discussions, interacts with pupils as they are engaged in hands-on activities, and provides comments on their workbooks and other written class work. Feedback of this kind should be serious, thoughtful, and honest. It is not useful to accept all responses as if they were equal with comments such as "That's an interesting idea" or "Thank you for your comment, Richard." It is better to ask for evidence, indicate that a response shows logical reasoning or "needs further thought," and tell a pupil, when necessary, that you will not accept silly responses. You should never be harsh, critical, or unkind, particularly to children who are shy or less able than others, but all children deserve to have their ideas taken seriously and to receive honest but gentle feedback.

It is only fair to have a short conference with each pupil when grades are reported. It should give the pupil an opportunity to ask questions about assessment methods and results and for you to explain what assessments were used in arriving at a grade. Elementary-school teachers will be discussing grades in other areas as well as in science, but these general principles apply to all. When pupils know that assessment and grading are fair, when they understand the bases for assessment, when feedback is clear and timely, and when they have opportunities to discuss their progress with their teacher openly and freely, assessment can achieve its most important purpose of promoting lasting learning.

# REPORT CARDS

Ongoing assessments that have been made during a grading period form the basis for reporting progress. Many schools do not use report cards that assign letter grades to children in the lower grades. Instead they use performance criteria, narrative statements, or other more descriptive ways to communicate progress and achievement in many areas. When a letter grade is required, it should be based on a variety of kinds of assessments, most of which should have been communicated to pupils. The grade on a report card should not come as a surprise; if it does, the matter can be discussed during the conference held with the pupil.

For report cards to communicate achievement effectively and to encourage rather than discourage pupils from striving for excellence, Stiggins (1994, p. 368) recommends a process that includes these steps:

*Each child needs honest feedback in order to meet the teacher's expectations.*

- Begin each grading period with a clear vision of the objectives to be met.
- Translate targets into assessments, aligning assessment methods to targets.
- Use the selected methods to assess attainment of objectives and keep accurate records.
- Combine data collected over time into a composite index of achievement, assigning grades that can be interpreted and understood by pupils and parents.

Make a determined effort to have a conference with parents or other caretakers of each child in your grade when report cards are issued. Parents need to know the basis for the grades, in what ways their child is making or not making progress toward meeting expectations, what the child's strengths and weaknesses are, and what they can do to help the child improve. Parents of a child who is meeting expectations like to hear about their child's success and can be given suggestions about ways to broaden their child's interests and skills. The conference may include the child and can be short if there are no major concerns—but you can't assume ahead of time that there will be no questions. If a face-to-face conference is not possible, try arranging to speak with a parent or caretaker by telephone. A sensitive and sometimes delicate approach is always needed when talking to parents or caretakers about their children. Remember that not all parents feel comfortable talking with teachers, that other parents will be very assertive in demanding more attention to their child's needs, and that for all parents the report card is likely to be an emotional issue.

# SELF-ASSESSMENT AS REFLECTIVE PRACTICE

The assessment process is not complete until you have taken time to reflect on the outcomes of a science activity and have asked yourself, "How well did I plan for instruction, implement the plan, and assess the results?" The answers to these questions need to be recorded regularly and systematically in a journal. The moment-to-moment demands of teaching are so great that it is easy to let the days and weeks go by without serious reflection unless you have a systematic plan and the resolve to follow it. The sources of data that you use for student assessment also tell you something about your planning, implementation, and assessment procedures. If pupils did not attain the objectives, was it because the activity was at the wrong level, too long for the time allowed, or not of intrinsic interest? Was the lesson well planned but not implemented as planned? Did the assessment procedure assess the wrong things? What should be done differently next time? Should this activity be used again? If the lesson, or unit, went really well, what were the factors that led to that positive outcome?

Engaging in serious thought about your teaching and working toward your own growth as a teacher is called *reflective practice*. The most important source of feedback is your pupils; they will let you know in both overt and subtle ways whether they are engaged and learning and whether the classroom is a pleasant and productive place for them. The outcomes of pupil assessment will also provide important data. Feedback from parents and from observations of administrators or colleagues are also useful and should be taken seriously. Your reflection on and response to all these things can be recorded in your journal. The amount of time you spend on your journal will depend on both your writing style and the time you can devote to it; notes can be as useful as well crafted sentences. The important thing is to do it.

■

## A CASE STUDY

## BUT WILL IT WORK IN THE CLASSROOM?

This narrative is a true story of one elementary-school teacher's implementation of authentic assessment in her science classes (Kamen, 1996). She used some, but not all, of the methods described in the preceding sections, and she added two that have not been mentioned. If you have been wondering whether these methods will work in the classroom, it should not surprise you that this teacher was sometimes frustrated and everything took longer than she had expected. But, despite problems and disappointments, her efforts led to a transformation of her teaching and her pupils' learning.

Virginia was a second-year teacher who was unhappy with her fourth-graders' performance in science and was always disappointed at the results of a test because the pupils missed questions that she had thought would be easy. Her frustration led her to enroll in a science methods class where she heard, for the first time, about authentic assessment. She had previously assessed her pupils' work the way her own work had always been assessed—with tests and homework.

She was already using active learning strategies because she believed that children should be physically active and involved in anything they were doing. To her, *hands-on* meant "giving the kids something to get their hands on." Then, in her methods class she heard, also for the first time, the term *minds*-on and came to understand the importance of minds-on as well as hands-on. As a result, her focus in teaching shifted from providing activities and giving grades to developing and assessing conceptual understanding. As she made this change, she soon realized that her assessment methods did not reflect her teaching goals and she decided to change the way she assessed her students. During the following summer she planned new science assessment strategies to use the following year and decided to keep a journal to record the outcomes of her experiments.

She began with portfolios with the idea that pupils would select one thing each week to put in their portfolios. At the end of the first grading period the only things in the portfolios were two tests. She had thought of portfolios as a way to collect other assessments, and the children had not thought of portfolios as a place to put creative work. So she abandoned portfolios for the time being.

Next she tried creative drama in a unit on animals. The children performed skits about predator–prey relationships, animals living in groups and symbiotic relationships. She developed checklists to document content understanding. Both Virginia and the children thought that this unit and its assessment were very successful.

Then she used an idea from language arts. First, she made a list of all the concepts in the animal unit. Then she asked each child to make one page. Each child chose an animal, wrote something about the animal related to each concept, and put the pages together to make a scrapbook. This approach also was successful.

When the children had a unit on snails they were allowed 10 minutes each day to write in their logs or workbooks. Another technique that she tried was to conduct interviews. She had groups of children prepare lists of questions about what they were studying; then she asked questions at random from the list.

In the spring she went back to portfolios but with a difference. This time the children kept all their work and wrote down what they had learned from each activity. At the end of the last unit Virginia asked the children to select the type of assessment they wanted, and she was surprised that those who chose interviews wrote very hard questions to be asked.

Her children did well on the Iowa Test of Basic Skills except for the multiple-choice questions. Many complained that the choices on the test were too simplistic or just boring. When Virginia developed and gave a multiple-choice test, several children came up to her and said that they didn't like any of the choices for answers. She told them that one answer was right and that they would have to pick the one that seemed best. But the next time she gave a multiple-choice test she changed her directions. "If you don't like any of the answers," she said "put your own answer in." When she graded the test she found that some children gave wrong answers because they didn't understand all the words used in the test items. By now, her focus had shifted from trying to help her pupils get the right answer to helping them explain what they knew. She then asked each child to submit five questions, and she chose the test questions from their lists.

It was hard for Virginia to accept the idea that assessment was taking up so much time. She still thought that she was supposed to teach a lesson and assess the outcome. It was a long time before she became comfortable with the idea that teaching and assessment can go on simultaneously.

By the end of her second year of using alternative assessment strategies she realized that she could never go back to the old methods. She had become a partner with her pupils in science inquiry. She now thought of assessment as an ongoing process in which she and her pupils could measure progress toward meeting learning goals.

Many factors helped her reach this point. She had the support of a university faculty member and a tolerant school administration. She worked with parents to win their support and acceptance of her approach.

Her transformation was summed up by Kamen: "Virginia's success in changing her practice came from a new understanding of what science teaching was all about. It was this shift to a conceptually based constructivist model that guided her reform" (p. 875).

# ■ SUMMARY

All classroom activity, including assessment, should be directed toward helping pupils achieve appropriate cognitive, affective, psychomotor, and social goals. Diverse data collection methods are replacing the traditional reliance on multiple-choice and other short-answer tests because of the limited ability of the traditional methods to measure many important educational objectives. A number of appropriate methods are available for assessing growth and achievement in elementary-school science. Foremost among them is the workbook that children use to record what they do, what they find out, and what they have learned from and think about the experience. Workbooks provide both a means of feedback to pupils and a means of keeping the teacher informed about pupil progress toward meeting learning objectives. Performance assessment is another method of letting pupils show what they have learned and whether they can put their knowledge to practical use. Other methods of assessment are portfolios and products. These methods can be modified as appropriate for students with disabilities or limited language proficiency. Including pupils in the assessment process in appropriate ways can help them become independent learners who can take responsibility for their own learning.

Communicating results to pupils, parents, or caretakers, and others is the final step in assessment. Ongoing communication with pupils lets them know whether they are meeting expectations and how to improve their performance if expectations are not being met. Grading for report cards should be a process that begins at the start of each grading period and includes setting and communicating clear goals, developing ways to assess attainment of those goals, gathering data, and compiling it to form a comprehensive index of achievement. The final step is self-assessment, a crucial part of reflective practice. As shown in the Case Study, assessment remains a demanding and complex part of teaching, and teachers still have to grapple with many unanswered questions.

# ■ Activities for the Reader

1. Develop performance assessments for three additional objectives in the electricity unit.

2. Develop a list of items to be included in a fifth-grader's science portfolio, covering one grading period, or about 8 to 10 weeks.

3. If your instructor hasn't assigned portfolios as a means of assessment in this course, develop a list of items that you would include in such a portfolio and design rubrics for grading the portfolio.

# ■ Questions for Discussion

1. Should effort be included as a grading factor? Assume that two pupils demonstrate the same level of achievement, but you know that one had to work much harder to reach that level. Should they both receive the same grade?

2. Should homework be graded and included in the composite grade? Some parents do homework for their children, others help their children, and others leave the children to do homework alone. But, if homework isn't graded and taken into account, children tend to ignore it. What is a fair way to handle this?

3. Should growth or achievement be the more important factor in assigning a grade?

4. On what basis would you like to be graded in this course?

# ■ References

Collins, A. (1992). Portfolios for science education. *Science Education, 76,* 451–463.

Kamen, M. (1996). A teacher's implementation of authentic assessment in an elementary science classroom. *Journal of Research in Science Teaching, 33,* 859–877.

National Research Council. (1996). *National science education standards.* Washington, DC: National Academy Press.

Novak, J. (1990). Concept mapping. A useful tool for science education. *Journal of Research in Science Education, 27* (10), 937–949.

Stiggins, R. (1994). *Student-centered classroom assessment.* Upper Saddle River, NJ: Merrill Prentice Hall.

Stoddart, T., Abrams, R., Gasper, E., & Canaday, D. (2000). Concept maps as assessment in science inquiry learning—A report of methodology. *International Journal of Science Education, 22*(12) 1221–1246.

CHAPTER

# 8

## *Planning for Achieving Goals*

In Chapter 1 you read a list of broad science goals for the entire span of the elementary-school years. To accomplish those goals, children need to have a consistent, coherent science program that builds, each year, on what they learned in previous years. The purpose of setting goals is to guide planning and implementation of instruction to maintain focus and stay on track. In a dictionary, you will find that the word *objective* has about the same meaning as *goal*. In this textbook, a *goal* is a general statement of purpose (the purposes of instructional units also are goals) and an *objective* is an expected outcome of an individual lesson. When all the objectives of the lessons in a unit have been accomplished, the goals of the unit will have been achieved.

A science program should flow from its goals. A program that leads to meaningful and long-lasting learning requires thoughtful, purposeful planning and evaluation that are tied to both short-term and long-term goals. Without long-term goals as a guide, a science program can easily degenerate into a collection of "fun" activities that give the children some miscellaneous and unconnected ideas. A series of unconnected lessons, no matter how interesting or exciting, does not constitute a good science program.

# GOALS

A general approach to articulating the goals of education—including, but not limited to, science education—was developed by Benjamin Bloom, who is widely regarded for his leadership in classifying educational goals by domain and, along with others, for developing taxonomies of the domains (Bloom, 1956; Krathwohl, Bloom, & Masia, 1964; Harrow, 1972). Bloom's three domains are cognitive, affective, and psychomotor. Adding the social domain expands the list so that it contains the following:

1. Cognitive Domain: knowledge, comprehension, and the ability to use knowledge
2. Affective Domain: feelings, attitudes, and values
3. Psychomotor Domain: motor skills and small and large muscle control
4. Social Domain: skills of getting along with others

For the purpose of planning instruction in elementary-school science, content and process goals are part of the cognitive domain. Each domain contains a hierarchy of educational goals. The lowest level is memorization of facts and vocabulary— that is, goals that require only memorization, not thinking. At the next level, children apply the knowledge they have gained to the task of solving problems. Higher level goals include analyzing situations, synthesizing information, and applying critical thinking and evaluation skills to real-world problems.

It is interesting to compare Bloom's goals of education with the Piaget-derived kinds of knowledge described in Chapter 1 because goals of education are tied to

*Children need time for quiet watching and thinking.*

knowledge. Arbitrary knowledge and logical knowledge are in the cognitive domain, physical knowledge is probably in both the cognitive and psychomotor domains, and social interactive knowledge is in the social domain. This comparison is a reminder that there are many ways to classify anything of interest, including goals of education.

Some cognitive scientists have classified knowledge as either declarative or procedural knowledge: Declarative knowledge refers to what a person knows about a subject, whereas procedural knowledge refers to the procedures used to solve problems or complete tasks. Cognitive content goals are similar to declarative knowledge goals, and cognitive process goals are similar to procedural knowledge goals. The difference is sometimes explained as the difference between "knowing that" and "knowing how." In most of your science lessons, you should try to have both kinds of goals.

## OBJECTIVES

A practical example may help you see how goals can be used as a guide in planning instruction. Consider how the goals from Bloom's taxonomy could be translated into objectives for a classroom science unit involving a series of lessons on electric circuits. In this series of activities, children work in groups of four, and each group is given the necessary materials. The overall goal is for pupils to learn how to construct a simple electric circuit and to begin to build a concept of the characteristics of electric circuits. Although you may not be familiar with the actual content of the activities, reading over the objectives should give you an idea of how goals direct teacher thinking and planning. The following is a partial list of objectives.

### Cognitive Content Objectives ("Knowing That")

- Know the elements of a simple circuit and their arrangement.
- Know the effects of adding resistance to a circuit.

### Cognitive Process Objectives ("Knowing How")

- Construct a simple electric circuit.
- Measure the brightness of a bulb with a simple meter.
- Make predictions about brightness of bulbs, and test the predictions.

Goals from the affective domain are not accomplished in isolation but simultaneously with the other goals of instruction. Part of your responsibility as a teacher is to model the behaviors exemplifying affective goals and to reinforce them as you observe evidence of their use by your pupils.

### Affective Objectives

- Show persistence in constructing a circuit when the bulb fails to light.
- Show curiosity by testing different arrangements of batteries, bulbs, and wires.

As hands-on activities are the heart of a good elementary-school science program, children need to learn to use equipment and apparatus with care and skill. That will be easier for some children than others, but the same can be said for cognitive tasks. As a teacher, you can have the expectation that all children except, possibly, those with physical disabilities will acquire increasing skill in the psychomotor domain while they also achieve the cognitive goals of a lesson.

### Psychomotor Objectives

- Handle circuit elements and connectors safely.
- Develop skill in manipulating small pieces of apparatus.

It is essential to promote social goals when children are actively pursuing cognitive and psychomotor goals through active work, often in groups. If children are to learn from each other, they must be able to work together in harmony, at least most of the time.

### Social Objectives

- Share equipment equally among group members.
- Take turns in doing the interesting group tasks.

# STANDARDS FOR ELEMENTARY-SCHOOL SCIENCE

The preceding example illustrates how general educational goals can be translated into specific objectives for daily classroom science activities. This section covers the specific cognitive content and process goals of the elementary-school science curriculum. These are the main ideas and concepts that scientists and educators think children should understand by the time they complete elementary school. These are neither general educational goals nor specific lesson objectives but are, rather, what can be thought of as the overall goals for science in the elementary school. To borrow a term from management, they can be considered as strategic goals. Most states have strategic goals or at least a framework for elementary-school science programs. And, as mentioned in Chapter 1, several national groups of scientists and educators have defined strategic goals for science learning as a guide for groups at the state and local levels. The content standards presented in *National Science Education Standards* (NRC, 1996) outline what students should know, understand, and be able to do and thus can be thought of as goals. You can review the standards for kindergarten through Grade 4 and for Grades 5–8 by referring to Tables 1.1 and 1.2 in Chapter 1. The standards shown are brief summaries; the actual NSE Standards are more elaborate and give examples and guidance for implementation. As you have already seen, throughout this textbook, many references to the NSE Standards are given in relation to the activities and experiments described. As you see how basic and simple the NSE Standards actually are, you will gain confidence in your ability to teach science to children. The standards will also spur you to begin thinking about the many interesting activities you can create to help your pupils accomplish these learning goals.

For other ideas about goals for elementary-school science, see *Benchmarks for Science Literacy* (American Association for the Advancement of Science [AAAS], 1993), mentioned in Chapter 1. That large volume explains what children at different grade levels should know about science, technology, and human society—and the associated values, attitudes, and thinking skills that should be developed.

# LONG-TERM PLANNING

One of the first things to do in planning a science program for the year is to look at the school calendar provided by your school or district. This calendar will show the beginning and ending of the school year, the dates when grades are to be turned in, the teacher work days or conference days when pupils will not be attending school, and the holidays and vacation days. You will notice that the school year is divided into grading periods and that the grading periods are punctuated by holidays and conference days. Thus there are natural divisions within the year that should be taken into account in planning.

A year-long science program is more meaningful when it is planned as a series of instructional or thematic units. A unit is a sequence of classroom activities that have a central theme or topic and are designed to lead children toward increased knowl-

*Teachers get ideas from each other as they plan together.*

edge and deeper understanding of the subject chosen. Instructional units have many advantages over stand-alone lessons. By staying with the subject of the unit for a longer time, pupils have more opportunity to experience and reflect, and the teacher has more opportunity to integrate the unit topic with other subjects and the lives of the children. These enhanced learning opportunities are more than enough justification for selecting instructional units rather than relying on one-day lessons. There is another advantage, however, that should appeal to busy teachers. Teaching instructional units is easier for the teacher and much more efficient in terms of both instruction time and evaluation time. The additional time and effort required initially to plan a unit is more than compensated for by time and effort saved later, during presentation and evaluation. Because of the continuity of materials and ideas, start-up time for individual lessons is reduced. The materials, once collected, require little additional teacher preparation time. When pupils are taught to manage materials, the teacher's preparation time is further reduced. Little time is needed to focus or motivate once the unit has been initiated because enthusiasm and interest not only carry over but also actually increase from lesson to lesson.

As you study the school calendar, you will see that there are blocks of time within which to fit instructional units, and you can estimate how many units to plan. A time frame of three to six weeks seems to work best for most units, with the shorter times for primary grade children and longer times for children in upper elementary grades. There will be time in the school year for perhaps six to eight units. Ordinarily, a unit can be planned to end just before a vacation or begin just after one. Holidays and vacations offer both opportunities and constraints on planning science units. Units about living things that need daily care should be scheduled so that they are not interrupted by vacation days. When interruptions are unavoidable, it will be best to plan a unit in which each lesson can provide a particular event without needing to hold over the actual setup for further observation on another day. The resourceful teacher always looks for ways to turn adversity into opportunity, however, and scheduling gaps are no exception. Slow changes that do not require daily attention are naturals for holiday periods. How much water will evaporate from an aquarium tank in two weeks? Which materials decompose most, or least, when buried in a terrarium? How much do various crystals dissolve when placed and left in water without stirring?

## CHOOSING TOPICS FOR UNITS

When you have studied the school calendar and decided how many units to plan for the year and what the special timing constraints are, the next step is to choose unit topics or themes. These may have already been set by a required curriculum, by a required pupil text, or in some other way. If the topics have been set, you may or may not be able to decide when you will teach the units. If the choice of topics is left to you, it is easy to be overwhelmed by the idea of having to start from scratch on your own. Until you have gained some classroom experience, it will be helpful to consult one of the resources listed in the Appendix and select topics for which there are activities that have been developed and tested by others.

Whether you're choosing a science unit topic or planning daily activities, always ask yourself, "What can my pupils learn by direct observation of real things, and what relationships and other ideas can they figure out based on those observations?" Science for children should depend mainly on real experience with actual objects and events, along with reflection on those experiences. Secondary materials, such as books, films, and speakers, should be used only to clarify and expand on direct experience. If a choice is open between two topics, the one lending itself more easily to direct experience should be selected. Topics that cannot be studied through direct experience, such as molecules, relation of the planets to each other, or cell division, should be postponed until mental maturation makes the possibility of learning from models, photographs, and written explanations more likely.

### Creating Balance and Variety

Science will be more interesting both to the pupils and to you if you have a balance between topics in earth science, life science, and physical science throughout the year, remembering to plan so that activities are appropriate to the climate and seasons. All science involves change; the type and speed of change vary, however, and require some thought during the planning phase. Units about living things, such as plant growth or animal life cycles, usually involve slow change. Children will make a series of observations over a period of days or weeks before changes are complete. Studies of physical or chemical topics usually involve rapid change. A popular unit for the lower grades is one in which pupils test common household powders (salt, sugar, baking soda, starch, etc.) with water, vinegar, iodine, and heat. The reactions occur immediately or within a few seconds. The child does something, and there is a quick result. Planning for this unit is different from planning for a unit on growing seeds in which the child plants a seed (or sets up a germination test) one day and the results of this action become apparent only days or even weeks later.

Both kinds of change, rapid and slow, are interesting and important for children to experience; each requires somewhat different planning considerations, however. Rapid-change topics are easier to plan in that there is immediate feedback to pupils from a particular activity. Data collection and data processing for a particular activity can occur during the same class period. You can make a list of activities and plan a discussion about each activity before beginning the next activity. With slow-change topics, several activities may need to be scheduled before the observations on the first activity are ready to be discussed. In this case you must plan something similar to a three-ring circus, with several lines of activity taking place more or less at the same time. While the children are waiting for seeds to grow or plants to mature, you can schedule other lessons that involve shorter time frames, such as dissecting soaked seeds, examining roots in germination jars (set up earlier), or observing colored liquids moving up celery stalks.

Plan the units that you will teach so that children have experience with both rapid and slow change. Slow change is especially useful for primary children as an aid to developing reversible thinking. When children keep daily records, especially in the form of pictures and simple graphs, they can look back over the records and mentally reconstruct past events. By thinking about how a plant grew taller bit by bit and how it was at the beginning compared to the present, they practice thinking about a series of events both forward and backward in time. This valuable kind of thinking practice is often lacking in the curriculum. In addition to the scheduling needs and opportunities that depend on the kinds of change involved, some topics have other special considerations.

A unit on light and shadows, for example, involves relationships among light sources, object position, and shadows. Some activities are done with artificial light, and some are done outdoors with sunlight. It is important to have several indoor activities well planned and ready in advance in case bad weather or heavy cloud cover makes an outdoor activity impossible on the day for which it was planned.

## A Teacher's Plan for the Year

If all this information seems too complicated to be practical, you may be reassured by seeing one teacher's plan for a year. An outline of a fourth-grade science program is shown in Table 8.1. It comprises seven units, grouped by science discipline. The sequence was arranged to fit into the school calendar and the seasons of the year. Each unit was selected in accordance with one of the NSE Standards that children are expected to meet by the end of fourth grade. The outline is the bare bones; from it the teacher will develop lesson plans that include the elements you have seen in lesson plans in earlier chapters.

**TABLE 8.1    Units for Fourth-Grade Science Program for One School Year**

| *Life Science* | |
| --- | --- |
| Living Things | Identify differences between living and nonliving |
| | Identify basic needs of living things |
| | Learn to care for animals and plants |
| | Classify animals |
| Mammals or Birds | Construct habitats |
| | Observe characteristic behaviors |
| Plant Structures and Functions | Observe and draw cells under microscopes |
| | Identify functions of parts of plants |
| | Compare plants grown in different environments |
| *Earth Science* | |
| Sun and Moon | Observe times of sunrise, sunset, and moonrise |
| | Observe night sky and find constellations |
| | Observe changes in shadows throughout day |
| Rocks and Minerals | Observe and analyze local geologic features |
| | Observe and report on stone used in local buildings |
| | Classify rocks and minerals |
| *Physical Science* | |
| Electric circuits | Construct circuits |
| | Represent circuits in diagrams |
| | Experiment with switches, bells, and different wires |
| Sound | Make and demonstrate simple musical instruments |
| | Experiment to change pitch, volume, and tone |

## Developing a Unit

When you have outlined a series of units for the year, the next task is to begin developing a unit. Start with the first unit, plan it in as much detail as you can, reflect on what is happening as you go along, and use what you learn from your experience to plan subsequent units. You will collect ideas and activities for the whole year from whatever sources you have available, but you are likely to be overwhelmed if you try to plan the whole year before it begins.

Although there are always decisions to be made on the spot while you are in the middle of teaching, other decisions can and should be made much earlier, during the planning stage. Lesson objectives, specific materials to be used, pupils who are to be involved, time of day to introduce the lesson, and many more such decisions should be settled during planning. Later in this chapter are guidelines for selecting teaching methods to achieve different goals.

Virtually everything that can be planned ahead should be. Does that lock you into decisions that you've made? Of course not. Once a lesson is underway, many contingencies of the real world may demand that the plan be modified. Whatever the purpose of a particular lesson, the main principle of instruction that always applies is this: Teaching is not merely transmitting information; rather, teaching is bringing together curriculum and the learner in a way that is appropriate to the learners' needs, thus enhancing meaningful learning. This principle means that you must constantly assess the pupils' understanding and fine-tune the delivery of the lesson as it unfolds. Occasionally, you will discover part way through a lesson that the pupils simply aren't ready for it. In that case, the best decision is to "abandon ship," or terminate the lesson. When the goal is understanding rather than information, this type of decision becomes possible.

## STEPS IN PLANNING A SCIENCE UNIT

A number of steps are involved in developing a science unit. Although there may be some variation, a common sequence is to

1. select a topic for the unit,
2. set goals and objectives,
3. outline a sequence of activities,
4. try the activities yourself with actual materials,
5. write the lesson plans,
6. provide continuity elements,
7. plan an ending, and
8. develop a means of assessment.

### Selecting a Topic

The topic that you select to start the first unit sets the tone for the year and should be one that lends itself to many opportunities for active engagement with materials. Because you will be able to use the out-of-doors early in the year (in most parts of the country that won't be possible later), topics from life science and earth science are often a good choice.

### Setting Goals and Objectives

The goals for the unit may come from one of the sources recommended earlier, or you may set your own goals, remembering to include goals from all four domains. Although you might think that developing a set of lesson objectives would be the next task to tackle after choosing a topic and determining the goals for your unit, in fact most teachers think about the particular lessons or activities before setting down the objectives. That's fine. You'll need objectives to guide development of evaluation devices, so goals and objectives should come early in the development of the unit—but you may work back and forth between lesson ideas and objectives. As long as there is a close relationship between objectives and lessons, the exact sequence of writing them isn't crucial. Just because the development of objectives is described first in this chapter doesn't mean that you must develop your objectives completely before thinking about lessons, but you should have them clearly in mind before you begin to teach the unit. Remember to include noncognitive goals and objectives in your planning. Ask yourself, what affective, psychomotor, and social goals can be achieved by the children as they carry out the learning activities?

## Outlining a Sequence of Activities

You may find yourself in a school where the science program is based on a specific comprehensive program such as Full Option Science System (FOSS), Science and Technology for Children (STC), or one of the other commercially available programs described in the Appendix. In that case the decisions about activities and sequencing have been made, and your task will be to carry out the program in a way that will meet the programs' goals as well as others that you may have developed for your own pupils. Another situation is one in which you will have curriculum guidelines that define topics and broad goals but give you some freedom to choose specific activities.

**Resource Materials Note.** Information, ideas, opportunities to meet other teachers, free materials, catalogs that list teachers' guides, materials, and equipment are all available at professional meetings of science teachers.

A third possibility is that you will have little guidance and will be left on your own to plan and implement a science program. That situation may seem overwhelming, but there are places to get help. Don't try to do it all on your own. Many sources of ideas and materials are listed in the Appendix. Look for teacher's guides that provide activities for whole units or outline a series of lessons. As you gain experience and confidence, you can develop your own science program by revising, changing, and supplementing these materials. You can help children develop ideas that they would like to pursue and then plan, with their help, investigations to answer their questions.

If you use the principles of constructivism as a guide, you will plan the lessons or units with as many opportunities as possible for the children to be engaged in activities that will stimulate their thinking and lead them to construct new knowledge for themselves. A unit should always have a variety of activities and may include lessons that integrate science with other subjects.

## Trying Activities in Advance

It is crucial to try in advance your planned activities with the actual materials to be used in the classroom. One reason for doing so is to deepen your own understanding of the phenomena involved. You probably found when you carried out the investigations in Chapter 3 that concepts that had been vague became clearer. Other reasons for trying activities ahead of time are to be sure that the materials behave in the way you expected and to watch for any unexpected difficulties the equipment may cause.

You can't prevent all problems no matter what you do—but you can minimize them. There are many horror stories of lesson failures caused by equipment malfunction. One student teacher who tried all the activities in an electric circuits unit still had a problem. Shortly before beginning, she bought additional wire at a different hardware store. None of the pupils could light the bulb in the first lesson unless the cut cross section of the wire was placed in firm contact with the appropriate circuit element. She discovered later that she had inadvertently bought wire that was covered with a thin film of transparent plastic, making electrical contact impossible except at the cut surfaces of the wire.

Other teachers have bought what they thought was iodine to use in a chemistry unit as a test for starch (iodine causes starch to turn purple). When the expected dark purple color didn't develop with starch, the "iodine" label was read more carefully. It turned out to be an iodide of some salt, that is, iodine that had already reacted with something else besides starch. It may have been fine as an antiseptic, but it no longer worked as a test for starch. Many teachers have tried activities of this unit at home in glass or ceramic containers and then bought paper soufflé cups or paper picnic cups for pupils to use in class. Sometimes they found that in class all the powders gave a positive reaction for starch! A bit of research revealed that it was the paper that was turning purple in the presence of iodine. Many paper products are made with starch added to give extra stiffness. Nobody, including scientists, can know all the facts about things that can cause a problem. What you can do is test the actual materials as the children will use them in order to be sure everything is as it seems.

You may be lucky enough to avoid spectacular problems and still have problems with untested materials. Children sometimes find equipment awkward to hold or have other problems that adults may not have noticed. Always observe your pupils carefully when they are working with new materials, not only to monitor their learning but also to assess the adequacy of the materials for the purpose at hand. Minor problems can often be corrected before the same or similar materials are used with the next class.

## Writing Lesson Plans

The next step in unit planning, writing lesson plans, was explained in Chapters 4 and 5. Therefore it is not repeated here.

## Providing Continuity Elements

Workbooks that serve as data books and journals provide a thread of continuity that unites individual lessons. You may duplicate some structured record sheets to make record keeping easier for pupils in some activities. Consider whether they should be pasted into the workbooks or bound into a booklet along with blank sheets. You may not want pupils to see some worksheets before they are needed. Sometimes the worksheets give away the discoveries that pupils are supposed to make or perhaps have other undesired effects. Regardless of whether and how you include structured record sheets, you should always supply plenty of blank sheets for drawings and free description and other writing.

## Planning an Ending

One or more activities should be planned to help pupils see how the individual lessons of a unit fit together to form a big picture and relate to other subjects as well as to life out of school. An important part of science is communicating with others what has been learned. You may have a culminating activity that becomes a regular lesson, or you may have other types of activities, including show-and-tell discussions. An example of a culminating activity might be as simple as a class discussion to review what was learned in the unit and to relate those learnings to life outside school. A field trip to a museum of science and industry or to a local place of interest may be a good way to link what has been learned in a unit to the lives of the children.

## Developing an Assessment

Evaluation includes both assessment of pupil learning and assessment of the learning potential of the unit and, as explained in Chapter 7, should be an ongoing activity for the entire unit. The purpose of assessment is to find out whether the pupils attained the cognitive, psychomotor, affective, and social goals that you set and what unexpected outcomes, if any, there were. Ask yourself, were the goals appropriate and attainable? Should the unit be kept as is, revised, or abandoned?

# DEVELOPING AUTONOMOUS LEARNERS

An overall goal of science teaching is to develop autonomous learners. You may be more familiar with the term *independent learners;* if that term is more meaningful to you, then think of *autonomous* as *independent*. The root meaning of *autonomous* is "self-governing." To be autonomous means to be inner-directed rather than outer-directed, to be responsible for one's own actions, to think independently, and to arrive at one's own conclusions. Science demands that people think for themselves. Science includes facts and theories, but its essence is the ability to consider evidence and draw a conclusion, an ability that requires independent thinking. In all your planning try to keep in mind the goal of guiding your pupils toward learning to think for themselves and to know that their own thoughts are worthwhile and valuable. You saw an example of this in the case study featuring the teacher named Virginia in Chapter 7.

## Promoting Autonomy

You can promote independent thought and responsible action—that is, autonomy—by the way you teach and interact with your pupils. Table 8.2 classifies the three teaching methods that have been described according to goals of instruction and

**TABLE 8.2 Autonomy Levels**

| | Level I Direct Instruction | Level II Guided Inquiry | Level III Independent Investigations |
|---|---|---|---|
| Goals for pupils | Learn and practice skills | Make skills automatic | Decide when and how to use skills |
| | Receive and remember information | Learn from direct experience | Design, carry out investigations |
| | Learn behavior standards | Internalize behavior standards | Cooperatively determine appropriate behavior standards |
| Type of instruction | Direct instruction | Guided inquiry | Group investigation |
| | | | Independent projects |
| Role of teacher | Provide knowledge, guide practice | Guide learning experiences | Motivate pupils |
| | Determine pacing and timing | Ask questions | Monitor progress |
| | Set and enforce behavior standards | Give students more responsibility for behavior standards | Assist with practical problems |
| | | | Monitor cooperative group behavior |
| | | | Plan and carry out learning activities |
| Role of pupil | Follow directions | Participate in learning activities | Devise questions to answer by investigation |
| | Answer teacher's questions | Ask questions, listen to others | Take responsibility for group behavior |
| | Maintain expected behavior | Take responsibility for own behavior | |

level of pupil autonomy. Remember that all classification systems are approximate and that there are always things in the real world that do not fit neatly into any category. Despite some overlaps and ambiguities, this table should help you see important differences in methods and be a guide in planning.

## Level I. Direct Instruction

Level I is essentially teacher-centered in that the teacher has responsibility for all instructional decisions. The teacher controls the source and flow of information, as well as pupil movement and behavior. The pupils have little or no voice in determining the content, methods, procedures, or pacing of the lesson. This method of instruction may be appropriate for a short lesson at the beginning of a unit, such as a lesson on identifying rocks and minerals or on learning to use instruments that will be needed later. Some units cannot be started until pupils have mastered certain essential procedures or learned some essential information.

Most beginning teachers find learning to teach at Level I easier than learning to teach at the higher levels because there are fewer variables to keep in mind and fewer decisions to make once the lesson has begun. Because pupils have fewer choices, they are less likely to get lost in sequence or procedure, which translates to fewer behavior problems for the beginning teacher to manage. There are, however, a number of limitations to teaching at this level, one of which is that it doesn't promote the goals of pupil independence and responsibility as teaching at the higher levels does.

## Level II. Guided Inquiry

Teaching methods that introduce more flexibility into the lessons have been classified as Autonomy Level II. The goals of the lesson are for the pupils to use the procedures in further learning, to learn from their own actions and experience, to learn to work with others, and to learn to talk about what they have learned. Guided inquiry is an appropriate way to accomplish these goals. The pupils (a) have more responsibility and independence; (b) work in groups, talk to each other, and ask questions; and (c) decide how to divide up the work, how to tackle the problems they are given, and to some extent how to pace their own work. The teacher acts as a guide rather than a taskmaster.

To the inexperienced observer, Level II lessons look deceptively easy. The pupils seem interested and businesslike; the teacher seems to take a back seat in running the lesson. But that inexperienced observer is like someone who has entered a theater in the middle of a movie. The beginning of the movie would show how the teacher developed this amazing increase in responsibility by means of deliberate instruction done in carefully thought-out stages. Children can learn to behave responsibly, to manage materials effectively, and to become independent learners if they are taught and have opportunities to practice those skills.

# Level III. Independent Investigations

A third level of pupil responsibility and independence comprises teaching based on group investigations and individual projects, in which pupils have more choice in what they will investigate and how they will do it. The exact division between any two levels is arbitrary, but each level can be illustrated with descriptions of appropriate activities.

Level III is the realization of the constructivist perspective in science teaching. At this level, children are well on the way to becoming autonomous learners who have confidence in their own abilities to select questions to investigate, to decide how to investigate, and to construct meanings for themselves. This level of autonomy is the goal toward which you will have been aiming as you worked patiently to help your pupils develop the attitudes, habits, and skills needed to learn independently, to be curious and creative, and to have confidence and initiative. Instruction at this level doesn't exclude other kinds of instruction; it includes them, but it also goes beyond them. The processes that were once themselves the goals of instruction have become the tools for reaching other, more inclusive goals.

# Comparing and Contrasting Levels

As you examine Table 8.2 and move across from Level I to Level II, note how the role of the teacher changes from the role of providing information and guiding practice to the role of motivating, stimulating, and encouraging pupils to do their own thinking and acting. The teacher's role also changes from setting and enforcing standards of behavior for individual pupils to assisting pupils in monitoring their own behaviors and to setting standards for group behavior.

Note, also, how the role of the pupils changes from answering the teacher's questions to asking questions and listening to other pupils' questions, and finally to thinking of questions to be answered through an investigation. The pupils' responsibility for their own behaviors increases from simply doing what is expected and defined by the teacher to taking responsibility for their behaviors, and, finally, to taking some responsibility for the group's behavior by reminding classmates when they are getting too noisy or disturbing others.

There are important similarities among the teaching methods at the various levels, as well as points of contrast. Concrete experience is always important. Real materials and firsthand experiences, as opposed to vicarious experiences, should form the basis of initial learning whenever possible.

Each level is useful for certain types of learning or lesson goals. The methods at Levels II and III require a greater number of judgments and other complex teaching skills. Much more is involved than just turning the children loose with materials. This textbook is intended to help you develop a repertoire of teaching skills and methods so that you can choose the method that will accomplish the goals of the lesson. Note in Table 8.2 the progression toward self-reliance and responsibility for one's own learning. If you follow the goals across from Level I to Level III, you will see that the goal in Level I is to learn and practice skills, the corresponding goal in Level II is to make the skills automatic, and the goal in Level III is to decide when and how to use the skills.

# LESSONS ON MEASURING AREA

**Note to Instructor.**
These activities can be used as a classroom activity. Although they are simple, they may clarify the concept of measurements for some students. It's also useful for students to experience different teaching methods and to see that a hands-on activity makes a class more interesting.

An example may help you understand how this progression works in practice. Suppose that your goal is for children to learn to measure area and to be able to use this skill independently. You might plan your lessons in the following way.

## LEVEL I. DIRECT INSTRUCTION

### OBJECTIVE

Learn and practice procedures for measuring area.

### MATERIALS

10 centimeter by 10 centimeter squares of tagboard
2 centimeter by 2 centimeter squares of tagboard
Pieces of tagboard cut to different sizes

### LEARNING ACTIVITIES

1. Teacher demonstrates using squares to cover an area (20 centimeters by 30 centimeters) marked on chalkboard or newsprint taped to wall. Counts squares, writes number on board.
2. Several children come to board and place squares on different areas marked on board or newsprint.
3. Children practice at their seats, using 2 centimeter by 2 centimeter squares to cover sheets of paper, all of which are the same size. Teacher asks for results.
4. Children receive pieces of tagboard of different dimensions and find areas.

If you look down Table 8.2 to the role of the teacher, you will see that the teacher should provide information, guide practice, determine pacing and timing, and set standards of behavior. These are direct instruction lessons, so the pupil's role is to follow directions, answer questions, and follow the rules set by the teacher. Children stay in their seats, but they have lots of materials and time to handle them. The teacher guides their practice of the measuring skills being taught. Over the following weeks, the pupils have many opportunities to practice measuring area. These lessons are all directed toward the goal of "learn and practice skills."

# LEVEL II. GUIDED INQUIRY

## OBJECTIVE

Make measuring skill automatic.

## MATERIALS

Squares used in previous lesson
Regular and irregular pieces of tagboard
Centimeter grid paper
Wrapping paper or newsprint

## LEARNING ACTIVITIES

The teacher explains that pupils will use the skill learned in last lesson to measure more areas. Some areas will be irregular, and the pupils will have to decide what to do if the area cannot be covered by a whole number of squares.

1. Children work in pairs to cover tagboard provided.
2. Class discusses results.
3. Children draw their footprints on paper and measure them by covering them with squares. Children who finish ahead of others find another object to measure or draw an outline and measure it.
4. Class discusses results.
5. Pupils receive grid paper and small pieces of tagboard to place on the grid paper and count squares covered.

Teacher explains that squares are marked in centimeters, each is one square centimeter, that this is a convenient measure and is used as a standard. They will use it to measure the pieces of tagboard, which may require a short Level I exercise at the beginning.

Pupils work in pairs to measure pieces of tagboard.
Class discusses results.

This approach may be continued for one or more additional lessons, increasing difficulty and complexity of measuring. Measuring will now become a part of their work in science.

At Level II the teacher's role is to guide learning experiences rather than just guiding practice. The pupils' goal is to use the skill to measure a variety of objects and in so doing to make the skill automatic. By practicing the measurement of area in many different contexts, pupils learn to make judgments more easily about which squares to count. They also come to understand which type of measuring device to choose for particular situations.

Making the skill automatic takes time and practice. (Think back to how complicated it all seemed when you were learning to ride a bike or drive an automobile, and you will appreciate this point. What is now automatic once took a great deal of concentration.) Children will have additional lessons on measuring area throughout the year. As measuring area becomes automatic, accuracy and estimation become part of the process. In that way care in measuring also becomes automatic, and estimation ensures that pupils notice large mistakes immediately. Because measuring is an integral part of many of the experiments and investigations that children will do later, this phase of learning is very important, as recognized in both the NSE Standards (NRC, 1996) and in *Benchmarks* (AAAS, 1993).

## LEVEL III. INDEPENDENT INVESTIGATIONS

If you look at the right-hand column of Table 8.2, Level III, you will see the goal "design and carry out investigations." When measuring can be accomplished with little thought given to the procedures, pupils can then make decisions about what and how to measure as they plan their projects and experiments. By that time, they will have moved up to a higher grade and will be able to assume more responsibility in many ways. That is, they can devise procedures for measuring because they have learned the basic processes and can focus on the investigation rather than on the procedures themselves.

For example, a group of pupils working together on a project may decide that they need to measure the area covered by the shade of a tree. To do so, they will have to devise procedures because this problem is new, requires the use of the skills they have learned, but is not a problem they have been taught to solve. Now the teacher's role is to motivate, monitor progress, and assist where necessary. The pupils are assuming the main responsibility for their own work.

## ANOTHER LOOK AT TABLE 8.2

As you study Table 8.2 again, follow each section across from Level I to Level III. You will see that each section shows a progression similar to that in the example of measuring area. Look at the pupil's role. The second line shows the place of questions in science instruction. At Level I, the pupil answers the teacher's questions; at Level II, the pupil is allowed and expected to ask questions and listen to other pupils' questions; finally, at Level III, the pupil participates in the group as questions are devised to be answered by investigation. Questions and questioning provide a powerful means of teaching and learning science at all three levels, but the responsibilities of pupils and teacher are different at different levels. If you understand these differences and learn to teach science at all levels, you will have a repertoire for science teaching that will allow you to motivate and engage pupils in discovering the excitement of science.

# ■ SUMMARY

A science program should be guided by both long-range and short-term goals, including goals in the cognitive, affective, psychomotor, and social domains. Examples of specific goals or objectives for lessons on electricity show how goals from each domain can be used in planning instruction. Cognitive goals, including both content and process goals, have been formulated by a group of scientists and educators and published as the *National Science Education Standards* (NRC, 1996). The standards presented in that volume can be used as guidelines in setting cognitive goals, but the instructional means for meeting the goals is left up to teachers.

Classrooms in which children are highly involved in interesting and meaningful learning activities are the result of careful planning, with attention to both overall goals and the details of daily activities. A year-long science program is more meaningful when it is planned as a series of instructional or thematic units—with topics chosen from earth science, physical science, and life science—spread across the year. Developing each of the units requires careful thought and planning of many elements, including cognitive and noncognitive goals, sequencing lesson plans for a series of learning activities that build on each other, and evaluation that provides useful information to the teacher and the pupil. The teacher's goal throughout planning and implementation is to engage children in learning activities that will help them build knowledge and an understanding of science without neglecting their growth in affective, psychomotor, and social dimensions.

Three levels of student autonomy, or independence, were described in terms of goals, type of instruction, role of the teacher, and role of pupils. A central goal of science teaching should be to lead pupils toward greater independence of thought and action, that is, toward becoming autonomous learners. Skill at teaching at all three levels allows the teacher to choose the most appropriate method for achieving any learning goal.

# ■ ACTIVITIES FOR THE READER

1. Make a list of behaviors that you would look for as evidence that (a) psychomotor, (b) affective, and (c) social goals are being achieved.
2. Select one elementary science program (e.g., FOSS, GEMS, or STC) from the Appendix. Find out all you can about it and report to your classmates.
3. Outline an instructional unit for a topic and grade level of your choice. Determine goals and outline a series of lessons in a manner similar to that presented in the text.

# ■ QUESTIONS FOR DISCUSSION

1. Should goals and objectives be the same for all children in a class?

2. React to this statement: "Science period should be for learning science. I don't see why I should be expected to teach children to get along with each other, and I can't help it if some children are awkward and clumsy with equipment."

3. Some college students are uncomfortable when the instructor teaches at Level III. Why do you think that this is so?

4. "Science Is Fun" has been a popular slogan for some science educators. Do you think that teachers should promote the idea that school science is fun? Why or why not? What does the word *fun* mean to you?

5. What developmental factors can help you determine whether a suggested science activity or unit is appropriate for a given grade level or age group?

# ■ REFERENCES

American Association for the Advancement of Science. (1993). *Benchmarks for science literacy.* New York: Oxford University Press.

Bloom, B. (Ed.). (1956). *Taxonomy of educational objectives: Handbook I, cognitive domain.* New York: McKay.

Harrow, A. (1972). *A taxonomy of educational objectives: Handbook III, psychomotor domain.* New York: McKay.

Krathwohl, D., Bloom, B., & Masia, B. (1964). *Taxonomy of educational objectives: Handbook II, affective domain.* New York: McKay.

National Research Council (1996). *National science education standards.* Washington, DC: National Academy Press.

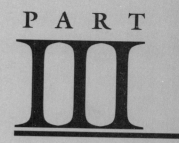
# Creating an Inclusive Science Program

# 9

# *Shaping the Classroom Learning Environment*

■    MR. NEWMAN:    What we have learned about teaching science as inquiry is really exciting, and though I'm anxious to get started with it, I'm concerned that my classroom will turn into chaos. How will I keep things under control when all the children are moving around, some of them doing what they are supposed to do and others off on their own, playing with the materials, or walking around aimlessly? To tell you the truth, it frightens me.

MS. OLDHAND:    I don't blame you for being frightened if that's the way you picture your science classroom when you begin to use inquiry methods. One thing to remember is that children crawl before they walk. If children have never experienced learning science, or any other subject, in this way, you can't expect them to know what to do in this sort of environment.

MR. NEWMAN:    That's exactly what concerns me. How will I get them to conform?

MS. OLDHAND:    I wouldn't say that what you want is conformity. What I aim for is to get the children to take responsibility for their own behaviors and to be so engaged in an activity that all their attention is focused on the tasks at hand. Of course, this ideal is never quite achieved, but on good days we come very close to achieving it.

MR. NEWMAN:    Yes, I have seen that in your classes. I just don't know how to get there myself.

MS. OLDHAND:    Well, if you knew everything you needed to know, you wouldn't be here. For me, the first place to start is at the beginning of the school year when you set up your classroom to welcome the children. Let's sit down after school today and talk about that.

**B**efore you begin this chapter, make a mental picture of what you would like a visitor to see and hear in your classroom in the middle of a science lesson. Choose a grade level and think about what the children would be doing. Would the visitor see all the children sitting quietly at their desks? Would children be dashing about the room borrowing equipment from other students and bumping into things along the way? Would boys be doing an experiment while girls sit and watch? Would a child with a speech impediment be sitting all alone? Or would the visitor see all the children busily engaged in an activity that you have planned as part of a series of lessons that will lead to understanding of an important science concept? The answer will be up to you when you have a classroom of your own. This chapter contains some guidelines to help you establish the kind of classroom that children are eager to enter each morning. Some of these guidelines apply generally to elementary-school classrooms, and you may have encountered them in other courses. Other guidelines are specific to teaching science.

Two main aspects of the classroom environment need to be considered in creating a setting in which children will be able to learn and will want to learn: the physical environment and the psychological, or affective, environment.

# PHYSICAL ENVIRONMENT

The way the classroom looks on the first day the pupils come to school and every day thereafter can play an important part in the way the teacher and the pupils feel about coming to school, teaching, learning, and being together all day. Certainly, a classroom should be a busy and happy place, perhaps even a neat and clean place. But there is still a great deal of variation in the way classrooms look.

## Making the Classroom Attractive

Consider two classrooms, room A and room B. Room A has colorful bulletin boards, busy learning centers, a reading corner with soft seating, and neat storage of many kinds of materials. The double desks are arranged in pairs so that four pupils form a natural work group facing each other. The teacher's desk stands in the back of the room, and a carpet covers the floor near the front chalkboard for group lessons. Fish, animals in cages, and plants occupy various corners and nooks. Room B has individual desks in straight rows with all the pupils facing forward toward the teacher's desk at the front. There are centers and bulletin boards, but there are no animals because the teacher thinks that taking care of animals makes extra work. All the children are at their desks.

In which classroom would you rather be a pupil? In which would you rather be a teacher? What do the differences say about the teachers' philosophies? Are there some situations that call for selecting more features of room A and other situations that call for selecting more features of room B? Deciding how to arrange and provide for a classroom environment that enhances instructional goals is more complex than the either/or choice described here. However, it is all part of creating an environment in which children can learn to the best of their abilities.

# ROOM ARRANGEMENT

Furniture and equipment should be arranged so that children can move about freely and have unobstructed pathways to the doors in case there is a need for everyone to leave the room. Make arrangements for assisting any children with disabilities in case of an emergency. Electrical outlets should be unobstructed; connecting cords should be short and in good condition. No electrical appliances should be placed near water.

## Accessibility to Children with Special Needs

Providing for children with special needs is more a matter of the teacher's and children's sensitivity to others than of rules about placement of furniture. A child in a wheel chair obviously can't move about a room that has no clear paths for such movement, and access to surfaces where observations are made or experiments are conducted must also be provided. Visually impaired children need more light than others, and they need special arrangements for taking tests that depend on reading. Hearing impaired children can't hear directions when the noise level is high, so the teacher should be sure that the room is quiet when giving directions and that the hearing impaired child is sitting or standing close to the teacher. Children take their cues from the teacher. If the teacher is sensitive to the needs of all children and molds the class into a cohesive group, the children themselves will become sensitive to the special needs of their classmates and will think of ways to ease the problems that arise.

## Equipment and Materials

Some science activities require only the materials that are available in an active elementary-school classroom. These materials include ordinary things such as scissors, string, plastic bottles, glue, paper, rulers, paper clips, small boxes or plastic containers, aluminum foil, and others that you may think of. You will need some specialized equipment—especially for pupils in the higher grades—for studying magnetism, light, electricity, and other topics that are part of a comprehensive elementary-school science curriculum. Some of the things that you will need are magnets, hand lenses, mirrors, balances, weights, pulleys, a hot plate, stop clocks or stop watches, thermometers, batteries, bulbs, wire, rubber or plastic tubing, and other items  required for special experiments. Much can be done with a modest amount of basic equipment, as pointed out by English educator W. Harlen (1993):

> Use of things that are familiar to children to help them explore and understand their surroundings emphasizes that they can do it through their own actions and thinking. . . . The directness of use of simple equipment emphasizes the point that answers can be found in the objects or situations themselves. The use of specialized equipment too early interrupts this message, makes science something distant and mysterious. When more precision is appropriate, later in the secondary school, then the equipment used has to allow for this [precision]. (p. 101)

Still other materials are things that are used up, including seeds that are planted or opened to expose what is inside, flowers that are pulled apart, and fruits and vegetables that are cut open. Some of these things can be obtained free; many of them must be obtained when needed because they cannot be stored.

Except for things that are perishable, storage is an important consideration. All other materials need to be safely and conveniently stored so that they are accessible when needed. Some teachers use shoe boxes for small items and plastic storage bins for larger items, making certain that all containers are well marked and returned

*Children learn to treat living things with care and respect.*

after use to a designated place. There is no time in a busy day to search for equipment or to open a box and find it empty.

## Animals in the Classroom

An elementary-school classroom is incomplete without animals, including fish, but there are several things to keep in mind about having them in the classroom. You have to protect both the animals and the children. Animals need a good place to live and daily care, including care on weekends, and need to be free from harassment or teasing. Children need to be protected from bites, scratches, and animal-borne diseases. Purchase animals for the classroom from a reputable dealer to ensure that the animals are healthy and teach the children how to handle each species. If you have questions about keeping or handling animals, ask a veterinarian or someone from the Humane Society or zoo if one is nearby. The Society for Prevention of Cruelty to Animals (SPCA) also has guidelines for safe and humane care and treatment of pets.

## Plants in the Classroom

The main consideration with plants is to prevent the pupils from coming into contact with plants that are toxic. Obviously, you wouldn't bring poisonous plants into the classroom, but some plants that seem harmless may cause an allergic reaction in some children—and some common houseplants such as philodendron and English ivy actually are poisonous. Caution children not to taste unknown plants and not to get sap on their skin. If you're unsure about a plant that you want to use, you may get advice from an agricultural agent, a knowledgeable gardener, or a botanist.

# MAKING THE CLASSROOM SAFE

Safety is placed near the beginning of this chapter because it is a special concern when planning science activities. You must consider safety in deciding how to arrange the classroom, what materials to use in science activities, and how to maintain an orderly classroom without restricting freedom to learn. Some science activities present situations that can be hazardous to children if you don't think ahead and take some sensible precautions. It is impossible to plan for every emergency, but you can prevent most serious as well as minor accidents by forethought and planning. Familiarize yourself before the school year begins with your school's or district's policies and procedures and any other regulations that relate to school safety. Many helpful ideas and reminders are included in the *Safety Booklet* published by the National Science Teachers Association ([NSTA], undated). Think about the following as you consider the children's safety.

## Fire and Heat

You can have an excellent elementary-school science program without the use of fire. If hot water is needed, tap water may be hot enough. If not, use a hot plate that you control or keep under your supervision (by fifth grade, most children can handle a hot plate with supervision). Avoid boiling water; it can cause serious burns because extra heat is given off as the temperature decreases on contact with the skin. Never leave a hot plate with red-hot coils unattended.

## Chemicals

You can also have an excellent science program without the use of hazardous chemicals. Instead of thinking about how to store hazardous materials, eliminate them. Be firm in setting rules for the use of all chemicals: no tasting, no touching, and no fooling around. When the pupils obey these rules, you can use many commonly available materials. If acid is called for, use white vinegar (acetic acid), lemon juice (citric acid), or a very weak solution of hydrochloric acid that can be obtained from a pharmacist. Rubbing alcohol, table salt (sodium chloride), baking soda (sodium bicarbonate), baking powder, a weak iodide solution, and weak ammonia water are other chemicals that can be used safely. Be aware that many household chemicals, such as chlorine bleach, drain openers, pesticides, and weed killers are *not safe*. The mercury in many thermometers is hazardous and should not be touched if the thermometer breaks; use thermometers with red liquid if possible. If you aren't sure about the potential hazard of any chemical, ask a high school science teacher, a scientist, or a pharmacist.

## Tools and Glassware

Beginning in kindergarten, children should be taught to use scissors. As they reach second or third grade, they can be allowed to use sharper scissors (the blunt-pointed scissors don't cut much) and other tools that require caution. Glassware should be handled with care; plastic containers and baby food jars can be used instead of beakers, sharp edges of mirrors should be filed off, and plastic tubing should be used rather than glass tubing if it is available. Be prepared to take care of minor cuts; they are seldom dangerous if handled promptly and treated to prevent infection.

## Eye Protection

All pupils should wear goggles when any of them are handling chemicals (even mild ones), sharp instruments, glassware, or other hazardous materials. A small cut on a finger from broken glassware is a minor problem, but a piece of glass in a child's eye is something you don't want to think about. Establish a routine for distributing, collecting, and cleaning goggles. *You must be firm about this and always wear them yourself.*

## Emergencies

Keep a fire extinguisher handy and in good condition and know how to use it. Keep a well-stocked first-aid kit. Develop a plan for getting a child with any injury to the school nurse or principal's office. (Will you leave the class to take the child yourself? Will you send one child with another child?) You must also have a plan for calling an emergency number in case a serious situation calls for immediate attention. Don't forget that you will also be responsible for the other children, so you must plan to keep them safe and calm. Be sure that the children understand what to do in an emergency but reassure them that they will all be safe. Once you have made these plans and have an emergency number close at hand, you can relax in the knowledge that you will be prepared for anything that may happen.

# THE AFFECTIVE ENVIRONMENT

Elliot Eisner, a professor of education, spent three months observing two third-grade classrooms in California. Eisner (1998) reported that one of the things he learned was that the teachers he studied created a common culture, which maintained the coherence of the group, and that pupils and teacher shared a comfortable, ongoing way of life:

> The maintenance of a class as a cohesive group is a pedagogical achievement. These teachers employed a variety of techniques to maintain such cohesiveness. . . . The teacher is indeed a planner, a producer, and a director. The most apt metaphor may be that of a chef. Like a chef, the teacher has to know how to use a wide variety of ingredients, how

to put them together, what level of flame is required, and when it is necessary to get back to the pots to keep them from boiling over. At times the teacher must innovate when ingredients are unavailable. All of this must be done with a sense of orchestration to keep the whole enterprise moving forward and working well. (p. 194)

## Pupil Engagement

Highly involved pupils are oblivious to things that normally distract them because they are very busy and locked into the task. Left to work on their own without teacher encouragement, they persist at the task much longer than at normal academic tasks.

Children who would not choose to spend their spare time at academic tasks may spend hours playing with construction sets, or watching bugs, or interacting with pets. Such activities are not just pleasant pastimes but important learning experiences of real and highly significant value children's mental and emotional development. Why would children voluntarily choose to educate themselves in this way? Because it is natural for children to be curious and to seek learning. Learning is unnatural only when removed from an individual's interests and curiosity. Teachers can make schooling more responsive to children's needs by trying to match methods and activities more closely to children's natural interests. Figure 8.1 is intended to help you think about how you can do this.

The types of learning activity listed are in the approximate order of difficulty that children have in maintaining attention over time. Some qualifications and exceptions apply to the sequence, but in general, the lower the activity is on the list and the less concrete, the harder it is for children to maintain attention. The two activities at the bottom of the list—listening and watching and listening only—make the pupil essentially a passive receiver of information. Even in reading, children have some control over pace and sequence. The top three activities involve real interaction; something happens in response to what the pupil does and vice versa. Remember that two factors—concreteness and interaction—are the main determinants of pupil engagement. Keep this chart in mind when you plan your science lessons and always try to think of a way to meet their objectives by planning to use methods as high on the list as possible.

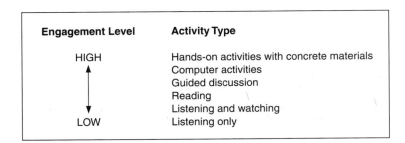

**FIGURE 8.1   Comparing Activity Types by Level of Engagement**

*Classroom management is not a problem when children are totally engaged in a task.*

## Firsthand Experience

The kind of learning that children seek is through firsthand experience. A beginning teacher once asked, "Do you mean there are things that you can't learn from reading?" The answer is Yes. From reading you can't learn how a banana smells or what color the sky is or how it feels to pet a kitten. You might learn the word *blue* from reading or from hearing spoken language, but unless you have had firsthand experience with things that are blue, the word conveys no meaning. Words, after all, are a wonderful way to communicate when they cause the reader or listener to recall a firsthand experience. If no experience lends meaning to the words, no real learning can occur.

Teachers must constantly remind themselves that the experience base of a child is limited. A child now in kindergarten was born only 60 months ago. There just hasn't been time for a 5-year-old to have had many experiences. Even older elementary-age children have amazing gaps in their experience that adults may not think to consider. For example, many children, even from affluent families, have never eaten or examined a fresh orange. That's true even in orange-growing regions, because many parents give their children frozen or ready-prepared orange juice. When teachers keep this limited experience base in mind, they are less likely to expect children to maintain attention for long periods of time during low-engagement activities such as listening. Without an extensive experience base, too many words and sentences seem meaningless. Extended listening is hard work even for adults; for children, even a very few minutes may be too hard.

You can minimize the amount of time spent in low-engagement activities in several ways. First, modify activities to increase the level of engagement. Instead of continuous talking, break up the information with questions to check for understanding. Invite children to ask questions or give comments. These changes move the engagement to a higher level. Carefully plan the use of spoken information to avoid unnecessary details and to keep things brief.

Second, spend more time in high-engagement activities. This textbook should help you learn to use these powerful methods with confidence and effectiveness.

Third, increase your own teaching efficiency. Learning time that is wasted waiting in line for supplies or waiting while the teacher finds a piece of chalk not only breaks the momentum and lowers the pupils' level of engagement, but it also sets the stage for inappropriate pupil behavior.

## CLASSROOM MANAGEMENT

Good science instruction involves many materials and pieces of equipment that are naturally attractive to children, making it easy for them to forget the purpose of their activities and to lose control of their behavior. Even well-behaved children will test the limits and sometimes break the rules, but they want to know that they will not be allowed to go too far. Most children seem to know instinctively that they need adult guidance and protection, and they become uncomfortable and nervous if they feel that no one is in control.

Many normal, acceptable home behaviors are disruptive when multiplied by 30 and packed into the confines of a small classroom. Thus restrictions on freedom become necessary to provide an appropriate environment for learning. Each pupil has to give up some freedom of movement to gain freedom from disorder and disruption of learning. Although the obvious goal of managing behavior is to provide an environment conducive to learning, a subtle goal is for children to practice controlling their impulses and to develop consideration for the needs of others.

Children know they are less effective in the world than adults. They yearn alternately to be more powerful and to be more secure. If they find no limits—or if the latitude of freedom exceeds their ability to manage on their own—they are likely to get into trouble. This generalization is closely related to the idea of overdoing in novel situations. Even while they are being disruptive or engaging in dangerous behavior, children are usually unconsciously asking for the security of adult control. They sense that they are not always able to control their behavior and that they need help from someone else.

### Effective Teacher Behaviors

Kounin (1970) reported on a pioneering series of research studies that examined how teacher behavior affects classroom management. A surprising finding was that, when teachers who were successful at managing behavior were compared to those who were unsuccessful, no particular differences were found in the way they

*A teacher makes her expectations clear.*

responded to pupil misbehavior. Later studies verified and extended these results (Anderson, Evertson, & Emmer, 1980; Brophy & Good, 1986; Doyle, 1986; Emmer, Evertson, & Anderson, 1980). Researchers were determined to find out what made the difference between successful and unsuccessful classroom managers. If it wasn't the action taken by the teacher when a child misbehaved, what was it? The answer turned out to be prevention of inappropriate behavior. Teacher behaviors that prevent discipline problems have been summarized from the research and reported by Good and Brophy (1987). They found that four teacher behaviors provide the most prevention of misbehavior and class disruption:

■ *Being aware of what is happening in the whole classroom at all times.* Awareness involves the teacher's use of ears and eyes to monitor noise level and take action when a crescendo is beginning to build. A teacher with this kind of awareness— and with a consistent history of intervention in potentially disruptive pupil behavior—conveys to pupils a sense of "with-it-ness" that prevents most problems from happening in the first place.

■ *Doing more than one thing at a time.* Being able to keep an eye on learning groups while holding a direct lesson with others allows the teacher to respond to outside questions and manage routine jobs without seriously interrupting the main activity.

- *Maintaining lesson momentum.* Being well prepared and organized enough to avoid stopping to look at notes or backtracking after false beginnings lets the teacher keep the lesson flowing. It means making judgments to ignore minor daydreaming but to intervene in situations that could escalate into disruptions. It also means minimizing the disruption to the lesson that teacher intervention itself causes.

- *Providing variety and challenge in independent work by assigning tasks that hold pupils' interest.* If a task is too hard or a procedure is unclear, pupils will give up. If the task is too easy or overly repetitive, pupils will be bored. Either situation means wasted learning time for the pupils and potential management problems for the teacher.

In summary, appropriate pupil behavior is achieved by teachers who are flexible, businesslike, aware of potential trouble building up, and sensitive to pupils' needs and abilities. You can't develop these traits simply by reading a methods book; they require the experience of being in charge of a real classroom. Experience alone is not enough, however; also essential is understanding the needs and abilities of pupils and reflecting on your own behavior and the results of your actions.

# PROMOTING APPROPRIATE PUPIL BEHAVIOR

The suggestions in this section are particularly important whenever children are introduced to inquiry-based teaching for the first time. These suggestions supplement those given previously, which are applicable to all teaching methods. The shift in roles from direct instruction to inquiry-based teaching means that pupils are expected to start learning to manage their own behavior and materials. Because the behaviors are new, pupils must be taught them. Teaching children how to manage for themselves is very much like the steps in a direct instruction lesson (though the time frame is much longer). The teacher gives motivation and then presents a procedure directly. The pupils practice, first with considerable guidance and later with less help. Periodically, the teacher may call a class discussion to involve everyone in evaluating progress. One difference between direct instruction and guided inquiry is that pupils are expected to take greater responsibility for themselves in guided inquiry.

## Standards and Consequences

*Standards* are a set of general rules of conduct; *consequences* are what happens when standards are violated. To begin, decide on a few absolute requirements that are not open to debate. Then, depending on the age and maturity of your pupils, you may decide to involve them in formulating additional standards and, possibly, identifying more consequences. The number of each should be kept to a few, however. Don't emulate the first-grade teacher, one of whose pupils went home after the first day of school and told her mother that school had been boring because "all we did today was listen to the teacher tell us all the rules." One way to involve children in the process is to discuss actual or potential disruptions and give them some alternative solutions to discuss and choose from. In any case, the pupils should be directly taught the few important standards that you will insist upon and the consequences of not meeting those standards. Instruction of this sort requires several interactive lessons at the beginning of the year, with regular reviews and reminders thereafter.

When your class is made up of children from diverse backgrounds, you must be especially careful to help all the children understand what the rules are and why they are necessary. Behavior expectations can be very different in different cultural groups; some of the behaviors that you expect may go against the cultural norms of some of your children. For example, some ethnic groups teach their children never to look an adult in the eye, whereas others teach their children just the opposite. For one child to help another is cooperation to some and cheating to others. Children with special needs comprise another group who will need your careful attention to be sure that they understand the rules and that they are capable of following them.

## Noise Level

Some teachers are uncomfortable with any level of noise, either because they feel that they are expected to maintain a quiet room or because they believe that noise will lead to serious disorder. The amount of noise that is tolerable varies from teacher to teacher. Experienced teachers are acutely aware of noise and of their own tolerance levels. There's no specific decibel level at which things always come unglued, but too much noise can have a contagious effect that leads to disruptive behavior. In the past, many principals expected silence, but now—with newer methods such as cooperative learning gaining acceptance—most principals do not insist on totally noiseless classrooms. With experience, you will find a noise level that feels right to you, that does not disturb other classrooms, and that is comfortable for the children.

## Using Psychology Instead of Coercion

Children like to do hands-on science activities, and they usually like to work together. You can use this affinity to keep order. Explain that working freely with the materials is a privilege for those who can control their own behavior but that if they forget, they will have to be separated from the work temporarily. (Because you need to tailor special standards each time the type of activity or materials warrants, you will need to remind the pupils of the standards occasionally—perhaps each day. What to include in the standards is up to you, but they should be specific and few. Some teachers like to include "Stay in your seat unless you are a monitor." Even if trips to the drinking fountain or pencil sharpener are allowed during other subject activities, you may want to try restricting them during science group work. Allowing both talking and walking around at the same time may be too much novelty to handle. If the children at one table discover something especially exciting, for example, their "oohs" and "ahs" may cause the rest of the class to leave their own work and crowd around that table.

## A Signal

You will need some kind of nonverbal signal to regain attention after group work begins. It could be a sound, reserved especially for this purpose, that can be detected over the hum of busy group workers, such as a chime or bell. Some teachers flip the light switch off and on. Some just flip the lights off and leave them off until they get attention. Other methods include rhythmic clapping (with which pupils join in) and simply raising a hand. Whatever signal you choose, talk it over with the pupils before using it—don't just expect them to know what it means automatically. Also, the signal may have been used for something different before you came. A student teacher once tried sounding a chime to get attention, and all the children stood up and sang "The Star-Spangled Banner"!

Another consideration for an attention signal is to use it sparingly. Consider a single science activity. After pupils begin group work, you will probably need to use your signal at least once—when it is time to stop working and to begin cleaning up. In addition, you may need to use the signal to caution the class if you feel that the noise level is increasing toward the "danger point." If such warnings happen more than once or twice, you should consider stopping the activity to review the standards. Another use for the signal is when you find it necessary to give additional directions for the activity. Clearly, this last use is undesirable. The activity will go more smoothly if interruptions of this type, or of any type, are minimized. Still, interruptions will be necessary occasionally for some unanticipated problem, so having a preestablished signal is important. Remember to plan carefully to minimize the need for using the signal. If used too often, as with any frequent stimulus, it will lose its effect.

## Distribution and Cleanup

Plan carefully for quick distribution of materials. A waiting child is not only wasting time but also getting restless and perhaps into trouble. On the first day of a new unit, some teachers like to set up all the tables while the pupils are out of the room, such as at lunch or recess. The problem of giving directions with materials already distributed can be handled by giving directions outside before the children come in or in a special discussion area of the room. After the unit is underway, a teacher should shift the setting-up and cleaning-up work to the pupils. They need to practice responsibility, and you need time to prepare your thoughts before beginning the lesson. A monitor system can be worked out, perhaps for a table captain of the week, on a rotating basis, for example. If necessary, special incentives such as extrinsic rewards can be used for groups showing responsibility in setting up at the beginning and cleaning up at the end of the class period.

## Dealing with Messes

Inquiry-based teaching is potentially messy. Although careful planning and good directions will minimize messes, they can never be completely eliminated. So a child spills something—that isn't the end of the world. The payoff from hands-on science is well worth an occasional mess. It is best to plan for the worst, though. Cover the tables with newspapers or towels and have sponges, mops, and buckets handy just in case. If there is a potential for spilled liquids on the floor, restricting pupil movement around the room may be desirable to prevent slipping and possible injury.

# PREVENTING INAPPROPRIATE PUPIL BEHAVIORS

Eisner (1998) noted "the degree of administrative acumen required to keep what is often a four-ring circus functioning in full gear and without a hitch" and added that the work of the elementary teachers he observed "relegates most university teaching demands to the minor leagues" (p. 195).

Some teachers use a comprehensive management system that they have learned through in-service training or through their own reading or course work. All such systems are based on the principles of behaviorism. As helpful as these approaches may be, many teachers have become excellent classroom managers without using any of them. Even though you may feel that you need such a system in the beginning, you may find that you no longer need it after gaining some experience in your own classroom. Whether you decide to use one of these approaches or develop your own, certain factors are common to all effective methods of classroom management, sometimes referred to as the three C's: clarity, communication, and consistency.

*Clarity* in your own expectations is essential. If you're not sure about what kinds of behavior to expect and what kinds of behavior you won't tolerate, you will have to settle each problem when it arises, a method that won't work for long. Planning is needed to develop general class behavior standards and the consequences of deviating from them. In any case, you must decide ahead of time how to present the standards and consequences to the class, and your thinking on the matter must be clear.

*Communication* is essential to transfer your expectations to the pupils. You can't assume that children know what you expect of them unless you let them know. Remember that children aren't just little adults. They have limited capacity to make judgments. It is unrealistic to expect children to regulate their own behavior by judging its appropriateness. During the elementary-school years, following clearly communicated standards is the first step and may be as far as some children can go toward the goal of responsible regulation of their own behaviors. Recall from Chapter 2 that young children accept the right of authority figures to exercise power and try to obey rules to avoid punishment.

*Consistency* in applying consequences is essential. If children see or believe that their teacher lets some children "get by" with behavior, for which they themselves have received negative consequences, it is only natural that they themselves will try to get by with such behavior the next time the opportunity presents itself. According to Kohlberg (1969), young children are very concerned about fairness and may be quick to point out other children's infractions of rules. It is very upsetting to children at this stage if they think that they have been treated unfairly or punished when someone else has escaped punishment. When there are exceptions to enforcement, infractions continue and even increase in number. When children aren't sure whether they can get away with something, they are tempted to test the limits of the system.

The secret to getting children to take responsibility lies in their learning a highly predictable sequence of cause and effect. The quickest and most humane way to teach responsibility while maintaining order is to enforce classroom standards by using prearranged consequences uniformly, immediately, and without exception. Remember to keep the number of standards to a few, or else you will be imposing sanctions too often and on too many children.

Once you have gained confidence in your ability to prevent or handle problems, you may want to develop your own methods. But one way or another, you must have a classroom in which children can go about their work without continual or major disturbances. The most effective way to prevent misbehavior and promote desirable behavior is to provide learning activities in which pupils will become completely and actively engaged.

## DEALING WITH MINOR MISBEHAVIOR

When inappropriate behavior is not serious and stops on its own, it's best to ignore it. Two examples are momentary pencil tapping and brief talking. If these or similar potential distractions continue for a longer time, an emotionally neutral intervention is called for, such as establishing eye contact, making a warning gesture, or standing near the pupil. With young children, a gentle touch often works, though this may be less effective with older pupils. Remember that the main idea is to continue the lesson or activity with a minimum of disruption. Calling on a pupil to gain renewed participation may be appropriate. None of these problems are serious and thus shouldn't be the cause of embarrassment. Embarrassment of the pupil in question is noticed by the others and can itself constitute a disruption of the lesson. A simple redirection of attention is all that is usually necessary.

## APPLYING CONSEQUENCES IN SERIOUS CASES

When inappropriate behavior becomes serious, you must intervene in a consistent, expected manner. If you apply penalties inconsistently, they will cease to be regarded as consequences and discipline will collapse. Because it is hard to foresee every situation, you may be apprehensive about using a system in which negative consequences are invoked in a seemingly automatic way. Shouldn't exceptions sometimes be made? First, a clarification is needed: Not all negative consequences are punishments. In fact, punishment should be used only as a last resort; although punishment can control behavior, it has little or no effect in changing attitudes or in teaching acceptable behavior (Bandura, 1969). A series of consequences of increasing impact on the pupil can be used. The first offense could call simply for a reminder. For many pupils, a reminder is enough. A second offense by the same pupil could entail a short conference with the teacher, during which the pupil is required to describe the unacceptable behavior and identify the class standard that has been violated. The penalty for a third offense could be to have the pupil devise a plan for correcting the problem. As this textbook is constructivist in its approach, you may wonder about using principles of behaviorism in classroom management. The reason is a practical one: These ideas usually work, and they prevent many of the problems that beginning teachers face.

## INVOLVING THE PUPILS AT HOME

Sending simple materials home with children has the potential for getting parents and others at the pupils' homes involved with your science program. Although such involvement sounds good, there are some possible drawbacks to consider. Your pupils may not have control over what happens to materials once they have left the classroom. Because materials may be lost or damaged, use caution in what you send home. For the same reason, if materials are sent home for children to use in homework assignments, don't penalize children who don't complete the assignment and don't depend on the work's completion as a prerequisite for a subsequent activity.

Sometimes teachers ask pupils to bring things from home. For example, if each child brings a working flashlight, you have most of the expensive materials for teaching activities on electricity. Also, you may have interested parents in what is happening in their children's science program. However, some children won't be able to bring a flashlight. Rather than penalize or call attention to those children, just have some extra flashlights on hand. Any time you ask for such materials, it is a good policy to send a note to parents or guardians. Similarly, certain kinds of materials sent home should be preceded by a request to parents for permission slips. Any living things that require care or that might cause consternation should be sent home only after parents have given written permission.

## ■ SUMMARY

Arranging a safe, attractive classroom is the first step in creating a physical environment that encourages children to learn and grow. A classroom that includes animals and plants as well as adequate equipment and supplies provides a setting for engaging children in a variety of science activities. A system for storage and management of materials and constant attention to safety are needed in every science classroom.

The affective environment of the classroom is created by the teacher working with pupils to develop a common culture in which pupils and teacher share a comfortable, ongoing way of life. The key to having an orderly but busy and active classroom is pupil engagement in activities that absorb them. Children are eager for firsthand experiences with everything. An inquiry-based science program takes advantage of this eagerness and builds on it by providing a classroom environment that stimulates and encourages it.

An active, inquiry-based science program gives children more freedom and demands more responsibility than more teacher-centered methods of instruction. Children who have never participated in inquiry-based learning may not be prepared to take responsibility for their own behavior and need guidance in learning to behave in ways that are appropriate and acceptable. The teacher sets the tone by establishing a few firm standards for behavior, by communicating expectations clearly, and by dealing with problems promptly as they arise.

## ■ ACTIVITIES FOR THE READER

1. Make a diagram to scale of a classroom planned for 25 pupils. Include and arrange whatever furniture and equipment you think is necessary or desirable for a specific grade level.

2. If you are working in a classroom as an intern, as a student teacher, or in another capacity, arrange to have a lesson or interaction with the pupils videotaped. Use the videotape to analyze your own behavior. (This activity will be more helpful if done in pairs so that each person gets another person's perspective.)

## ■ QUESTIONS FOR DISCUSSION

1. What are your greatest concerns as a prospective or beginning teacher?

2. If you have visited different elementary-school classrooms, you probably noticed a wide variety in the amount of pupil movement, accepted noise level, and general impression of order (or disorder). What are some of the factors involved? What do you think would work best for you? Why?

3. If you were planning to introduce science activities with concrete materials for the first time to your class, what are some safety considerations to keep in mind? Some behavior considerations to keep in mind?

4. Describe two different ways by which you might introduce behavior standards with a new class.

5. What are the differences among penalties, negative consequences, and punishment? If any of these actions are required, which are most effective for controlling behavior? For teaching responsibility?

## ■ REFERENCES

Anderson, L., Evertson, C., & Emmer, E. (1980). Dimensions in classroom management derived from recent research. *Journal of Curriculum Studies, 12,* 343–356.

Bandura, A. (1969). *Principles of behavior modification.* New York: Holt, Rinehart & Winston.

Brophy, J., & Good, T. (1986). Teacher behavior and student achievement. In M. Wittrock (Ed.), *Handbook of research on teaching* (3rd ed.). New York: Macmillan.

Doyle, W. (1986). Classroom organization and management. In M. Wittrock (Ed.) *Handbook of research on teaching* (3rd ed.). New York: Macmillan.

Eisner, E. (1998). *The kind of schools we need.* Portsmouth, NH: Heinemann.

Emmer, E., Evertson, C., & Anderson, L. (1980). Effective classroom management at the beginning of the school year. *Elementary School Journal, 80,* 219–231.

Good, T., & Brophy, J. (1987). *Looking in classrooms* (4th ed.). New York: Harper & Row.

Harlen, W. (1993). *Teaching and learning primary science* (2nd ed.). London: Paul Chapman.

Kohlberg, L. (1969). Stage and sequence: The cognitive developmental approach to socialization. In D. A. Goslin (Ed.), *Handbook of socialization theory and research* (pp. 118–140). Chicago: Rand McNally.

Kounin, J. (1970). *Discipline and group management in classrooms.* New York: Holt, Rinehart & Winston.

National Science Teachers Association. (n.d.). *Safety Booklet.* Washington, DC: Author. (Available from the National Science Teachers Association, 1742 Connecticut Avenue, Washington, DC 20009.)

# Including All Children in Science

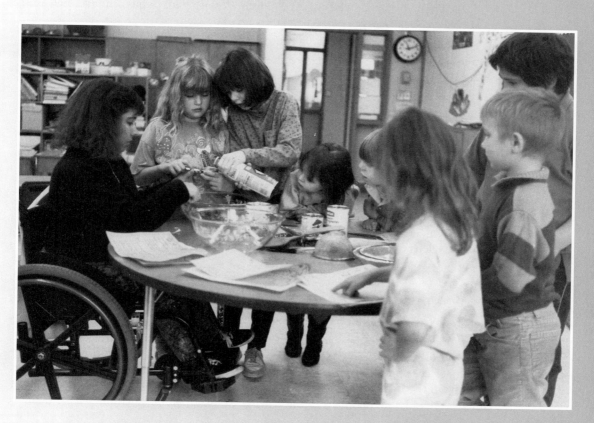

**T**his chapter challenges you to consider what it means to create a truly inclusive classroom; that is, to be sensitive to the special needs and problems of some children and, at the same time, to expect each child to achieve at the highest level possible for that child. The first part of the chapter focuses on issues of gender, ethnicity, and handicapping conditions in relation to learning in science; the second part focuses on the way teacher expectations influence learning outcomes for all children.

Before you begin this chapter take a few minutes to write your responses to the following statements and requests. Record your responses and put them aside. You will be asked to come back to them later.

## A SURVEY

A. Respond to the following six statements. For each statement, choose one of these reactions: (a) strongly agree, (b) agree somewhat, (c) disagree somewhat, or (d) strongly disagree.

1. All pupils can achieve success.

2. When you have a class of 25 children, dealing with pupils as individuals isn't feasible.

3. Some children just don't want to learn.

4. Some children will disregard the rules no matter what the teacher does.

5. It is unreasonable to expect children from poor families to keep up with those from families that are better off.

6. If a teacher has the same high expectations for all pupils and communicates these expectations effectively, all pupils will meet them.

B. On a plain piece of paper draw a picture of a scientist. You won't be judged on your drawing ability. The drawing should include a few details but should not take more than five to ten minutes. Put the drawing aside or hand it in to your instructor to be used later.

C. Make a list of five or more scientists who lived during the twentieth century. They may be from any field and may include those in fields closely related to science, such as engineers. Put the list aside until later.

## DIFFERENT WORLDVIEWS

Science as it is taught in American schools from the elementary level through graduate school is based on the science that arose in Western Europe and is embedded in the Western view of the world and of reality. Students absorb this worldview and are seldom, if ever, reminded that it is not the only possible worldview. Children who come from the many countries of Africa, Asia, and South America—as well as Native American children—may have to deal with confusing contradictions between their families' beliefs and those they encounter in school science. Even within a specific culture, subcultures may define themselves by specific beliefs and patterns of action that are not congruent with the Western worldview. Atwater (2000) describes this problem as follows:

> All students in science classrooms in the United States bring their culture into their classrooms. What the problem continues to be in science classrooms is that the White, middle-class, Protestant culture is considered the norm and every other culture is considered "deficient" and has no relevancy in science classrooms. (p. 172)

## THE MULTICULTURAL CLASSROOM

If you teach in the United States, you will probably teach a multicultural group of children. In many parts of the country, almost all public school classrooms contain students of more than one race or ethnic identity; for some of these students, English is not their first language. In addition to cultural differences, there are often wide differences in family income and social status among the children in a class. Atwater (2000), an African-American educator, writes of problems that desegregation has brought for many African-American pupils. Urban schools have become

*The diversity of American life is reflected in the classroom.*

segregated, with few white students, and black students in predominantly white schools may face "invisibility, hostility, discrimination and racism" (p. 172). You may think of this diversity as a difficult problem, or alternatively, as an opportunity to help children learn to live in a democratic society. Some of the children you teach may have been the targets of prejudice; others may have been brought up in homes where racial bias or antipathy to immigrants is considered normal.

## Different Cultural Norms

Behavior expectations can be very different in different cultural groups; some of the behaviors you expect may go against the cultural norms of some of your children. Recall from Chapter 9 that some ethnic groups teach their children never to look an adult in the eye, whereas others teach their children just the opposite, and for one child to help another is cooperation to some and cheating to others. In her 1995 book, *Other People's Children: Cultural Conflict in the Classroom*, Lisa Delpit, who grew up as one of a few minority children in a predominantly white school, pointed out that turning a directive into a question is a polite form of speech in mainstream, particularly female, culture. First graders from this culture will respond when the teacher asks, "Would you like to sit down now?" or "Isn't it time to put the scissors away?" but those from a different background will not respond because commands are not couched in those terms in their culture. Teachers have to learn to say "Sit down now" or "Put the scissors away *now.*"

## Different Languages

In addition to different languages you may find that different dialects of some languages are spoken by children in your classroom. *Dialect* is the word linguists use to denote patterns in the way people use language. Differences in pronunciation, or *accent,* in vocabulary, and in grammar reflect the user's cultural and regional background. Well-intentioned people who would not make overt remarks about race, gender, or class openly mock and disparage people who speak differently from themselves. Children's ability and intelligence are often judged on the basis of a sentence or even one word. Children as young as three to five years show strong preferences and prejudices based on the way other children speak and may tease and belittle those who speak differently from themselves (Wolfram, 2000).

## The Need for a Multicultural Curriculum

The curriculum should reflect the multicultural nature of the classroom as much as possible. Banks and Banks (1989) outlined several approaches to the integration of ethnic content into the curriculum. The first and lowest level is the focus on people who have made important contributions to American life and culture, including noted scientists and engineers of color. Holidays and special cultural elements are highlighted. This approach is the easiest, but it is limited in impact because students are apt to see it as an addendum or appendage to the "real" curriculum. This approach is further limited because young children are not much interested in and can hardly appreciate the contributions of major scientists of any ethnic group.

The second approach is what Banks and Banks call the additive approach. Examples are the addition of books about children from diverse groups or a unit on Native Americans. An example in science might be the addition of a unit on native medicines used in the Southwest United States or in Mexico. The second approach is still additive rather than integrative, but it does go beyond the first approach and is a practical way for teachers to recognize the different backgrounds of the children. It may be all that a teacher can do, and it is certainly worth doing.

The third approach is called *transformative* and differs fundamentally from the first two. The emphasis is not on how different groups have contributed to main-stream culture but on how the common culture of the United States emerged from the synthesis and interaction of the diverse cultural, racial, and ethnic groups that make up American society. Science was once thought of as a neutral subject, uninflu-enced by the forces that have shaped other aspects of culture, but that view is no longer widely held. Over the past half century attitudes and beliefs about many sub-jects related to science have moved closer to those of Native Americans and other groups from non-European cultures. Three examples are attitudes about the con-sumption of natural resources, about the relation of human beings to the natural world and about the use of alternative medicines. Although many of the science activities suitable for elementary-school students are culturally neutral, be on the lookout for opportunities to let pupils know that the contributions of their diverse cultures to American life are recognized and valued.

## Cross-Cultural Science and Technology Units (CCSTU)

Another approach to curriculum building is exemplified by the CCSTU Project, a curriculum developed in Canada, (Aikenhead, 2000) with the goal of

> making Western science and engineering accessible to Aboriginal students [those who would be called Native American or Indian in the United States] in ways that nurture their own cultural identities; that is, so they will not have to set aside their culture's view of the material world when they study science at school. (Aikenhead, 2000a)

A collaborative team of teachers, a science educator and people from each teacher's local community explored what it would mean to develop culturally sensitive science teaching materials and strategies. They started from the perspective that science is part of Western culture, developed with a worldview that is different from the worldview of Aboriginal peoples and that it is as if children were crossing a border when they entered the Western worldview in order to learn science. The participants wanted chil-dren to learn Western science without having to be assimilated into Western culture. One result of the project was development of a process for producing culturally sensi-tive instructional and assessment strategies and curriculum materials that support learning within any particular community. The process that the group developed can be used in designing curriculum materials for pupils from any cultural and/or ethnic group whose values are different from those of the predominant group.

Many of the beliefs and values of Canadian Aboriginals are similar to those of Native Americans in the United States. Some of these differences may be summarized as follows.

1. *Attitude toward nature.* Native Americans want to accept and live in harmony with nature, whereas Western science has sought to control nature and change the course of natural events.

2. *Understanding other creatures.* Native Americans ask, "Who are these animals?" whereas Western science wants to classify and categorize them.

3. *Our place in nature.* Native Americans feel personally related to what is observed, whereas Western science seeks to be an objective observer, removed and remote from the thing observed.

4. *Ways of knowing.* Native Americans seek to understand things as wholes, whereas Western science reduces everything to its smallest parts and studies the parts.

Six CCSTU units, each dealing with a theme that is significant to one community, have been developed and are available on the Internet, as are articles detailing the developmental process. Because each unit speaks to the unique culture of a particular community, the materials aren't transferable. The process, however, is transferable and can be used in other contexts with other groups. The teachers' guide for cross-cultural science teaching is also applicable in any multicultural setting.

## DISADVANTAGED CHILDREN

As teachers we must be careful in attaching the term *disadvantaged* to children. That term and *inner-city* have come to be used as code words for urban African-American, Hispanic, or other children, many of whom, but certainly not all, are truly disadvantaged by poverty and discrimination. But pupils who are culturally or ethnically different from the majority of children in a school may be advantaged in some ways rather than disadvantaged. They may have the advantage of strong family ties and cultural traditions that give them strength and ambition in spite of lower incomes than the majority. Teachers must take care to have high expectations for all children and to help them achieve at the highest levels they are capable of.

The children who are truly disadvantaged are those who are homeless, living on the streets, or in shelters for the homeless; those whose parents are migrant workers and must travel from state to state, following the crops and taking the children with them; those whose family incomes are so low that there isn't enough money for basic necessities, let alone the expensive backpacks and clothes that other children wear; and those who are abused by alcoholic or drug-addicted parents and come to school hungry and frightened. You may encounter these children in unexpected places. Economic well being doesn't protect children against alcoholism and abuse, schools built in new developments with houses for affluent families may enroll migrant children from farms that remain close by, and every city has homeless mothers with children. There is little that you as a teacher can do to change the basic facts of their lives, but you can treat them with kindness, respect, and sensitivity. For example, don't expect a migrant or homeless child to bring things from home; don't be careless with food in front of children who never have enough to eat. Remember that more than a tenth of American children live in poverty.

# THE CHALLENGE

Approximately 90 percent of K–12 teachers in the United States are white, but more than a third of the school population are pupils of color. "Science for all" has become a national goal and a rallying cry for science educators. There is a widely held belief that all children can learn science if they are given access to adequate resources and taught in ways that reflect the true nature of science. This view is challenged by Barton (1998), who believes that it puts students and science in a relationship whereby only students can change while science remains static. She argues for a science that shifts from the traditional view that places science at the center, as a target to be reached by students, to a science that takes students' histories, identities, and differences into account. She asks, "how science—and the teaching and learning of science—can be constructed in schools in ways that demand attention to the social, historical, political, and physical contexts of the lives of teachers and students" (p. 526).

A 1999 survey of more than 1000 teachers (Holliday, 2000) found that the teachers surveyed believed that, despite much progress over the past several decades, there is still racist, sexist, religious, and homophobic bias in their schools. The bias is shown in comments by students, colleagues, and parents, many of whom are not even aware of their own biases.

Whatever your own race, ethnicity, or cultural background, you face the challenge of teaching children whose backgrounds, beliefs, native languages and life experiences may be very different from your own.

# PREPARING FOR THE CHALLENGE

The following recommendations and some of the suggested activities at the end of the chapter are drawn from the work of Geneva Gay (1989).

1. Become aware of and reflect on your own attitudes and behaviors toward different ethnic groups. Find out how your behaviors and responses are perceived by pupils and what effects they have on pupils' self-concepts and academic achievement. Self-knowledge is the first step.

2. Do not tolerate comments and jokes that reflect bias and prejudice whether it is directed at the way a child dresses, speaks, or interacts with others.

3. Learn to see the differences in cultural values and behavioral codes between yourself and those from other ethnic, cultural, or economic groups. Remember

that there are vast differences within each of these groups; economic disparities often create greater barriers than ethnic or cultural differences.

4. Develop instructional skills that take into account the diversity in learning styles, life experiences, and interests of pupils. The ability to use a variety of teaching strategies, curriculum materials, modes of presentation, and assessment methods is essential.

5. Learn to communicate and interact with parents and other adults from groups that are different from your own. Remember that school is very intimidating to parents who have little command of English and may feel socially and economically inferior to their children's teacher.

6. Watch for cultural bias in textbooks assigned to your students and take care to use curriculum materials, pictures, videos, and other materials that include representatives of minority groups.

7. Believe that the most important thing of all is for *you to accept all children and model this behavior for your class.*

## Pupils with Disabilities

Legislation passed by Congress titled the Individuals with Disabilities Education Act (IDEA) requires that all pupils with disabilities be provided a free public education and that they be taught in the least restrictive environment. Another requirement is that schools collaborate with parents in designing educational programs for students with special needs. One result of this legislation is that many students who were once taught in special education classes are now enrolled in regular classrooms, a practice that is often referred to as *mainstreaming* or *inclusion*. An estimated 15 percent of children have a disability of some sort, so the likelihood is high that you will have at least one child with a disability in your class.

### Adapting the Environment to Meet Children's Needs

A child with a severe disability may have an aide who accompanies the child to class and works with him or her in appropriate ways; most children with disabilities will receive some form of assistance, but, in practice, it may be minimal. Thus you, the teacher, will have to try to adjust the environment or the activities to meet the needs of children with disabilities without sacrificing the needs of the other children. Children with handicapping conditions may need your careful attention to ensure that they understand the rules and that they are capable of following them. It is important to help all children understand the rules of the classroom but especially so for children with special needs.

Children with visual, hearing, or motor impairment have one less avenue through which to learn about the world and are deprived of much of the incidental learning that other children naturally acquire. Every disability affects the way children learn and what they learn. Children with visual impairments or who are blind can see or feel parts but not the whole and don't have the same concept of space as children who see. Children with hearing impairments do not hear speech clearly and

thus don't develop normal speech patterns. Children who have emotional disturbances or who have mental disabilities have their own special learning problems that
often lead to difficulty in interacting with other children.

## Science for Pupils with Disabilities

Science may be the curriculum area that is most amenable to adaptation for students
with disabilities. Hands-on activities and group work—both a natural part of an
elementary-school science program—provide opportunities that are seldom available
in other subject areas. Science curriculum materials adapted or specially designed for
children with hearing impairments, visual impairments, and mental handicaps have
been shown to be effective in both regular and special education classrooms. Some of
these are listed among the references at the end of this chapter and in the Appendix.

Adaptations include many commonsense ideas such as the use of motors or
buzzers, rather than light bulbs, for students with visual impairments to use in testing electric circuits. For students with hearing impairments, teaching methods that
emphasize communication through pantomime, pictures, and careful explanation of
terms have been effective.

A comprehensive review of research involving science education for students
with disabilities (Mastropieri & Scruggs, 1992) found that activity-centered science
curricula were generally effective in facilitating science content learning, manipula-
tive skills, and process skills. Their recommendations for teaching learning disabled
(LD) students include (a) repeated practice with new problems, (b) a wide array of
instructional strategies, (c) continuous assessment of progress and (d) extensive
structure and guidance for working cooperatively with others.

The cumulative results of studies that examine science teaching for students with
disabilities indicate that adaptations of science education methods and materials can
be effective for students with sensory, physical, intellectual, behavioral, or learning
disabilities. More intensive teaching practices, more highly structured presentations,
and more use of pictures and mnemonics are strategies that appear to improve learning for students with disabilities. In addition to paying attention to teaching strategies, teachers can adapt curriculum materials by reducing peripheral content, enhancing concrete experiences and incorporating additional practice and review activities.

## FOCUSING ON ABILITIES

Whatever changes or adaptations you make, the focus should be on the child's abilities rather than disabilities. The following attitudes and strategies are generally
applicable, regardless of the specific disability.

1. Show by your actions and words that you accept the child with disabilities as a
   valuable member of the class.
2. Encourage the children to offer help to the special child when needed but to
   allow the child to be as independent as possible.

3. Use group work and cooperative learning for science activities and place the child with disabilities in an appropriate group.

4. Give all explanations and directions clearly and explicitly. Be sure that the special child understands what is to be done and why.

5. Maintain contact with the parents and work with them to provide the best learning opportunities for the child.

If you try these suggestions, you may find that they will help all your students, not only those with disabilities.

# GENDER EQUITY

By the time they enter first grade most children have clear ideas about gender and about what is appropriate for children of their own sex. In the early grades, most girls appear to like science as well as boys do, but boys have consistently scored higher than girls on such large-scale standardized tests as the National Assessment of Educational Progress in 1978 and 1989 and the Third International Mathematics and Science Study in 1994–95.

A report by the American Association of University Women (1992) provides evidence that by middle school girls' attitudes toward science begin to decline and by the senior year in high school, science, except for biology, has become predominantly a boys' subject. By senior year there are large gender differences in future career plans with more boys than girls planning to pursue careers in every field of science except biology. (AAUW, p. 44)

## Gender Stereotyping in Textbooks

A factor that may have contributed to the attitude that science is more appropriate for boys than for girls is the gender stereotyping found in many earlier textbooks and other curriculum materials. Pictures showed men as scientists and women as laboratory assistants, men as doctors and women as nurses, and men as engineers with no women in the picture. With the single exception of Marie Curie, women scientists' pictures were not included in science textbooks. This situation has changed over the past decade: Most up-to-date science textbooks for elementary-school students use illustrations that are balanced by gender and also by ethnicity, but inclusiveness is something to keep in mind if you are in a position to choose a textbook. You should also be aware of these considerations in choosing other books and materials for your pupils.

## Differences in Science Experiences

Early experience has been suggested as a contributing factor to gender differences in science achievement. In general, boys have more experiences with electric toys, tools, pulleys, gears, and microscopes and more boys have visited a factory, a weather station or an electric plant. These differences may carry over into the classroom. Many teachers have noticed that when boys and girls work together on science activities, the boys more often set up the equipment and take the measurements while girls watch and record the data.

Although the reality of gender differences has been well established, researchers don't know whether they are due to choice or to different societal expectations. That is, do girls and boys voluntarily choose different activities and experiences or do they simply play with the toys they are given and accept the experiences they are offered? Whatever the reason, gender differences will be reinforced if teachers allow children to select science activities based solely on familiarity or interest.

## Differences in Teacher Attention

The most disturbing finding that has emerged from 20 years of research on gender differences in school is that teachers pay more attention to boys than to girls. Although differential treatment of pupils by teachers is found in all subjects, teacher bias in favor of boys is particularly noticed in science classes. Teachers pay more attention to boys than to girls, giving boys more praise, acceptance, criticism, and remediation. Teachers give boys more precise—and therefore more helpful—comments on both academic work and conduct than they give girls. Teachers also wait longer for boys than for girls to answer questions, and reward girls more than boys for obeying the rules than for having good ideas. When teachers need help in carrying out a demonstration, they more often call on boys than girls.

A multicultural classroom does not guarantee equal treatment of pupils. Limited data indicate race differences as well as gender differences in teacher–pupil interactions, with white boys receiving more teacher attention than girls and more teacher attention than boys of any other racial or ethnic group. (AAUW, 1992 pp. 118–122).

Another difference between boys and girls is that girls are more likely to attribute their success in school to hard work or effort and their failures to lack of ability, whereas for boys the reverse is true. Many studies have found that boys attribute their success in science or math to ability and their failure to lack of effort, even though the actual ability of the boys and girls is the same.

## Gender and Power in the Classroom

The result of the evidence just cited is that science classes tend to be dominated by boys. Gallas (1998), a first-grade teacher and researcher, set out to provide a description of how children "do gender" but found that gender could not be separated from race and class and came to believe that the real issues in her classroom were those of power and social control, rather than gender. "Classrooms are more than rooms full of children waiting to be taught" she wrote. "They are dialogic communities where understandings of texts and social relations are collectively forged, with and without the teacher's assistance" (p. 3). Gallas found that power

*Girls and boys learn together in this classroom.*

and control are issues even as early as first grade and that some children, both girls and boys, in her classroom try to gain control and exert power in different ways. Other children, particularly girls, are passive and accepting and concede power and control to those who are seeking to establish it for themselves.

## Creating a Gender-Equitable Classroom

Most teachers do not want to be biased in their treatment of the children in their classes and are often surprised to learn that they have treated boys and girls differently, usually in subtle ways. The following are some suggestions for creating a gender-equitable classroom, based on strategies that teachers have used successfully.

1. Eliminate sexist language and make it clear that you will not tolerate sexist language or jokes in your class.
2. Assign the same science activities to boys and girls. Do not allow boys to handle the equipment and make the measurements while girls sit by to record results.
3. Give as much attention to girls as to boys. Ask girls the same kinds of questions you ask boys and give them as much time to answer. Granting equal time is very important in discussions that take place at the completion of science investigations or other activities.

4. Emphasize collaboration rather then competition. Most girls work best under noncompetitive conditions.

5. Be aware of the ways children try to exert power and do not allow individual children, either boys or girls, to dominate discussions or take sole charge of science experiments or activities in their groups.

## Checking Your Assumptions

Now it's time to look at your drawings of scientists and your lists of scientists. Display your drawings so that all members of the class can see them and write the names of all listed scientists on the chalkboard. Examine the drawings and lists and answer these questions:

1. What percentage of the drawings depict white males?
2. What percentage of the drawings depict women?
3. What percentage of the drawings depict people of color?
4. What percentage of the drawings depict persons with handicapping conditions?

Answer the same questions for the total number of scientists listed. Reflect on the answers to increase your awareness of unconscious assumptions and biases.

# TEACHER EXPECTATIONS

## ■ A CONVERSATION

Ms. Sanchez, a beginning teacher, was talking over a problem with her mentor, Ms. Oldhand.

MS. SANCHEZ:  Ms. Oldhand, I need some help with one of the pupils in my class. Stephen's record shows that his grades have always been among the lowest in the class, beginning in first grade. He's a nice kid and has never been a behavior problem, but lately he doesn't even seem to be trying, and he is beginning to be a little bit of a show-off. I'm afraid that he'll start being a behavior problem as well as a low achiever unless I can do something to change his attitude.

MS. OLDHAND:  Well, you have a good start on the problem because you assume that you can do something to turn the situation around. Would you like for me to sit in on your class and see whether I can come up with some things for you to try?

MS. SANCHEZ:  Yes, I think that's a very good idea.

The next day Ms. Oldhand observed the class.

| | |
|---|---|
| MS. SANCHEZ: | I'm glad you could observe my class this morning. You could see for yourself that Stephen isn't interested in what's going on in class and that he tries to call attention to himself. |
| MS. OLDHAND: | Yes, I did see that, and I agree with you that something needs to be done to help Stephen. I noticed several things that I wonder whether you are aware of. I noticed that, when you asked Stephen a very easy question, you gave him only a second to answer. When he hesitated, you turned to another pupil and asked her to give the answer. Why didn't you give Stephen more time? |
| MS. SANCHEZ: | It seemed clear that he didn't know the answer, and I didn't want to embarrass him. |
| MS. OLDHAND: | But when you asked a question of Rita who is a very bright girl and she hesitated, you gave her a clue and waited long enough for her to think of a reply. Why did you give her more time than you gave Stephen? |
| MS. SANCHEZ: | I gave her more time because I knew that she could come up with an answer if she just thought about it. |
| MS. OLDHAND: | In other words, you expected Rita to be able to answer the question you asked her, but you didn't expect Stephen to be able to answer the question you asked him. Stephen may not be the brightest student in the class, but he's smart enough to figure out that your expectations for him are very low. |
| MS. SANCHEZ: | Are you suggesting that Stephen could do as well as Rita? |
| MS. OLDHAND: | No, I'm not suggesting that. I am saying that I believe Stephen knows that you don't expect him to be able to master the work in this class and that makes him think, "What's the use? Even the teacher doesn't think I can do this work." If he thought you believed he could do the work and expected him to do the work, he might try harder to live up to your expectations. That way he could get positive feedback and wouldn't have to try to get attention by showing off. |
| MS. SANCHEZ: | It's hard for me to believe that my expectations influence the way I interact with Stephen, but I think I'll tape record the next question-and-answer session and listen to the tape to see whether you're right about this. |

Everyone has expectations about what will happen in certain circumstances, and people often have expectations for both themselves and for other people. Most people have felt at some time that they had to do something to live up to someone else's expectations.

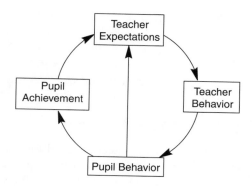

**FIGURE 10.1  Pupil Achievement Affected by Teacher Expectations**

In a famous book, *Pygmalion in the Classroom,* Rosenthal and Jacobson (1968) reported the results of a research project in which researchers told a group of teachers that certain children in their classes were "late bloomers" and would make a spurt in achievement during the year. Actually, the children had been chosen at random, and the researchers had no objective reason to believe that they were different from any of the other children in the classes. But the teachers believed that those children were different and thus raised their expectations for the children. As a result (according to the researchers), the designated children actually did achieve at a higher level than they had before. A valid conclusion seemed to be that when the teachers expected them to do better, the children did do better.

The results have been questioned by other researchers and have led to some controversy, but the book was important because it focused attention on teachers' expectations and led researchers to ask how teacher expectations could influence pupil achievement. Now there is evidence that a teacher's expectations for a pupil affect the teacher's behavior toward that pupil and that the teacher's behavior has an effect on pupil achievement. Several popular television programs have been based on the idea that teachers who expect a lot from their pupils raise the level of achievement of the whole class. Figure 10.1 shows how the process might work.

## TEACHER EXPECTATIONS AND TEACHER BEHAVIOR

Suppose that a science teacher doesn't expect girls to be as interested in science as boys are and therefore doesn't expect girls to do as well in science. How might this expectation unconsciously affect the teacher's behavior? One thing a teacher might do would be to give different assignments to boys and girls when groups are formed. Girls might be assigned or "allowed" to be recorders while the boys do the experiments. This division of tasks would give boys an active role and girls a passive role. Because children learn by doing, not by watching, the result likely would be that the girls would not learn as much as the boys, and the teacher's expectations would be confirmed. This type of outcome is what is called a *self-fulfilling prophecy;*

that is, the teacher's behavior brought about the result the teacher expected. Suppose that the teacher, taking a different tack, had thought, "Why shouldn't girls do as well as boys in science? I'm going to be careful to see that girls and boys have the same opportunities to learn in this class, and I'll expect all of them to do well." The teacher would organize the class so that all the pupils did some of the experiments and all took a turn being recorder.

## High and Low Achievers

It may seem natural for teachers to have lower expectations for low-achieving pupils than for high-achieving pupils, but this attitude can be discouraging and even damaging to the low achievers, who know they are being treated differently in class. Sometimes teachers assume that children with disabilities or minority children or those whose families are recent immigrants will automatically be low achievers.

Johanneson (1999) tells the story of Veronica, a daughter of migrant workers who moved with her family as they followed the crops from place to place. She was able to remain in one school for most of her high school years, was an honor student and is headed for college. She tells of her experiences in classes in which teachers expected less of migrant children than of other children.

> A lot of teachers assume that we are not as smart as other kids because of the fact that we are migrant," says Veronica "For example, we'll be studying a certain topic in class—say politics—and the teachers will think we know nothing about it. They ask other students and skip over us. If we nag at them they'll start asking us. But it shouldn't take us nagging. Instead of challenging you more, they give you the answers and that's sort of disappointing. . . . I don't like people handing me things because I'm a migrant. I like to work for what I have. (Johanneson, 1999. p. 36)

Some of the ways that teachers treat high and low achievers differently include

1. calling on low achievers to answer questions in class less frequently;

2. waiting less time for low achievers to answer questions asked by the teacher (the teacher doesn't expect the pupil to know the answer and so moves on quickly to someone else);

3. dismissing low achievers' ideas (the teacher doesn't expect low achievers to have good or useful ideas, though creativity and school achievement aren't necessarily related); and

4. giving briefer answers to questions of low achievers (the teacher doesn't expect low achievers to understand anyway, so less time is spent explaining).

In all these cases, the teacher's behavior communicates to the low-achieving pupil that the teacher does not expect that child to know the answer, to have good ideas, or to be able to understand the learning task. These expectations can cause the pupil to become discouraged and lose interest, and the teacher's expectation becomes a self-fulfilling prophecy.

Some educators have suggested that teachers should neither look at pupils' previous records nor talk to other teachers about individual pupils in order to prevent forming negative expectations. Such denial seems unreasonable. What a teacher does with the information is the important thing. Information from the past can be useful in helping a teacher diagnose a pupil's problems and plan instruction that will meet the pupil's needs. Teachers should trust their own judgment and good intentions. All of us as teachers have unconscious assumptions and expectations that are often based on false premises. The way to avoid harmful expectations is not to restrict information but to become more aware of negative, unconscious assumptions and expectations and the behavior that signals them to pupils.

## RESPONSES TO STATEMENTS ON TEACHER EXPECTATIONS

Now that you have thought about the effects of teacher expectations, let's return to the statements on teacher expectations on page 232. My responses to these statements are as follows.

1. All pupils can achieve success. (Strongly agree)

Teachers should expect all pupils to meet minimum standards. These standards should be set so that all pupils who work hard at the tasks and assignments can succeed. Although all pupils cannot be expected to do equally well, a teacher can establish reasonable minimal objectives for everyone. Many pupils will be able to exceed the minimum, and the teacher should try to provide learning tasks that stimulate each pupil to go as far as possible.

2. When you have a class of 25 children, dealing with pupils as individuals isn't feasible. (Strongly disagree)

As a rule, teachers should think, talk, and act in terms of individual pupils. Doing this does not mean that teachers should not practice grouping or that terms such as *low achievers* should not be used. Teachers do sometimes lose sight of the individual, however. There are certain teacher behaviors to watch for as warnings that a stereotype has begun to structure a teacher's perception of a pupil. Among these behaviors are continual references in speech to group names to the exclusion of individual names ("the boys in this class" or "the kids from the projects") and an overemphasis on differences between groups. These warning signs are especially important when the groups in question are the more permanent ones of economic status, ethnicity, or gender.

3. Some children just don't want to learn. (Strongly disagree)

The teacher should assume that children enjoy learning—that each child wants to learn, is able to learn, and is hoping to learn. The teacher's job is to create a classroom environment in which each child *can* learn. A teacher who doesn't recognize or accept this responsibility may act as if the pupils are expected to learn on their own with no help from the teacher. If a pupil doesn't catch on immediately after one demonstration or doesn't do the work correctly after hearing the instructions one time, the teacher reacts with impatience and frustration. The real goal of teaching is *not* accomplished by giving information, although that is often a part of it. Rather, it is by listening to pupil responses and observing pupil behaviors as sources of information and then using the information to design further learning experiences. A child is always ready to learn something; the art of teaching lies in finding out what each child is ready to learn and helping each child take the next step.

4. Some children will disregard the rules no matter what the teacher does. (Disagree)

The teacher should expect all pupils to follow the rules. Some teachers have a hand in creating serious discipline problems, usually by failing to establish and enforce appropriate rules of behavior. Adherence to rules is usually obtained rather easily by teachers who (a) establish fair and appropriate rules, (b) are consistent in what they say, (c) say only what they really mean, and (d) regularly follow up with appropriate action whenever necessary. Appropriate action produces credibility and respect; the pupils are clear about what the teacher expects of them and know that they are accountable for meeting these expectations. Children are not born difficult; they learn that behavior if adults around them do not sufficiently respect their potential for growth and their current limitations. Children who have been taught to be difficult can usually be untaught. Exceptions to this generalization include children with certain learning disorders or intellectual disabilities. Until a problem child is diagnosed by a specialist, however, the regular classroom teacher should not hold lower expectations for that child than for any other pupil in the class.

5. It is unreasonable to expect children from poor families to keep up with those from families that are better off. (Strongly disagree)

Intelligence and motivation to learn are not distributed according to family income or gender or ethnicity or physical condition. The teacher's expectations are especially important for children who come from families who are in difficult circumstances or are thought to be different in some way. It is true, however, that children from poor families do not have the same opportunities for travel and some other experiences that children from middle- and upper-income families have. For this reason, the experiences provided in school may be even more important for their future than for the future of those who have wider opportunities.

6. If a teacher has the same high expectations for all pupils and communicates these expectations effectively, all pupils will meet them. (Disagree)

The keyword here is *same*. Children are not all the same and cannot all meet the same high expectations no matter how hard they try. It will be one of your challenges to know your pupils well enough to set high but reasonable expectations for each one.

Although positive expectations go a long way toward improving student achievement, they are not magic. Some pupils will still have difficulty in meeting the learning objectives. To the extent that positive expectations initiate behavior that does lead to positive effects, they encourage students to work hard and do their best. All teachers, however, are sometimes disappointed; to expect perfection of yourself as a teacher or of your pupils is unrealistic. You can only try to do your best.

# ■ SUMMARY

This chapter is divided into two parts. The first section examines the problems and challenges of including all children as equal participants in all the science activities that take place in the classroom. Children from racial, ethnic, or religious groups that aren't part of the predominant culture are now found in classrooms throughout the United States and challenge the teacher to make science interesting and meaningful to children from all groups and backgrounds. Perhaps the most difficult children to reach are those who are severely disadvantaged because of poverty, abuse, or other problems that leave children vulnerable and unprotected. Questions are raised about even the possibility of including all children when science is seen as unchanging and unrelated to pupils' lives and experiences.

Multicultural science education seeks to take into account children's differences in behavior norms, languages, worldviews, and family values. Several methods are suggested, including a rather superficial inclusion of references to scientists from various racial and ethnic groups. A more useful approach is inclusion in the curriculum of scientific ideas generated in different cultures. A third, and more truly inclusive approach, is to help pupils understand how the mainstream culture of the United States emerged from the synthesis and incorporation of diverse points of view, social customs, vocabularies, and experiences. Finally, a cross-cultural curriculum project is described.

Federal law requires that children with disabilities be taught in the least restrictive environment. Most children with severe disabilities are still taught in special schools, but children who are able to benefit from being part of the regular school population are taught along with nondisabled children, a practice called *mainstreaming* or *inclusion*. Strategies that have been shown to improve learning for children with physical, emotional, and intellectual disabilities include more intensive teaching practices, more highly structured presentations, more use of pictures and mnemonics. Other strategies include adaptations of teaching materials by reducing content, enhancing concrete experiences, and incorporating additional practice and review activities into the curriculum.

The problem of persisting gender differences in science achievement in school and in pursuing careers in science has been attributed to gender bias in textbooks, differences in early experiences, and differences in the amount of attention paid to girls in the classroom. Guidelines to help teachers create gender-equitable classrooms are presented.

The second part of the chapter focuses on teacher expectations, explaining that teachers' expectations of pupils can influence pupil achievement in subtle ways. High expectations create an atmosphere for learning in which children have the motivation and incentive to succeed. That is particularly true with children who have traditionally been thought of as "different"—children with disabilities, minority children, poor children, or any others who may have been labeled as "problems." Sometimes girls are not expected to do as well as boys in science because science has not been a traditional subject or career for women. As teachers increase their awareness of the role of expectations in pupil achievement, they also have to be realistic and not expect all children to have the same abilities and interests. Teachers can set reasonable expectations and work with children so that they can all gain confidence in their abilities to learn and grow.

A questionnaire for education students was designed to help you examine your own ideas and learn ways to communicate your own positive expectations so as to encourage all pupils to strive to do their best.

# ■ ACTIVITIES FOR THE READER

1. Find out what cultural groups, other than the one to which you belong, live in your community. Did any groups arrive within the past 10 years? What language do they speak? Is there a close-knit community or only isolated families?

2. Interview a mother or caretaker of a child with disabilities about the school experiences of the child. Make a careful list of questions before you attempt an interview.

# ■ QUESTIONS FOR DISCUSSION

1. What would it mean, in practical terms, to take into account pupils' histories, identities, and differences?

2. How can science be taught in ways that give attention to the social, historical, political, and physical contexts of the lives of children?

3. Food was mentioned as something that has different meanings to different children. What other topics for science activities may be sensitive to some children. How can you handle them?

4. How do you feel about mainstreaming children with severe disabilities? Do you believe that they are better served in a regular classroom or in a special class or school? (This subject is controversial, so you should feel free to give your honest views, provided that you have arrived at them thoughtfully.)

5. A growing body of literature examines science from a feminist perspective, suggesting that women's lived experiences and ways of thinking have not been incorporated into science as it has developed from a Eurocentric male viewpoint. Read and respond to the article by Roychoudrey, Tippins and Nichols (1995).

6. Suggest some ways not mentioned in the text that expectations could affect achievement by (a) minority students, (b) students with disabilities, (c) boys, and (d) girls.

# ■ REFERENCES

Aikenhead, G. (2000a). Rekindling traditions. Cross-Cultural science and technology units (CCSTU) project [On-line]. Available: http://capes.usask.ca/ccstu.

Aikenhead, G. S. (2000b). Students' ease in crossing cultural borders into school science. *Science Education, 84.*

American Association of University Women (AAUW) Educational Foundation. (1992). How schools shortchange girls: The AAUW Report. New York: Marlowe & Company.

Atwater, M. (2000). Equity for Black Americans. *Science Education, 84*(2), 154–179.

Banks, J. & Banks, C. (Eds.). (1989). *Multicultural education: Issues and perspectives.* Boston: Allyn and Bacon.

Barton, A. (1998). Reframing "science for all" through the politics of poverty. *Educational Policy, 12*(5), 525–541.

Delpit, L. (1995) *Other people's children: Cultural conflict in the classroom.* New York: New Press.

Gallas, K. (1998). *Sometimes I can be anything.* New York: Teachers College Press.

Gay, G. (1989). *Ethnic minorities and educational equality.* In Banks, J. & Banks, C. (Eds.), *Multicultural education: Issues and perspectives* (pp. 167–188). Boston: Allyn & Bacon.

Holliday, J. (2000, Spring). Survey says? *Teaching Tolerance, 17,* 50–51.

Johanneson, A. (1999, Spring). Follow the stream. *Teaching Tolerance, 15,* 32–39.

Mastropieri, M., & Scruggs, T. (1992). Science for students with disabilities. *Review of Educational Research, 62*(4), 377–411.

Rosenthal, R., & Jacobson, L. (1968). *Pygmalion in the classroom.* New York: Holt, Rinehart & Winston.

Roychoudrey, A., Tippins, D., & Nichols, S. (1995). Gender-inclusive science teaching: A feminist–constructivist approach. *Journal of Research in Science Teaching, 32* (9), 897–924.

Wolfram, W. (2000, Fall). Everyone has an accent. *Teaching Tolerance, 18,* 18–23.

# *Integrating Science with Other Subjects*

■ Mr. Newman was nearing the end of his student teaching assignment and had just finished teaching a fifth-grade science lesson. He found that he was unable to finish what he had planned for the day, even though the period had gone longer than scheduled. At the next opportunity, he talked about the lesson with Ms. Oldhand.

MR. NEWMAN: The children really enjoyed their science lesson today, and I think they learned a lot. But I feel very frustrated because there is never enough time for the children to do all that I want them to do.

MS. OLDHAND: That's a problem that we all have and one that I'm afraid you will always have to live with. The school day is never long enough for all the things that need to be done.

MR. NEWMAN: Well, you always seem to be able to get a lot more done in science than I can manage to do. When you teach, the children move along through the curriculum in math and language arts as fast as all the other classes, and you still have time for special science projects that I can't seem to find time for.

MS. OLDHAND: (Laughing) I can assure you that I sometimes feel frustrated, too, but teachers learn to become more efficient as they gain more experience. I certainly don't have any secrets that I'm keeping from you, but I think the one thing that has helped me the most is learning to build interdisciplinary units combining science with other subjects.

MR. NEWMAN: What does that mean?

MS. OLDHAND: That means taking one important idea or theme and using it as the basis for activities in several subjects so that what the children learn in one area adds to their understanding in the other areas. You know that we talked about integrating content and processes in science; building interdisciplinary units takes that idea a step or two further. There are many obvious ways to integrate two areas of the curriculum, such as using science books in reading and using examples from science when you make up word problems in arithmetic. A less obvious way to do so is to use the various science processes in other areas of the curriculum. After all, the processes of observing, measuring, communicating, and hypothesizing aren't confined to science. Those skills are needed in all areas of the curriculum, as well as in everyday life. Actually, science is such an important and pervasive part of our lives that I find it just works its way into the curriculum all the time.

**I**n previous chapters, many ideas for extending science lessons or units into other areas of the curriculum have been suggested. This chapter, goes a step further and demonstrates ways to develop integrated, or interdisciplinary, lessons and units to expand and deepen children's subject-matter understanding and skill development. *To integrate* means to combine things in such a way that together they form a unified whole; the aim is to interweave subjects so that children's understanding embraces several subjects as if they were one.

## RATIONALE FOR AN INTEGRATED CURRICULUM

Integration of science with other subjects is an opportunity and a challenge for you to make science more meaningful to children and to help them integrate knowledge learned in one context with knowledge learned in another context. The world did not divide itself up into distinct subject areas; these divisions have been made by human beings who have classified and categorized what they found in the world in order to make it more comprehensible. One result has been that subjects are taught in school as isolated bundles of knowledge, applicable to a narrow range of life experience. Many simple, though important and even profound, ideas cut across disciplines. In fact, most powerful ideas are not confined to one subject but cut across the range of human experience.

Inquiry-based science teaching by its nature overlaps in many ways with other subjects. For example, writing in a workbook or journal reinforces skills learned in language arts, and making measurements and constructing graphs reinforces concepts and skills learned in mathematics. An integrated, or interdisciplinary, curriculum goes beyond those activities, however, in that neither subject is incidental to the other. Both (or several) subjects receive equal emphasis in setting objectives and other aspects of planning. Each contributes to understanding of a concept, building a theme, or learning a skill or process.

Building integrated interdisciplinary units will be easier for a teacher in a self-contained classroom than for one who teaches science as a special subject. In the latter case, the science teacher needs to work with classroom teachers to plan units and coordinate the lessons taught by the science teacher with those taught by the other teachers. According to Jacobs, (1989), what makes the effort worthwhile is that "students' understanding within the subject matters can become deeper, their understanding of the relationships among the subjects can become sharper and their thinking can become more insightful and systematic, in school and out" (p. 3).

There are both practical and theoretical reasons for building units that incorporate science within the unit. Four good reasons are:

- *Time pressure.* As Ms. Oldhand explained, it's hard to find the time to do everything that needs to be done in elementary school, and science is sometimes the subject that gets neglected. By integrating science with other subjects when appropriate, the teacher can accomplish the objectives of the science lesson along with the objectives of one or more other subjects.

■ *Fragmentation of the curriculum.* A rigid schedule allowing 30 or 40 minutes for reading, followed by 30 minutes for math, followed by a lesson in writing, does not help children see the connections between subjects nor the purpose of learning the skills that they are taught. This approach can lead to what has been called *inert knowledge,* or knowledge that can be delivered on request but that is not used spontaneously in solving real problems. For example, a pupil might be able to work exercises in addition and subtraction during arithmetic class but not be able to figure out differences in mileage between two points on a map during social studies class. In contrast, integration of subjects requires that children use their skills and knowledge in multiple contexts.

■ *Pressure for the Three R's.* Some parents and others believe that teachers should spend most of their time on reading, writing, and arithmetic. Teachers who feel that they are required to emphasize these subjects at the expense of all others can kill two birds with one stone by using science activities and concepts as the basis for work in other subjects.

■ *Explosion of knowledge.* There is so much to be learned in science that no one can hope to teach everything that children need to know. It is more useful if teachers can help them learn how to learn on their own. When subjects are integrated at the concept and process levels, children begin to understand how knowledge in one area is connected with knowledge in another area. This understanding will be helpful when they start to learn something new because they will know that new knowledge can be tied into knowledge they already have.

## CONCEPTS AND SKILLS ACROSS THE CURRICULUM

Curriculum integration includes not just the interweaving of subjects, such as science and social studies, but also the interweaving of concepts and skills. Many important concepts in science have counterparts or similar concepts in other subject areas. An example is the concept of a network or web. In science it is an important ecological concept, used particularly in teaching about the interdependence of organisms. Network is also an important concept in social studies as children learn that people are interdependent and that they themselves live in a network of family, friends, and others.

Integration of subjects helps children acquire higher order concepts that are applicable and important in more than one, and often in many, contexts. Children deepen their understanding of topics and concepts by seeing things from different points of view, making comparisons, and seeing connections. A well-integrated unit is seamless; in other words, children aren't aware that one part of the unit is science and another part is social studies or literature. The teacher has planned the unit to integrate these subjects and meet the various learning objectives, but in the minds of the pupils, all the parts come together to make the topic more interesting and meaningful.

Both symbolic skills and process skills can be enhanced and made more meaningful when they are taught and used in several subjects. Symbolic skills include mathematics, writing, drawing, graphing, and mapping. When children watch a butterfly emerge from its cocoon and then write about it, the writing has immediacy and meaning. Using mathematics in science brings abstract numbers on a page into the children's world. Both writing and drawing as ways to represent knowledge should be part of every science program.

Observing, classifying, inferring, hypothesizing, and various higher order thinking skills have been discussed earlier in this book. Once you begin to think about using these science processes in teaching other subjects, you will see that they are applicable across the curriculum. In a reading lesson with even the youngest children, you can read a few lines of a story and then ask, "What do you think will happen next?" and "Why do you think that?" When you ask those questions, you are asking children to form hypotheses based on evidence in the story, a process similar to forming hypotheses in science.

Classification can be used in reading, writing, mathematics, social studies, art, and music. As children see that they can classify things in all subject areas, they will begin to consider this a tool for understanding and a useful way to think about the things they encounter in their daily lives. In doing so they are acquiring metacognitive skills; that is, they are learning how to learn, probably the most important thing they can learn in school.

In thinking about embedding skills in a lesson, your chain of reasoning may be something like this:

1. What are the content objectives of the lesson?
2. What activities will the pupils be carrying out?
3. What skills will they use in order to meet the content objectives?

Or you might focus on a skill and follow this line of reasoning:

1. What are the skill objectives of the lesson?
2. In what areas of the curriculum is that skill needed?
3. In what activities can the skill be used to meet content objectives?

In either case, the skill is taught and practiced as a tool to aid learning.

## CRITERIA FOR INTEGRATING SCIENCE WITH OTHER SUBJECTS

An integrated unit is one that integrates several subjects in a unified plan for a series of lessons with broad goals. Sometimes only two subjects are integrated to form a unit of study, and sometimes it seems best to focus on a science concept alone. Before you decide to teach an integrated lesson or unit, you should ask yourself these questions:

- Does the lesson or unit meet important goals or objectives in both science and the other subject(s)? It serves no useful purpose to include unimportant facts or something far outside of the science curriculum just to have an integrated lesson.

- Does the integrated lesson or unit do a better job than you could do in a single-subject lesson or unit? Does it lead to more understanding or a higher level of performance of a skill? If not, why are you doing it?

Whether you are in a self-contained classroom or working as a special science teacher, planning and gathering materials for any lesson take time and energy. It probably takes more time to plan integrated units or lessons than single-subject units or lessons. When you need to coordinate your work with that of other teachers, as you will if you are a special science teacher, even more time and energy are needed for planning. That is why you must ask yourself those questions and try to give honest answers. Unless you can answer "yes" to those questions, it may be best to teach a single-subject lesson or unit.

## Science and Reading

As one of the three R's, reading has always consumed a major portion of the school day in the primary grades and has received serious attention all the way through the elementary-school. Learning to read is a major developmental task for young children and of great concern to teachers and parents. If you are a teacher in a self-contained classroom, you will spend a good deal of your time teaching your pupils to read—from the early stages of emergent literacy, through skill at decoding and comprehension, and finally to the ability to use reading as a means of learning other subjects and understanding the world. Classifying, inferring, and hypothesizing—processes needed in science—also have a place in reading. As children get past the earliest stages of learning to read and begin to read for comprehension, these processes become important in their progress. Because reading consumes so much time in the elementary school, it seems sensible to integrate science and reading as much as possible. In the early grades, that is most easily accomplished by the use of science experiences as a basis for the experiential approach to teaching reading. In the intermediate grades, it can be done through the use of books as supplements to classroom science experiences.

### Using Science as the Basis for Reading

Use of basal readers remains the primary means of instruction in beginning reading, but language experience and whole language approaches are other methods now in use (McGee & Lomax, 1990; Schickedanz, 1990; Stahl & Miller, 1989). These personalized, reality-based approaches encompass listening, speaking, reading, and writing—and

*Reading has a place in every subject, including science.*

children are encouraged and guided to use language in regard to a shared experience of the group. All these methods can use science experiences as the basis for narratives constructed by the children. In the older, language experience method, children tell their experiences to the teacher, either individually or in a group, and the teacher writes down what they say. In the whole language approach, the children write their experiences themselves, spelling the words however they can. A science lesson on observing and classifying objects, for example, can form the basis for a language experience or whole language lesson.

## Reading about Science

Although science should be taught primarily by means of an active, hands-on, experiential approach, that does not mean there is no place for books and reading. Reading can make experience more meaningful and can provide vicarious experiences that cannot be had directly. The problem arises when reading becomes the primary means by which children learn science. *Reading should supplement experience, not take the place of it.*

A wonderful variety of books on every imaginable science subject is available for readers of all ages. These books range from the lowest vocabulary level to detailed, accurate treatments of subjects of interest to those upper elementary–school children who by this time are excellent readers and have a special interest in science. Between these two extremes are many science books that have wide appeal. All pupils should be required to read and report on, either orally or in writing, books about science subjects, along with works of fiction, history, and other areas of interest.

It is useless to require pupils to produce book reports unless you are willing to put thought and time into how they will carry out the assignment. To make the assignment is easy, but to follow through can prove difficult. The pupils will have to take a number of steps, and you will have to monitor their progress, in selecting a book (in this case, a book on a suitable science subject), having the book approved, reading the book and taking notes, submitting for approval an outline of the report, and getting the report in on time. In effect, the reports become independent projects, similar to those described in Chapter 6. You can determine whether writing a book report will be growth-promoting or only a frustrating process for most of your pupils.

Books will also be needed for information on subjects studied in class, particularly in the case of group investigations and independent projects, such as for a science fair. School librarians are always ready to cooperate, within the constraints of their budgets, in securing books that children need for carrying out science assignments. You will need to let them know ahead of time what your pupils will need for their science projects and assignments.

## SCIENCE AND WRITING

**Materials resource note.**
*Science and Language Links* by Johanna Scott and *Science through Children's Literature* by Carol and John Butzow, distributed by Cuisenaire Company of America, are useful resources for ideas for integrating science and language arts.

Writing is included in the *National Science Education Standards* (NRC, 1996) in the statement that students should be able to "gather, store, retrieve and organize data" (p. 145) and to communicate results to others. Writing has been incorporated as an integral part of the science lessons you have studied in previous chapters of this textbook in several ways. Two of these are workbooks and scrapbooks.

### Workbooks

When children keep workbooks to record their work in science they are meeting writing standards as well as the science standard just cited. Writing standards for pupils in kindergarten through second grade (Mid-continent Research for Education & Learning, 2000) include the following

**Discusses ideas with peers, draws pictures to generate ideas, writes key thoughts and questions, rehearses ideas, records reactions and observations.**

For children in Grades 3 through 5 the following applies:

**Uses graphic organizers; groups related ideas; takes notes; brainstorms ideas; organizes information according to type and purpose of writing.**

All these skills are used when children keep workbooks. It is difficult to think of another way of teaching these skills that better meets the standards.

Workbooks encourage children to think of writing as a way to explain to someone else what they have seen and done and, in the process, to understand it better themselves. Grammar and spelling are important, but their purpose is to aid communication,

*An investigation is not complete until it has been recorded.*

not inhibit it. Note that spelling and grammar aren't included in the writing standards cited. If you choose to grade the workbooks, grade them for completeness, organization, and evidence of thinking but not for spelling, grammar or penmanship.

To become autonomous learners, children have to be able to work on their own without constant adult guidance. For that to happen, they have to have tasks, both in science and in writing, that they can manage mostly on their own. When science lessons become too abstract or too complicated or keeping workbooks becomes too difficult, children are forced to rely on adults and can't grow toward autonomy. As children get older, science experiences can provide the basis for the development of clarity and accuracy in writing, but the important thing for younger children is to learn to write in their workbooks with confidence in their ability to express themselves.

## Scrapbooks

Scrapbooks were mentioned briefly in the story of the teacher called Virginia in Chapter 7. A scrapbook is a collection of pages that children create to provide additional details about a topic they have studied. The example given in Chapter 7 was a scrapbook on animals. A scrapbook is a useful way to learn more about a topic such as trees, insects, flowers, or seeds for which there are many examples that can be used to illustrate a concept.

Each pupil or pair of pupils creates a page that describes one animal or tree or flower—whatever the topic may be—and answers several questions posed by the teacher. Questions about animals, which each page must contain, might include:

- What are the specific needs of food, water, and temperature that determine this animal's habitat?
- What behaviors and body structures help this animal survive in its habitat?

After the pages have been put together, they are available for all members of the class. When the teacher has provided guidance about available resources for this information and has encouraged the children to use drawing and other means to create interesting pages, the scrapbook will be read and enjoyed by many members of the class.

# Science and Mathematics

Mathematics is too often taught as algorithms to be learned and problems for which there is only one right answer that can be arrived at by only one correct method. Doing mathematics is identified with searching for the unique solution to a problem that is stated in a uniquely acceptable way. Because mathematics is usually first taught in mathematics class and then applied in science class, it is natural to assume that a problem in science must first be mathematically formulated and then solved by some means of automatic processing.

## Mathematics as a Tool

To integrate mathematics and science in the elementary-school classroom, a different approach is needed—an approach that teaches and uses mathematics within the context of classroom experiences in science. Mathematics may then be considered a useful and necessary means of representing observations that have been made and working out problems that have presented themselves.

Science workbooks in which pupils record their observations, experiences, experiments, and conclusions should also contain notations of the mathematics associated with the work done in science, including measurements, graphs, and the calculations necessary to understand the observations made.

## Mathematics as a Science

The relation of mathematics to science usually focuses on the use of mathematics as a way of representing and analyzing data collected during science activities. But these practical uses and representations of the physical world aren't all there is to mathematics. Mathematics is a science as well as a tool. From the constructivist point of view, an understanding of mathematics depends not only on experiences in the real world but also, and importantly, on logical thinking.

In the primary-school grades, mathematics and science merge in many ways. Children learn to identify shapes, come to understand one-to-one correspondence, begin to recognize patterns in numbers and in objects, start to classify numbers, and come to understand concepts of area and volume. Learning activities associated with these processes and concepts are truly integrated, as mathematics and science are one at this level. Science and mathematics also merge in some more advanced but basic concepts in physical science. For example, by the fifth and sixth grades, children are beginning to understand proportional reasoning, a mathematics concept related to displacement volume and density.

# SCIENCE AND SOCIAL STUDIES

Both science and social studies are complex subjects comprising many areas of knowledge. Science includes biology, chemistry, physics, geology, meteorology, and other branches, each of which has its own history, methods, and traditions. Social studies include geography, history, civics, economics, and other subjects, each of which also has its own history, methods, and traditions.

## Application of Science Processes

By now you are familiar with the science processes of observing, collecting data, classifying, measuring, predicting, and inferring, among others. Many of these processes are as applicable in social studies as in science. Classifying, for example, is as useful to the historian and the geographer as to the biologist, the chemist, or the physicist. Classification is a thinking process that can and should be used in many contexts and with many kinds of objects, characteristics, and ideas.

There is another very practical reason for integrating science and social studies (and teachers have to be practical). Because the elementary-school curriculum is now focused so heavily on skills development, very little time may be allotted to either science or social studies. To fit these important subjects into the curriculum, many teachers schedule their class time so that science and social studies are taught at the same time on different days. For example, social studies might be taught at 1:30 on Mondays, Wednesdays, and Fridays and science taught at 1:30 on Tuesdays and Thursdays. The advantages of building an integrated unit are readily apparent if you have that kind of schedule. Instead of teaching social studies two or three days each week and science the other days, one integrated unit is taught every day.

## Curriculum Topics

The most obvious connections between social studies and science are history and geography. Some ideas for units that integrate these subjects will be given later in this chapter. A less obvious connection is between science and civics, or government, which is one of the branches of knowledge that comprise social studies. Civics is integrated into science teaching in an unconscious way by teachers who establish and manage classrooms where active learning can take place, as explained in Chapter 10. The need for rules of conduct and mutual respect among people who live and work together is the beginning of understanding of what it means to live in a democratic society.

When you establish and enforce fair and uncomplicated rules for behavior in science class you are giving children a practical lesson in two basic premises of democracy: protection of the rights of individuals and promotion of the common good. If you intend to use pupils' experience in science as part of a lesson in civics, you should make these ideas as explicit as possible with examples and discussion. Without spending too much time on talking about rules, you need to be sure that children understand why rules are necessary when people are living and working with other people. When you help children learn to work together in harmony, to respect each other, and to respect rules that are fair and fairly enforced, you're giving them a lesson in democratic living that transcends curriculum content in science or any other subject.

## SCIENCE AND THE EXPRESSIVE ARTS

There are many examples of trivial exercises planned in an effort to extend science lessons into other areas. In art, for example, teachers have been known to hand out marked sheets of paper that are to be cut out and pasted together in some way to represent a small animal or plant. Other teachers give first-grade children outlines of dinosaurs or farm animals to be colored in. It only takes a moment to reflect that these activities do not meet the criteria provided at the beginning of this chapter and thus are appropriate for neither art nor science.

*Young children express their ideas and feelings through drawing and painting.*

There is no need to resort to such devices when there are so many ways that children can express their feelings. Recall the little girl mentioned in Chapter 6, who said that she liked to follow and observe an animal, like a worm. It's easy to imagine that she would want to express her feelings about the worm she had followed in writing, drawing, or dancing.

## Visual Arts

All styles of drawing and painting can be integrated with science lessons. Children can often represent more of what they know in a drawing than in writing (Howe & Vasu, 1989) and should be encouraged to include in their notebooks drawings of the animals, plants, and other things that they've studied. They can also be encouraged to express their feelings about other subjects that they're studying.

Structural patterns found in nature have inspired artists through the centuries and can stimulate your pupils to respond in their own creative ways. For example, a science unit on insects can be extended to explore spider webs, honeycombs, or wasp nests as stimuli for drawing, painting, or ceramics. For older pupils, optics is a topic that can be the basis for an integrated unit on light, color, and design.

## Music

A unit on sound is often included in the elementary science curriculum. The unit begins with the physical properties of sound and ends with making simple musical instruments and investigating the relationship between physical characteristics of the instruments and characteristics of the sound produced. Learning to recognize patterns in sound reinforces the process of pattern recognition by using it in another context.

## Creative Movement

Children can use their bodies to represent the movements of animals, moving sideways like a crab, hopping like a kangaroo or rabbit, and walking like a bird, among many others. These activities are often treated as trivial, or more suitable for young children on the playground than in the classroom. Indeed, the playground may be the appropriate site; however, these activities are not trivial. They are ways of taking another point of view and increasing children's understanding and appreciation of the other creatures with whom they share the earth.

The lessons on the mealworm in Chapter 5 offer examples of including drawing and dance (moving like a mealworm) in a science lesson. These clearly meet the three art objectives of using

- visual structures and functions of art to communicate ideas;
- locomotion movements (e.g., walk, hop, leap, gallop, slide, skip) in different directions (e.g., forward, backward, sideward, diagonally, turning); and
- kinesthetic awareness, concentration, and focus in performing. (Mid-continent Research for Education and Learning, 2000)

The integration of subjects in the mealworm lessons wasn't a deliberate attempt to do so but seemed natural because drawing and movement appeared to be the best way for pupils to understand the content and processes that were the lesson objectives. Drama can also be used effectively by children playing out roles and interactions—observed or from reading—of animals in their natural habitats and social groups. An example cited earlier was of children playing out predator–prey relationships. A child shouldn't think of the day in elementary school as a period for this and a period for that but as a day filled with a variety of interesting and challenging things to do.

## Writing Poetry and Stories

Children should be given opportunities to write about their experiences in whatever ways they want to. Many scientists have written poetically and expressively about the beauty of nature and of science and their feelings about it. Some children have an immediacy and perceptiveness of expression that adults have lost and should be encouraged to use this talent in science as in other areas.

# A SCIENCE-BASED LANGUAGE ARTS LESSON

The following example lesson is a simple activity that illustrates how a science experience can form the basis for a writing and reading lesson or series of such lessons. Almost any of the common topics of the kindergarten and first-grade curriculum—animals, parts of the body, the five senses, the seasons, shadows, magnets, floating and sinking, and balancing—can be used as the basis for an approach to teaching language arts.

LESSON PLAN 11.1

## CLASSIFYING LEAVES

### NSE STANDARD

Objects can be described by properties, and those properties can be used to separate or sort a group of objects (NRC, 1996, p. 127).

### GRADE LEVELS: K–1

### OBJECTIVES

By the end of these activities, the pupils should be able to

1. observe and classify leaves, and
2. represent their own experiences in writing and read what they have written or dictated.

### ACTIVITIES

When the leaves have begun to turn in the fall, the teacher brings a few leaves to class, shows them to the pupils. The teacher then asks questions to allow the children to tell what they know about leaves—for example, that some trees have leaves that change color in the fall and that other trees stay green all year.

An alternative is to do this lesson late in the spring after leaves have appeared on local trees. In that case, the questions are about leaves coming out in the spring. (If you are in an area where there are few trees, you may have to use some other local natural material.)

After a brief discussion, the children go for a nature walk on the school grounds or nearby where leaves can be found. All the children should collect a few leaves to bring back. In the classroom, the children examine the leaves for color, shape, and size—perhaps with small hand lenses. Then they sort the leaves by color, shape, or other characteristics. Next the teacher draws from the children a story about the walk (including the kinds of leaves they found) and writes that story on the board or on large paper. Alternatively, the teacher could have the children write their stories. Finally, children are asked to read from the board or from their papers. This lesson could be the beginning of a unit on trees or on changes in seasons in which a series of related experiences forms the basis for a class book on the chosen topic.

## INTEGRATED UNIT ON INSECTS AND BUGS

This unit can be planned as group investigations to be carried out in the same general way as the group investigations of trees in Chapter 6. The teacher and the children choose a topic, the children develop questions, the teacher helps them organize their thoughts and ideas, and they then carry out group investigations and record and present their results. Assessment and feedback follow as in the unit on trees.

Drawing or painting, writing poems and stories, and counting and estimating in math are integrated throughout this unit. Studying the habits and ways of social insects could also be incorporated into the unit and lead into a social studies emphasis. One class of younger pupils who studied caterpillars and butterflies made up a dance that represented butterflies flying over a field.

INVESTIGATION 11.1

## INSECTS AND BUGS

### NSE STANDARD

Life Science. Diversity and adaptation of organisms (NRC, 1996, p. 158).

## GRADE LEVELS: 3–6

## OBJECTIVES

Science objectives for this investigation are generally the same as those listed for the group investigations of trees.

## MATERIALS

Jars with lids or plastic insect boxes
Butterfly nets
Cages
Magnifiers

## MOTIVATION

A child brings an insect to class or the teacher can bring some kind of interesting insect. The insect should be placed in a cage or terrarium for safekeeping and easy viewing. A better approach is to plan a field trip for the children to collect a variety of insects and other creatures that they will bring back to the classroom to study.

## PLANNING

Planning for a field trip should include instructions in safety, discussion of some things to observe about insects in the field, discussion of how to capture the creatures that will be brought back, and development of questions pupils want to ask about the creatures when they return to the classroom.

## GROUP ACTIVITIES

In this investigation, each group will first focus on the insect(s) or other creature(s) they find and observe in the field and then focus on those collected and brought back. Different groups may be asking the same questions, but they will have different answers because their insects will be different.

Children may need some suggestions at first for places to look for insects, slugs, spiders, and other interesting invertebrates. This depends to some extent on the time of year. As long as the weather is warm, insects can always be found in grass or weeds, and interesting creatures live under stones and logs. In the fall, insects can be found in fallen and rotting fruit, spiders can be found in webs in corners around buildings, and galls appear on trees after leaves have fallen. In the spring, pupae can be uncovered in the soil under trees, and caterpillars can be found on leaves, later, butterflies can be found around flowers, and moths can be found resting on trees.

On the field trip, each pupil will take a small notebook so that observations can be recorded, including:

*Size and appearance.* What color is it? How big is it? What special features does it have?

*Habitat.* Where was it found? Was that place dry or wet? Light or dark? How many were in one place?

*Behavior.* What was it doing? How does it move? Did it react if you touched it?

The easiest way to observe insects and other small creatures at close range is to keep them indoors in jars or petri dishes for a day or less. Most species will tolerate short periods away from food and normal surroundings. Short-term captives can be observed for general behavior, such as locomotion and grooming. With the help of a magnifying glass, structural features can be observed. Each child will draw his or her special creature, which may be an insect, a snail, or an insectlike creature. If the diet is known and can be provided, feeding behavior can be observed.

If the proper conditions are maintained, the captured creatures can be kept for longer periods in the classroom, allowing children to observe changes and carry out experiments. Some events to watch for are egg laying and hatching, eating, molting, mating, and life-cycle stages. Pupils can determine the foods preferred, effects of changes in light or temperature, and reactions to various stimuli.

Children's drawings are displayed and discussed:

Does anyone know the name of this creature? How can we find out?

Tell us what you have learned about it by watching and listening.

Show us how your little animal moves.

An important part of this project is the children's use of reference books to identify their creatures and to check their own drawings and information against what they find in books. Children who become particularly interested may want to learn how to catch and keep insects at home (Keidel, 1994).

### CLOSURE AND ASSESSMENT

Pupils should have an opportunity to display drawings, observations, and results of experiments. A special time for parents to visit might be arranged.

## Extension

Writers and artists—as well as naturalists and scientists—have found insects, spiders, and other bugs to be endlessly fascinating. One of the favorite children's books of all time is E. B. White's (1952/1980) *Charlotte's Web,* a story about Charlotte (a spider) and a friendly pig. Some teachers do not use books in which animals have human characteristics in conjunction with science lessons. Others believe that children understand that animals do not actually talk or behave like humans and are able to move easily from reality to fantasy. This choice is a matter of individual judgment and cannot be decided objectively.

## AN INTEGRATED UNIT ON WEATHER

The following example is an outline of plan for a unit on weather. Now that you have studied examples of many lesson plans, the details of the lessons in this unit are left for you to work out. As you study the outline, note the ways in which other subject areas are incorporated into this unit. As presented, the unit is intended for Grade 3 or 4, but weather can be, and is, studied at all levels up to and including high school. Studying one subject at all grade levels is an example of Bruner's (1966) idea of the Spiral Curriculum, explained in Chapter 2. Bruner believed that there is an appropriate version of any skill or knowledge that may be imparted at whatever age one wishes to begin. Moreover, he believed that an important topic could be returned to later as children were able to understand more and more difficult and abstract concepts. Thus observations of changes in weather can be the topic for a class project at a wide range of grade levels. Younger children can make simple observations and keep very simple records, using symbols that are easily understood. Older children can make their own measuring instruments for a weather station, with groups taking responsibility for different aspects of recording and reporting weather changes. You may make this a major project or keep it simple, at any grade level, using it in addition to other science activities going on every day in class.

As you study this example, note that the unit—which is usually taught as a science unit—(a) incorporates writing as the children fill in the chart and use symbols to represent data; (b) uses mathematics in calculating averages and making graphs; (c) meets goals of social studies as children learn how climate affects all aspects of people's lives; (d) includes writing and drawing; and (e) relies on reading throughout the unit as children use books to identify clouds, read newspapers to check their own data, and read about the effects of climate in other parts of the world.

## INVESTIGATION 11.2

## WEATHER PATTERNS AND RELATIONSHIPS

The basic idea is to keep a daily record of the weather over a period of four to six weeks and to use the weather data to look for patterns and relationships, to consider the effect of weather on people's lives, and to express feelings about weather.

### GRADE LEVELS: 2–4

NSE Standard: Weather can be described by measurable quantities such as temperature, wind direction and speed and precipitation (NRC p. 134).

### OBJECTIVES

1. Measure temperature and rainfall, identify clouds, and estimate wind speed.
2. Record data on charts and graphs.
3. Use graphs and charts to analyze data, look for patterns, and discuss day-to-day changes in the weather.

4. Consider how climate affects the way people dress, the work they do, the kinds of houses they live in, and the food they grow and eat.
5. Express feelings about weather in poetry, song, painting, or other art form.

Begin the project with an open discussion in which you ask questions to find out what the children already know about various aspects of weather. Tell them that the class will start keeping a watcher chart and ask what information will be on the chart. Depending on the pupils' ages and abilities, either make a large chart yourself or ask for volunteers to make one under your guidance.

Place the chart on the wall and ask all the pupils to sign up for the days they will collect weather data. Two pupils will collect data at the same time each day and enter the data on the chart. For a simple weather chart, the data that might be gathered are temperature, sunshine, rainfall in 24 hours, type of clouds, and windspeed.

For collecting temperature data, a centigrade thermometer should be located in an area protected from direct sun and at a height comfortable for all the pupils to read. The amount of sunshine can be indicated simply by "sunny, light clouds, heavy clouds, rain, snow," and so on. Rainfall can be measured by placing a Mason jar or a similar container in a protected place but open to the sky and measuring with a metric ruler. You need not worry that this is not a really accurate measure; if children are interested, they will start checking their measurements with those published daily in the newspaper.

Clouds can be identified by reference to a book, or you can have a direct instruction lesson on cloud forms. Here again, accuracy is not a major concern; let the children decide among themselves what to record. Windspeed can be indicated simply as 0 (no wind), 1 (moderate) 2 (strong) and left up to the children to determine. If the children want more detail, a weather vane or wind sock can be used for wind direction and a scale can be devised for speed, but that isn't necessary for this simple activity. Figure 11.1 is an example of a weather chart made by one third-grade class.

Remind children, as necessary, when it is their turn to collect data and be sure that the data are being obtained and recorded. Some children will not need to be reminded but others will.

After several weeks, the class will have enough data to start working with it. The children can calculate average temperature, average rainfall, and days of sunshine and use the averages to construct graphs. The children may compare their data to that published in the local newspaper. Figures 11.2 and 11.3 are examples of graphs that pupils produced, using 1-cm graph paper.

Use the chart and graphs as the basis for a discussion of changes in weather and relationships between clouds and rainfall, between temperature and rainfall, and between length of day and temperature.

If the pupils have access to the Internet, you can expand this unit to include the use of weather information from around the world. Local, national, and international weather reports and satellite maps are available with almost constant updates.

| Weather | Day | | | | | | | | | | |
|---|---|---|---|---|---|---|---|---|---|---|---|
| | M | T | W | Th | F | – | M | T | W | Th | F |
| | 1 | 2 | 3 | 4 | 5 | | 8 | 9 | 10 | 11 | 12 |
| Temperature °C | 19 | 17 | 14 | 15 | 18 | | 20 | 22 | 18 | 17 | 15 |
| Rainfall (ml) | 200 | 120 | 10 | 0 | 0 | | 50 | 100 | 10 | 0 | 0 |
| Wind | 2 | 1 | 0 | 0 | 0 | | 1 | 2 | 1 | 1 | 0 |
| Sunny/rainy | ¦¦¦ | ¦¦¦ | ⊠ | ☼ | ☼ | | ¦¦¦ | ¦¦¦ | ⊠ | ∂ | ☼ |
| Clouds | st | st | ci | cu | cu | | st | st | st | st/ci | cu |

Key:   Clouds
    cu  cumulas
    st  stratus
    ci  cirrus

Wind
  0  calm
  1  mild
  2  strong

Sun/Rain
  ☼  sunny
  ∂  overcast
  ⊠  cloudy
  ¦¦¦  rainy

FIGURE 11.1   A Weather Chart Made by a Fourth-Grade Class

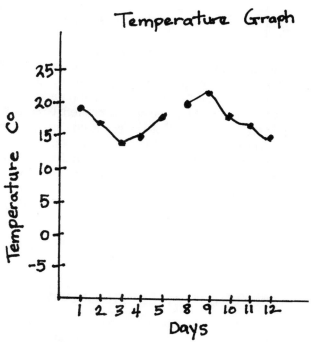

FIGURE 11.2   A Pupil-Produced Temperature Graph

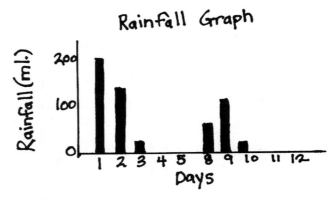

**FIGURE 11.3    A Pupil-Produced Rainfall Graph**

After discussion of the data, begin a follow-up investigation with this question:

How does weather (climate) affect the way people live? Ask the pupils to think about kinds of clothes, work, houses, food grown and eaten, and recreation as they answer the question.

At some point during the investigation, give the children an opportunity to express their feelings in writing, drawing, or painting about some aspect of weather—changing seasons, snow falling, a rainy morning, a sunny day, or clouds racing by.

This unit can continue in any of several directions. Books, films, and the Internet can be used to find out how animals and people protect themselves in the extreme climates of the Arctic, the Sahara, and the Amazon rain forest. Field trips to a local park will add interest and knowledge, particularly if you can arrange several trips to the same spot at different times of the year. The emphasis for fifth and sixth graders can be on technology as pupils make weather instruments that can become a weather station. Children in the upper elementary grades who have had a weather unit at a lower grade can focus on rainbows, sleet and snow, violent weather such as hurricanes and tornadoes, or other special topics related to weather.

## AN INTEGRATED UNIT ON TECHNOLOGY

Children have used tools and instruments to collect data in most of the investigations you have studied so far. The investigation described below is different only in that the emphasis is on technology rather than on the science objectives. For this unit the objective is taken from *Benchmarks for Science Literacy* (AAAS, 1993) which prefaces the objective with this statement: "Students can become interested in comparing present technology with that of earlier times, as well as the technology in their everyday lives with that of other places in the world" (p. 54). Simple machines are often included in the elementary science curriculum, usually at fifth or sixth grade, with content and process objectives in technology as well as science. This topic lends itself to integration with social studies by planning from the outset to meet the history objective of knowing about the achievements of people and cultures of the ancient world, an objective that is commonly included in elementary social studies curriculum. The investigation is outlined below with the expectation that you can now write lesson plans that include all the parts listed in Chapter 5.

INVESTIGATION 11.3

## Simple Machines in the Ancient World

### Grade level: 5–6

Standard: Know that technology has been part of life on earth since the advent of the human species. [T]echnology is an intrinsic part of human culture and it both shapes society and is shaped by it. (Benchmarks, AAAS, 1993, p. 54)

The unit may start with either technology or social studies and may plan it as a group investigation, as described in Chapter 6, or guided inquiry, as described in Chapter 5.

If you start with machines you will use the six that are considered basic, simple machines. These are the lever, the wedge, the screw, the pulley, the inclined plane and the wheel-and-axle. It is essential to have a good supply of these in sizes that fifth graders can use. Strong hooks should be screwed into the ceiling so that pulleys can be attached and used for hands-on activities, including measuring and comparing the force needed to lift loads by various combinations of pulleys.

Books on machines by St. Andre and Macaulay and books by Macaulay on pyramids and cathedrals are listed in References at the end of this chapter. You may be able to obtain free or inexpensive building materials from lumber yards and locally-owned hardware stores.

Levers of several kinds should be available, as well as bricks or rocks to lift. Children will first learn about these machines by using them to lift real weights and by measuring forces and masses. After pupils have had enough experience to achieve some understanding of how the machines work each group may choose one kind of machine to observe and explore. Building models and demonstrating the uses of each kind of machine lead to learning experiences of more variety and depth than might be accomplished through other teaching methods.

If social studies is the starting point the focus can be on the ancient Egyptians who built the Pyramids, the Greeks who built the temples of Athens, the Britons who built Stonehenge, or the medieval architects and artisans who built the cathedrals of Europe. There are many other possibilities, including temples built by the Aztecs, the Incas and peoples of the Far East. Constructing a model of a pyramid or temple, combined with reading about the construction, can lead to the question of how such imposing structures were erected before the invention of the steam engine or the discovery of electricity, when the only power available was supplied by humans or animals and the only machines were versions of the simple machines that your pupils are now familiar with.

This unit provides many opportunities for children to use and improve their skill in using metric units for measuring. In addition to measuring forces and masses they must make careful measurements of the sides of the bases of the model of a pyramid or temple or whatever structure they build.

Drawing and drama could also be integrated into the unit. There are so many available resources and so many interesting possibilities for this unit that some restraint will have to be exercised to keep it within a reasonable time frame.

## ■ SUMMARY

Science may be integrated with other subjects in a variety of ways to increase understanding, make better use of time, and make schoolwork more meaningful for children. Subjects may be integrated by topic, by concept, or by using a skill from one subject in learning activities from another area. In all cases, it is important to identify objectives for both subjects and to plan the lesson or unit so that both sets of objectives are met.

Science processes can be thought of in a broader sense as thinking processes and thus are applicable to all subject areas. The integration of science and language arts may include using writing as a way to represent science experiences and using science as the basis for reading and writing. Although firsthand experiences are the primary way for children to learn science, many experiences are available only vicariously through reading. These experiences can be memorable and valuable and should be a part of the science program in elementary school. Books of information are also required for a well-rounded science program. Social studies and science share concepts and processes and provide many opportunities for integrated units and projects.

Mathematics is an indispensable tool for representing and understanding science. Both geometry and arithmetic are so interwoven with science at the elementary-school level that it is hard to separate them in a good science program. Although this chapter focused on the uses of mathematics in collecting and analyzing data, mathematics is also concerned both with applications to real-world problems and with ideas based solely on logical reasoning.

This chapter contained many ideas or suggestions for lessons or units that were not fleshed out into lesson plans with objectives, lists of materials, activities, and evaluations. You are encouraged to refer back to them when you're searching for ideas that you can develop and use in your own teaching. Your success as a science teacher will depend, in part, on how creative you are in taking a simple idea and developing it into a focused, activity-centered, goal-oriented unit of study.

## ■ ACTIVITIES FOR THE READER

1. Select a topic, concept or skill and outline an integrated unit for a subject area of your choice.
2. Outline a lesson for first grade that integrates reading and science. Give objectives for both subjects.
3. Make an annotated list of 24 science trade books. Select 4 for each grade level from the first through the sixth grades, giving the correct citations for each. Write a short paragraph describing each book.(Exchange lists with your classmates to form a valuable resource for the future.)

## ■ QUESTIONS FOR DISCUSSION

1. Many teachers hand out prepared sheets with blanks to be filled in rather than have pupils keep science workbooks. Their reasons are that pupils cannot write well enough, it takes too much time, pupils lose the workbooks, and workbooks take too much time to grade. What arguments can you give to justify the use of workbooks?

2. Explain and discuss the meaning of this statement: "Reading should supplement experience, not take the place of it." Do you agree?

3. Should children experience the school day as a continuum or as separate periods for each subject? Explain your answer.

4. What is your understanding of Bruner's famous statement that there is an appropriate version of any skill or knowledge that may be imparted at whatever age one wishes to begin?

5. Discuss the pros and cons of self-contained classrooms as opposed to having content specialists in elementary schools.

## ■ REFERENCES

American Association for the Advancement of Science. (1993). *Benchmarks for science literacy.* New York: Oxford University Press.

Bruner, J. (1966). *Toward a theory of instruction.* Cambridge, MA: Harvard University Press.

Howe, A., & Vasu, E. (1989). The role of language in children's formation and retention of mental images. *Journal of Research in Science Teaching, 26*(1), 15–24.

Jacobs, H. H. (Ed.). (1989). *Interdisciplinary curriculum: Design and implementation*. Washington, DC: Association for Supervision and Curriculum Development.

Keidel, S. (1994). Pet bugs. A kid's guide to catching and keeping touchable insects. New York: Wiley.

Macaulay, D. (1981a). *Cathedral*. Boston: Houghton Mifflin.

Macaulay, D. (1981b). *Pyramids*. Boston: Houghton Mifflin.

Macaulay, D. (1988). *The way things work*. Boston: Houghton Mifflin.

McGee, L. M., & Lomax, R. G. (1990). On combining apples and oranges. A response to Stahl and Miller. *Review of Educational Research, 60*, 133–140.

National Research Council. (1996). *National science education standards*. Washington, DC: National Academy Press.

Mid-continent Research for Education and Learning [McREL] (2000). K–12 Standards. www.mcrel.org/compendium/Benchmark.

St. Andre, R. (1995). *Simple machines and how they work*. White Plains, NY: Cuisenaire.

Schickedanz, J. A. (1990). Critique of Stahl and Miller's study. *Review of Educational Research, 60*, 127–131.

Stahl, S., & Miller, P. (1989). Whole language and language experience approaches for beginning reading. *Review of Educational Research, 59*, 87–116.

White, E. (1980). *Charlotte's Web*. New York: HarperCollins. (Original work published in 1952).

# Taking Science beyond the Classroom

■ Mr. Newman was usually smiling and cheerful when he arrived at school, but one morning Ms. Oldhand noticed that he seemed concerned about something.

MS. OLDHAND:    You seem to have something on your mind this morning. Is there anything I might help you with?

MR. NEWMAN:    Well, I do have something on my mind, but there's nothing anyone can do. You know that I live in an off-campus student apartment—not exactly the Hollywood Hilton. We had a large tree on the lot that shaded the building and was a home to birds and squirrels. Some of the pupils in this class got data on the tree for a group investigation. I really loved that tree, but when I got home yesterday I found that the tree had been cut down to make room for more cars in the parking lot. That made me really sad.

MS. OLDHAND:    That seems like a shame. Did you talk to the owner of the building?

MR. NEWMAN:    Yes, I did. He said that people who live in the building had gotten parking tickets for leaving their cars on the street overnight and that he had to provide more off-street parking. The only way to get more parking space was to get rid of the tree.

MS. OLDHAND:    That's a good example of why science teaching is no longer confined to the classroom. When I first started teaching in the 1970s we were excited about the new science curricula that focused on concepts and processes with many interesting classroom activities. Now we know that's not enough; we must help children see the connections between what they learn in science and what's happening all around them. I'm sure the children will be very sad to learn that the tree has been cut down.

The title of this chapter intentionally has a double meaning. One meaning of taking science beyond the classroom is literal; it means using the schoolyard, taking children on field trips, and visiting museums. Its other meaning is less literal; it means relating science in the classroom to the world outside its four walls; it means bringing larger societal issues down to the local level and studying problems that are of concern and interest to children.

One of the primary goals of American education is to prepare students to become responsible citizens of a democratic society. Science education plays an important role in meeting this goal because responsible citizenship in today's world requires knowledge and understanding of issues related to science and technology. A broad, general purpose of science education is to provide experience in gathering data, analyzing it, and understanding its meaning so that students will be prepared

address issues of public and personal concern when they have the background
maturity to do so.

This idea was expressed in *Science for All Americans* (AAAS, 1989) as follows:

> For its part, science education—meaning education in science, mathematics and technology—should help students to develop the understandings and habits of mind they need to become compassionate human beings able to think for themselves and to face life head on. It should equip them to participate thoughtfully with fellow citizens in building a society that is open, decent, and vital. (p. 12)

## EXPLORING YOUR SURROUNDINGS

In previous chapters you have considered examples of lessons or units that took children outdoors. The emphasis, however, was not on learning about the environment but on teaching methods or integration of science with other subjects. Examples are the group investigations of trees in Chapter 6 and the investigation of bugs in Chapter 11. This chapter focuses, instead, on exploring the world just outside your window.

The investigations in this chapter follow the recommendation of a panel of experts who wrote:

> Start with questions about nature. Sound teaching usually begins with questions and phenomena that are interesting and familiar to students, not with abstractions and or phenomena outside their range of perception, understanding or knowledge. Students need to get acquainted with the things around them—including devices, organisms, materials, shapes and numbers—and to observe them, collect them, handle them, describe them, become puzzled by them, ask questions about them, argue about them, and then try to find answers to their questions. (AAAS, 1989, p. 147)

Science education for children once consisted almost entirely of nature study. Nature study was intended to develop children's appreciation for the natural world and to increase their knowledge of it. Few schools had organized programs but many teachers included studies of native plants and animals in their curricula. Children learned about birds, wild flowers, trees, and other parts of the local environment. About 50 years ago, as science shaped people's lives more and more, educators realized the need for organized, systematic instruction in all areas of science for children and older students alike. The result was the development of curriculum materials based on science concepts and processes in physics, chemistry, earth science, and biology. Today, many excellent curriculum materials are widely available, as indicated in the Appendix of this textbook.

As these materials were being developed, nature study became passé and was dropped from the curriculum. Now educators realize that children can use science processes in a broader context and can study nature—that is, the natural environment—with the same mental tools that they use to study electricity or magnets. For children in the primary grades, the goals of taking science beyond the classroom are (a) to develop an appreciation of the natural world, (b) to learn concepts related to the environment, and (c) to develop science process skills that are appropriate for their ages. Children in the intermediate grades can develop a fuller understanding of interrelationships of organisms that they find in the environment to the impact of human activities on the environment. Some of the investigations in this chapter suggest ways that you can help children make connections between what they learn in school and what they encounter in their lives outside school.

# PREPARING TO TAKE INSTRUCTION OUTDOORS

The units and lessons that you plan will depend on the part of the country you live in; whether your school is in an urban, suburban, or rural area; and, of course, the grade level you are teaching. There may also be school rules and regulations about taking children out of the classroom that you will have to deal with as creatively as you can. The lesson plans and suggestions in this chapter can be used in some locations and not in others. Let those that you cannot use stimulate your thinking about other possibilities in your own situation.

Before your pupils can explore an area or investigate a phenomenon, you will need to know the area yourself. Walk around and look for physical hazards such as uncovered drains or environmental hazards such as poison oak. If there is nothing but blacktop surrounding your school, try to find an interesting area close enough for children to walk to within a few minutes.

None of the lesson plans or unit plans that follow contain all the details necessary for successful implementation. You will have to make lesson plans that are appropriate for your pupils and your circumstances.

INVESTIGATION 12.1

## FINDING INTERESTING THINGS OUTDOORS

### GRADE LEVEL: K–1

Children who haven't yet learned to read and write learn best, like others, from their own experiencing of the world, but they need ways to sort out, clarify, and communicate their experiences and their ideas. A common activity in kindergarten and first grade is a nature walk on the school grounds or a natural area close to the school. The following are some ideas for turning nature walks into focused science activities for kindergartners and first graders.

#### 1. TREASURE HUNT

This activity can be an introduction to the school grounds or natural area that you and your pupils will visit many times during the year.

*Objectives*

1. To learn about the school grounds
2. To sharpen skill in observation
3. To describe observations to others

*Materials*

Prepare 3″ × 5″ cards with a color, shape, or texture on each card. Give one card to each child before you leave the classroom.

Tell the children that they are to look for something outdoors that looks or feels like what is on their card. As they walk out, they are to think about what they might find that will match the card. The object can be but doesn't have to be brought back to the classroom. If a child couldn't find a match, the child should ask for help.

The children search for objects in a designated area. After about 10 minutes, gather them together in a circle to tell what they have found. (Adapted from Roth, Cervoni, Wellnitz, & Arms, 1988, p. 46)

## 2. Getting to Know a Tree

Gather children around a tree as closely as possible and do the following:

Ask the children to feel the bark. Why does a tree need bark? Compare bark to their skin.
Ask them to close their eyes and smell the tree. What does it smell like?
Ask them to listen for sounds. What do they hear?
Ask them if there is a place that an animal could live in the tree. What kind of animal might it be? Why would an animal live in a tree?
Ask them if there are signs that animals might use the tree but not live in it. What kind(s) of animal?
Ask them if birds live in the tree. How can they tell?
Ask them if insects live in the tree. How can they tell? Can they find any?

Either outdoors or back in the classroom have the children sit in a circle and have each child tell the most important thing (only one per child or it will go on indefinitely) they learned.

You can close by reading a book (e.g., *The Great Kapok Tree* by Lynne Cherry), or the children can draw pictures of something they saw or found that you will display somewhere in the room.

## 3. Learning about Tiny Creatures

Chapter 11 has a unit plan for a study of insects and bugs for older children. This plan is a simpler version for kindergartners and first graders.

*Many interesting things can be found in the schoolgrounds.*

*Materials*

Hand lenses

Small white shallow boxes and/or box tops

A flat white box of the kind shirts or blouses are packed in. (The purpose of the box is to hold it under a shrub or bush to catch small insects or bugs.)

Take the children for a walk in an area you have previously visited and where you have seen evidence of insects.

Ask the children to look for insects or bugs on the ground, in a tree trunk, on weeds or shrubbery. After they have had time to explore the area, explain that they are to see whether there are insects or bugs in the shrubs or bushes that will fall out when the bush is shaken.

Several children shake the bush while you catch insects or bugs; then take them inside. Distribute hand lenses and distribute insects (or bugs) in the small white boxes to the children, one insect (or bug) in a box to each pair of children. Then ask these questions:

How many legs does their insect (or bug) have? (Explain that insects have six legs.) Is it a bug or an insect?
What else can they see? Eyes? Antennae? (Explain these words.)
Where do insects (or bugs) live? What animals eat insects (or bugs)? How do insects (or bugs) hide from bigger animals that will eat them?

The children then draw their insects (or bugs), and you post the drawings.

## 4. SHADOWS

Wait for a bright sunny day to take the children outdoors at midmorning or midafternoon to make and observe shadows.

*Materials*

Large box
Large cone
Other objects that can be used to make shadows

Gather the children in the classroom and ask whether they know what makes shadows. Give a simple explanation—that light comes from the sun but that it can't pass through objects, so the light doesn't shine on the other side, the side away from the sun. (Use you own words but keep it simple.)
First the children will look for shadows. Then ask:

What shape are the shadows?
What side of the tree or bush or object are they on?
Are they all on the same side? Why?

Stand children in a row so that their shadows fall evenly in front of them. Spend a moment for discussion.
Stand them one behind the other so that one shadow is formed in front of the first child. Spend a moment for discussion.
Stand them in a circle; have them notice that the shadow is in front of some children and behind others.
Hold up a box and ask what shape the shadow will be. Put it on the ground and observe the shadow; then turn it and have them observe what happens.
Use your imagination for other activities. Two children can make their shadows touch when the children aren't touching. You can take the children out another day at a different time or later the same day and observe the differences in shadow length and direction.
Follow-up activities in the classroom can be to make shadow puppets or shadows with hands to represent animals (using a bright light and a white surface).

## ANT POPULATIONS IN THE SCHOOLYARD

This investigation may be part of a unit on insects, in which case the emphasis will be on close observation of the ants and differences between them. Alternatively, the activity may be part of a unit on distribution of populations, in which case the emphasis will be on differences in the number and kind of ants found in various locations, results with different kinds of traps, investigation of an ant hill, and other related activities.

Before starting this activity, obtain permission from the principal or other administrator to take the children into the school yard to place and monitor ant traps.

### NSE STANDARD

Life science: Populations and ecosystems (NRC, 1996, p. 155).

### GRADE LEVEL: 5

### OBJECTIVES

1. Develop knowledge of a population of ants.
2. Use an appropriate method to collect biological specimens.
3. Construct a graph to present data.

### MATERIALS

Plastic container with lid for each pupil
Labels or permanent felt-tip pen for labeling
Squirt bottle for filling traps with liquid
Supersaturated salt solution
Wetting agent of the kind used in dishwashers
Trowel or bulb planter
Cloth or plastic for flags to mark traps
Meter stick or measuring tape
White paper or plastic plates
Toothpicks
Forceps
Magnifiers

### MOTIVATION/REVIEW

"Who has taken a really close look at an ant? What did you notice? Do you know where ants live when they aren't visiting your picnic?" Explain that ants are found all over the world and that you are going to take a close look at some of those that live around the school.

## DATA COLLECTION

Pupils work in pairs. The basic procedure is as follows. Small straight-sided plastic containers are filled with a salt solution and placed in the ground as ant traps. After 24 hours, the traps are collected, tops are placed on them, and they are brought back to the classroom. The containers should have straight sides; 35-mm film canisters and medicine bottles work well, but you may think of others. There must be a sufficient number of containers of uniform size, shape, and color for each pair of pupils to have one. Prepare a saturated salt solution by adding table salt to hot water until no more salt will go into solution. Strain the solution through cheesecloth or a disposable dishcloth to remove solid residue. Add 4 to 5 ml of wetting agent per liter of salt solution. (The wetting agent makes ants fall to the bottom of the solution rather than float on top and perhaps escape.)

Discuss with the pupils where the traps should be placed. You may place some in grassy areas and others in bare areas, or you may place them at varying distances from a walk or building. Traps in the same area (same site) should be placed about 2 m apart. Take the pupils into the school yard to determine where they will place traps, and place numbered flags to mark the spots. Have students make a map or diagram for each area (site) to show where the traps have been placed. (You may have to make a quick map for reference, depending on the age of the students, time, and other factors.)

Continue if there is time (otherwise, wait until the following day to continue), but do so on a day when no rain is expected for 24 hours. Now dig a hole with a trowel at each spot, set the dirt aside (away from the hole), and save it for replacement. Each pair of children puts a number, corresponding to the number on the flag, on their container and places it in the hole, with the cover on.

Traps are placed so that they are flush with the ground as shown in Figure 12.1. Pack dirt under and around the trap to hold it steady. When a trap has been

**FIGURE 12.1   An Ant Trap in Place**

set properly, the lid is removed and the squirt bottle is used to fill the trap one-third full of salt solution. There should be little or no disturbance or leftover dirt around the traps.

Traps are collected after 24 hours; the covers are replaced, and the containers are taken to the classroom.

The contents of each container are poured onto a paper plate or piece of heavy white paper. Toothpicks and forceps can be used to separate the ants.

## DATA PROCESSING

Pupils count the ants collected, and each pair record their data on a class chart such as the one shown in Figure 12.2. Engage the children in discussion of the data table later, after they have completed the table; they should record the data without interruption before the ants dry out.

Pupils now sort their ants into groups based on size and color. Small black ants go in one group, large red ones in another group, and others may be in a miscellaneous group unless there are several with similar characteristics. The numbers are recorded in their workbooks and used to make a graph similar to that shown in Figure 12.3.

## CLOSURE

Display the class data and pupils' graphs. The direction of the discussion will be determined by pupil interests and the goals of the unit. Pupils will have many sug-

### ANTS CAPTURED

| Trap Number | Number of Ants | Names of Students |
|---|---|---|
| 1 | | |
| 2 | | |
| 3 | | |
| 4 | | |
| 5 | | |
| 6 | | |
| 7 | | |
| 8 | | |
| 9 | | |
| 10 | | |
| 11 | | |
| 12 | | |
| 13 | | |
| 14 | | |

**FIGURE 12.2   Data Table for Ants Captured**

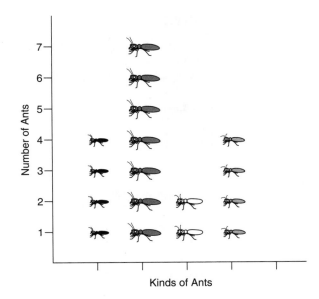

**FIGURE 12.3    Pictograph of
Ants Captured**

gestions for further investigations, and you may use your judgment as to where to
go with this. Finding other ways to observe and/or count ants, finding other ways
to trap ants, making closer observations, and drawing individual ants are all possible follow-up activities. Many books on ants are available at all reading ability
levels.

### ASSESSMENT

Observation of pupils in the school yard provides the basis for the assessment of
cooperative behavior. Workbooks and graphs can be assessed.

*(From* Investigating Ant Populations in the School Yard  *[pp. 4–8] by N. A. Anderson, 1996,
Raleigh, NC: SCI-LINK/GLOBE-NET, North Carolina State University. Copyright © 1996 by
North Carolina State University. Adapted by permission.)*

INVESTIGATION 12.3

# ACID RAIN

This unit integrates science, social studies, math, language arts, and art, but it
emphasizes the integration of science and social studies. The lessons are
described in general terms, leaving the details for you to work out.

## NSE Standard

Science in personal and social perspectives: Human activities can induce hazards through resource acquisition, urban growth, land-use decisions, and waste disposal (NRC, 1996, p. 168).

## Grade Levels: 5–6

### Objectives

Children will learn

1. meaning of the term *acid rain,*
2. how acid rain affects living organisms,
3. what causes acid rain,
4. how people contribute to acid rain,
5. possible future consequences of current behavior and policies.

### Materials

Acids (weak solution of hydrochloric acid, vinegar, or lemon juice)
Bases (ammonia, baking soda, or antacid tablets)
Indicator papers (pH paper and others)
Radish or bean seeds
Potting materials
Prepared inventory sheets
Reading materials
Overview of activities

## Lesson 1

Acids and bases, including vinegar, baking soda, antacid tablet, lemon juice, and other materials, are tested with pH paper and classified as to pH above or below neutral. (It isn't necessary for pupils to know the definition of pH—only that it is a way of testing whether something is an acid, a base, or neutral.) Explain to the children that they will be collecting rain samples to test for acid rain and begin preparations for testing on the next rainy day. (Be prepared to deal with the possibility that the rain in your area is not, in fact, acidic.)

## Lesson 2

Seedling response to acid rain is tested. This investigation is to be conducted as a controlled experiment. Children plant radish or bean seeds (two to a pot) and watered with water of varying acidity (pH from 3 to 6). Three weeks after the seeds were planted, pupils measure and record plant height, number of leaves, and leaf midrib length. (Other suitable activities are to find the effect of acidic water on leaves and on the tiny organisms found in pond water.) Their measurements should be carefully recorded and used to make simple bar graphs.

## Lesson 3

Introduce the idea of acid rain and some information about its effect on trees. Ask: What is the evidence that acid rain has caused trees to die? This question will lead the children to search for sources of information. Your next questions should seek to relate the results of acid rain to social concerns. How would it feel to live near a forest where the trees are dying? This could be an opportunity for creative writing or role playing.

## Lesson 4

Where does acid rain come from? Ask questions about sources of air pollution. Questions and discussion follow about the meaning and origin of fossil fuels, what happens when they burn, and how they provide usable energy. (Children of this age all know something about dinosaurs and other prehistoric animals.) Pupils are assigned to collect pictures of sources of air pollution from magazines, newspapers, and other publications to bring to class. You or a committee will make these into a collage and add pictures as more come in.

## Lesson 5

Sources of energy in the pupils' homes and in your city or town are addressed next. Begin by making a list on the board or overhead projector of machines and appliances that pupils used before coming to school that day. Then discuss where energy comes from. Does the electricity in your area come from water power, coal, or another source? Pupils take worksheets home and, with the help of parents, list all energy users in and around their homes and what they think the source of energy is. These lists form a basis for discussion the following day.

## Continuing Activity

Throughout these lessons, don't neglect preparations for and actual collection of rain samples. When samples have been collected, the pupils test them to determine whether they are acidic. For this activity, have pupils work in pairs or cooperative groups; each pair or group has samples of the water collected and access to the available acids, bases, and pH and other indicator paper. They enter the results of testing in their workbooks, and the class discusses the results.

## Lesson 6

Wrap up the unit by forming groups to discuss "What if" questions that you will assign: What if there weren't any more fossil fuels? Would that be good or bad? What if people continue to pollute the air as they are now doing? What if the United States makes laws prohibiting air pollution and other countries do not? What effects will that have on the environment and relations with other countries? What if people have to pay higher taxes and lose jobs in order to lower pollution? Each group writes out answers on big sheets of newsprint, and these answers are read and discussed by all.

*(Activities adapted from Hessler & Stubbs, 1987. Acid rain: Science projects. Raleigh NC: The Acid Rain Foundation.)*

INVESTIGATION 12.4

## RUNOFF OF WATER ON SCHOOL GROUNDS

When rain falls on earth that is covered with vegetation, the water soaks into the ground. It is then available to support the lives of the plants that live there, which, in turn, support many forms of animal life. When the earth is covered with pavement or buildings, the rain that falls cannot soak into the ground but runs off into gutters or along streets (or wherever there is a way for it to go) into storm drains or ditches, streams and rivers, and eventually the ocean. Runoff has been increasing ever since people began to build buildings and make roadways, but the pace of this process has increased rapidly in modern times because of the amount of earth being covered with highways, parking lots, and large buildings. Runoff of rainwater and melting snow is a problem in many localities. A sixth-grade class in one school selected this problem to investigate.

### QUESTIONS

What happens to the water from rain and snow that falls on the parking lot and roof of the school building?
How does runoff affect the environment?

### OBJECTIVE

Increase awareness of how the needs of modern life affect the natural environment.

### INVESTIGATION

The study began in the fall, soon after school opened. Immediately after the first substantial rainfall, the children noticed that water was rushing through a small stream close to the school grounds, and they saw that ditches and a culvert were leading water in that direction. Soon after, pupils who had cameras brought them to class, and the teacher took the entire class out to look at the stream and to take pictures from spots that could be identified later. (Standing against a certain tree or a signpost, for example.) A few children made sketches of the stream, the banks, and nearby trees. A few small rocks and samples of dirt were taken back to the classroom.

When the pictures had been developed, the teacher assigned pupils to cooperative groups and gave them the task of selecting a few photos—from among the large number of those available—that gave the best views of the banks of the stream. These photos were put aside for later use. Several science periods were spent identifying the earth materials (rocks and soil) that the pupils had brought back and learning something about their resistance to erosion.

Meanwhile, the math teacher had assigned the sixth graders the task of determining the area covered by the parking lot and the school building. Later in the year, they determined the total volume of water that had fallen on that area. That involved finding out what the rainfall was from the date they began until the investigation ended in May and multiplying the area by the rainfall, which is given as a height. (Snow is converted to the equivalent amount of rain in official statistics.)

This investigation was carried out in an area that has a heavy snowfall every year and therefore has a runoff of water from melted snow in the spring. When spring came and the snow had all melted, the teacher took the pupils, with their cameras, back to the place where they had taken pictures in the fall. They were careful to stand in the same spots and use the same angles they had used when they took the photos in the fall.

When they compared the two sets of photos, they found that the banks of the little stream had been eroded, a result that didn't surprise them because they had considered the nature of the soil that formed the banks and the total volume of water, much of which flowed into the stream.

The pupils made charts and graphs, mounted their before-and-after photos on a foam board, and made a presentation at Parents' Night and to an assembly. No immediate follow-up action was to be taken, but this investigation gave meaning to a topic in earth science (stream erosion) and increased the pupils' awareness of the fragility of the environment.

INVESTIGATION 12.5

## An Ecosystem at My Feet

### Grade Levels: 3–6

The purpose of this investigation is to develop an understanding of the concept of *ecosystem.* The project requires an open area that you and your pupils have access to. The ideal is for the area to be on the school grounds or close by. It is more interesting if the spot selected has some variety in the amount of sunshine received or in the moisture content of the soil, but any spot will do.

Each pair of pupils measures off a square meter of earth, labels it with their names, and investigates this area intensively. Their investigations should address questions such as:

What plants grow in your plot? How many varieties?
What insects or other small animals can you find?
What kind of soil is in your plot?
How many hours of sunshine does it get?

*What are they measuring?*

Suggest other things for them to look for, ways to measure, what to collect, and some general ideas. However, leave the details of deciding what to observe, collect, and measure to each pair of pupils to plan cooperatively.

In deciding how long to continue the observations and collection of data, you will have to be guided, as always, by the age and skill of your pupils and the time available.

Each pair of pupils will draw a map of their plot and use it at the end of the unit to characterize their plot. Observation and measurement data are recorded in workbooks on each visit to the plot by writing, drawing, making charts, and in whatever other ways the pupils choose.

After sufficient data have been collected, students will compare and contrast findings from their plots. They can make charts or graphs as appropriate and look for patterns and relationships, such as:

What is the relationship of amount of moisture and amount of sunshine to the
    number and variety of plants?
Their relationship to the number and variety of insects?
Their relationship to the presence of worms?

Introduce and explain the term *ecosystem*.

## CLOSURE

Place a large map of the area on a wall, showing the locations of predominant plants, insects, and other features identified. Use class discussion to broaden and reinforce the pupils' understanding of the tiny ecosystem that they have studied.

---

Investigation 12.6 describes an extension of Investigation 12.4 during the following year when the pupils used the information they had gathered to estimate the loss to the environment when part of the school grounds was torn up to make way for a road.

## INVESTIGATION 12.6

## WILDLIFE LOST TO ASPHALT

### BACKGROUND

Any open space covered with vegetation supports a variety of plant and animal life. When the area is paved over, the plants are destroyed and the animal life is destroyed or has to find a new home. The impetus for this investigation was the building of a new access road beside the school property to accommodate traffic into and out of the school grounds. In addition to the paved roadway, bulldozers cleared shoulders on each side of the roadway.

### QUESTION

How much wildlife was destroyed or displaced when a road was built alongside the school property?

### OBJECTIVE

Increased awareness of the trade-offs that are made as the population increases and urban areas reach farther into the countryside.

### INVESTIGATION

The year before this unit began, fourth-grade pupils had carried out an investigation of the plant and animal life in an open space behind the school that sloped down to a marshy area. This activity had given them an appreciation of the great number and variety of organisms that can share a small space.

When the pupils returned to school and saw that a road had been built alongside the school during the summer, they asked whether they could use some of their science and math time to estimate how many organisms had been destroyed or displaced and then present this information to parents and other students. The teachers agreed that this activity would be a good way to reinforce math skills and to increase awareness of the trade-offs that must be made between preserving the environment and meeting the need for safe, efficient transportation. The children planned the investigation and decided to carry out the work in cooperative groups.

First, they obtained a map of the school grounds. They divided the area covered by the roadway and the shoulders so that each group had approximately the same area to measure. One period was spent transferring the lines on the map to markers on the ground. When this task had been done, the groups set about to measure the assigned areas. They soon found that the measurements could not be exact; they decided to measure as best they could but recognized that the final figure would be only an estimate. This discovery increased their understanding of the use of estimation in solving real-world problems.

When all the areas had been measured, the results were added to give an estimate of the total area of the natural environment that had been destroyed. Using their previous year's results, they could now estimate how many plants, insects, worms, and other organisms had been destroyed or—in the case of some animals—forced to find another home.

The teacher did not ask them to decide whether the road should have been built, leaving that as an open question. You might decide to have a debate, with each side basing its arguments on data.

### INVESTIGATION 12.7

## A CREEK THAT RUNS NEAR THE SCHOOL

### BACKGROUND

Many streams that were once clear and full of fish have become polluted by runoff from farms, industrial wastes, and inadequately treated sewage that contains harmful bacteria and chemicals. This investigation helped pupils understand the nature and importance of a stream.

### QUESTIONS

What are the characteristics of the stream?
What changes occur over time?

### OBJECTIVES

Increase the children's knowledge and understanding of a stream and the area that surrounds and supports it; reinforce and improve skills in math, science, social studies, and language.

**TABLE 12.1   Environmental Survey**

| Myself | | | Parent | |
| Agree | Disagree | | Agree | Disagree |
|---|---|---|---|---|
| | | 1. The United States has enough natural resources to last forever. | | |
| | | 2. All pollution in our streams is caused mainly by business and industry. | | |
| | | 3. Everyone is affected when the environment deteriorates. | | |
| | | 4. Saving jobs is more important than saving a few rare birds. | | |
| | | 5. The increasing amount of garbage is an environmental problem. | | |

## INVESTIGATION

A team of sixth-grade teachers took advantage of a creek near their school to plan and carry out an interdisciplinary investigation that spanned the entire school year. The school is not in a rural area, as you might have supposed, but is in a large urban district. Some of the ideas for the investigation came from *City Science* (Perdue & Vaszily, 1991), a book of science activities that can be carried out in urban areas. Weekly walks to the creek, when the weather permitted, were part of the plan.

To arouse interest in the unit, the teachers took a survey to determine the views of pupils and their parents about environmental issues. The survey contained some 20 questions similar to those shown in Table 12.1, with spaces for pupils and their parents to indicate agreement or disagreement.

After pupils wrote their responses, they took the forms home and asked a parent to respond. The following day, a teacher put a transparency of the questionnaire on the overhead projector and asked for a show of hands of those who agreed and disagreed with each statement. She marked the numbers on the chart but didn't indicate right and wrong answers because the purpose was to get the children to think about the issues.

Plans for the first trip to the creek were discussed in several classes. In social studies, each pupil was given a copy of a map of the area through which the creek runs and a copy of a street map of the city. Before going to the creek, they plotted on a separate piece of paper the route that they would take to reach the creek. After walking to the creek, they worked in small groups to refine their maps and transfer them to grids. Historical sites, which had been discussed in class and pointed out on the walk to the creek, were marked on the maps. Later, the pupils learned to use topographical maps to relate or "match up" a map of the area to the actual features they could observe when they visited the creek.

On the first walk to the creek, the children observed the plants and animals living in the creek and surrounding area, took water samples, and measured the temperature of the air and the water. The pupils recorded their observations in their own logs, which they kept throughout the unit. These observations formed the baseline data for comparisons to be made later.

A park ranger accompanied the children on a geology walk along the creek. They observed rocks in and along the banks of the creek and selected samples of rocks to take back to the classroom. On this trip, as on all others, they collected water samples, determined the temperature of the water and air, and recorded their observations, both in writing and in sketches, in their logs. Back in the classroom, they identified the rocks they had collected, using an identification key and comparing them to samples provided by the teacher. They learned that rocks may affect the water that passes through or over them on the way to the creek and that the results may be beneficial or harmful to aquatic life. They found the pH of the water samples, using pH paper, measured the turbidity of the water, and recorded the water and air temperatures on a computer spreadsheet.

To investigate another aspect of water quality, the class collected samples of the insects and other invertebrates that lived in or on the water. The kinds of organisms found in a stream are bioindicators of water quality, providing information as to whether fish can live in it. The children collected fallen leaves from several kinds of trees and prepared mesh bags with an equal weight of leaves in each bag. They labeled the bags with waterproof labels, attached them to bricks or rocks, and suspended them in the water. The pupils monitored the bags each week and collected them after six weeks. They then put the mesh bags in plastic bags, carried them back to the classroom, and examined them by scooping the contents onto newspapers spread on tables. The children identified the organisms they had found by using a chart provided by the teacher. The chart identified organisms that could live under various water conditions. A preponderance of certain organisms indicates good water quality; a preponderance of others, including worms and leeches, indicate a high level of pollution.

By the end of the year, the sixth graders had a record of water and air temperature, pH, and turbidity, which showed the changes that take place as the seasons change. Table 12.2 shows average air temperature above the water and at its surface by month.

The data collected by the pupils were converted into graphs (see Figure 12.4) and charts to help them understand the changes. These graphs and charts could also be used in a presentation of results to others.

The pupils had indicators of water quality, both the pH data and the bioindicator data. They had learned to make and use maps. They had improved their writing skills in describing their observations and the results of their investigations. They had collected, analyzed, and interpreted data in geology, biology, and social studies. They were ready to present what they had learned to parents, other classes, and administrators.

**TABLE 12.2    Air and Water Surface Temperature at Indian Creek**

| Month | Max. Air Temp. °C | Avg. Surf. Temp. °C |
|---|---|---|
| September | 26.7 | 23.5 |
| October | 20.6 | 16.6 |
| November | 15.0 | 12.1 |
| December | 8.3 | 6.6 |
| January | 5.6 | 2.3 |
| February | 7.8 | 4.4 |
| March | 13.3 | 7.1 |
| April | 19.4 | 11.6 |
| May | 24.4 | 17.6 |
| June | 29.4 | 22.6 |

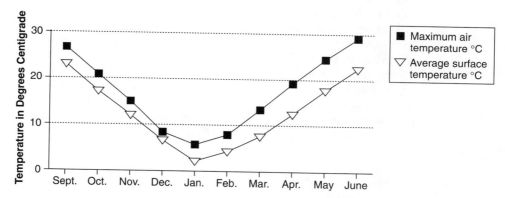

**FIGURE 12.4    Air and Water Surface Temperature Change, September to June**

# FIELD TRIPS

A field trip is a trip away from school, usually in a bus or van provided by the school system, to a site that has some particular relevance to the lesson or unit that the pupils are studying at school. A visit to an appropriate site can make classroom learning come alive and can be an experience that children remember all their lives.

Preparation for a field trip includes getting permission from the school administration, arranging for transportation, and getting written permission from the pupils' parents or guardians for them to go on the trip. You may have to secure permission to visit the site and set up a time for the trip. You will need to recruit several adults, usually parents, to help you keep the children together and to ensure that none of the children strays away from the group. If you will be away all day, you will have to make preparations for lunch.

Plan the time carefully so that you do not have more time at the site than you can use profitably. In most school districts, field trips are a lot of trouble to arrange, so you shouldn't go to all the trouble unless you believe that the trip will provide your pupils with a learning experience that will be worth the effort and could not be gained any other way.

Preparation in the classroom is even more important for the learning value of the trip than making the arrangements. A field trip may be the culmination of an investigation or unit, or it may come at the beginning of a unit or at any other time. Children should learn about the site, know what to expect, know what to look for, and know what they will be expected to do or report upon their return.

Preparation may begin with an announcement that the trip will take place, or it may be initiated by children who feel they need to visit a site to gather information for an investigation underway. A discussion of why you are going, what you may see or do, and how you will use the firsthand knowledge of the site may be the next step. Children may be assigned to get specific information about the site and report it or make it available to others in some way. Some teachers hand out a list of questions as a guide for making observations or collecting data. The goal is to prepare children so that they will know what to look for and what they are seeing when they are on the site.

Whether the field trip comes at the beginning, the end, or somewhere in the middle of a unit of study, it should be treated as a means of making observations and collecting data. The discussion that follows the trip will be similar to a discussion that you might lead during any investigation. The suggestions in Chapter 5 for leading an interesting discussion are applicable. By talking about an experience and listening to others talk about it, children come to understand its meaning.

## ■ SUMMARY

To take science beyond the classroom means to use the school yard, other areas close by, and field trips to provide experiences that will help pupils reach science content and process objectives. It means motivating them to *think* beyond the classroom and to relate what is learned in school to the larger world. It also means bringing larger societal issues down to the local level and letting children study problems that are of concern and interest to them.

The focus of this chapter is on practical ways to accomplish those goals. Kindergarten and first-grade children can pursue many science activities in the school yard or in a nearby natural area. The suggested activities include questions that will make young children think about what they have observed and learn to observe carefully and thoughtfully.

Investigations for older children follow the patterns established in previous chapters and leave it up to you to flesh out the details of lesson plans. Subjects investigated are ant populations in the schoolyard, the causes and effects of acid rain, the effect on the environment of increasing water runoff from paved areas, the ecology of a meter of earth, organisms and animals lost to roads, and the seasonal changes that occur in a nearby creek. Many of these investigations integrate science with other subject areas. Three of them have been carried out successfully by school children in several parts of the United States.

Guidelines are offered for field trips. Field trips are expensive, require a great deal of teacher preparation, and take time away from other classes and activities. For these reasons they should be planned carefully and used for maximum benefit.

# ■ ACTIVITIES FOR THE READER

1. Work in a group to develop an investigation for which data have to be gathered outdoors. The investigation should include data analysis and a plan for presentation of results.

2. Visit the grounds of an elementary school and look around for ideas of projects to use with younger (K–2) children. Develop a simple plan for carrying out such a project.

3. Determine the procedure in a local school for getting permission to have a field trip. Make a detailed plan for a field trip, including a time line for following procedures, what you will do to prepare students to get the most from the trip, and how you will follow up.

# ■ QUESTIONS FOR DISCUSSION

1. A grandfather reported that his grandson was afraid to go out in the rain because he had heard that acid rain was very dangerous. Do you think there is a danger that adult talk about environmental problems may frighten children? If so, what can you do about it?

2. Explain what this quotation means to you: "As science educators in Western societies, it is difficult to divorce ourselves from the right (scientific) answer syndrome, which tends to see learning as positivistic and/or empirical in nature" (Bloom, 1992, p. 412).

3. Behavioral objectives tend to be narrow and limiting. How can investigations remain focused and, at the same time, allow pupils the freedom to explore and develop habits of independent thought?

# ■ REFERENCES

American Association for the Advancement of Science. (1989). *Science for all Americans.* New York: Oxford University Press.

Bloom, J. (1992). The development of scientific knowledge in elementary school children: A context of meaning perspective. *Science Education, 76*(4), 399–413.

Cherry, L. (1995). *The great Kapok tree.* New York: Harcourt Brace.

National Research Council. (1996). *National science education standards.* Washington, DC: National Academy Press.

Perdue, P., & Vaszily, D. (1991). *City science.* Good Year Books.

Roth, C., Cervoni, C., Wellnitz, T., & Arms., E. (1988). *School ground science activities for elementary and middle schools.* Lincoln, MA: The Massachusetts Audubon Society.

# Learning Science with Computers

■   Mr. Newman, who had now graduated and had a class of his own, dropped by
to see Ms. Oldhand.

MR. NEWMAN:  I came by to get some ideas from you about how to use the
one computer that I have in my classroom.

MS. OLDHAND:  Oh, there are lots of ways to use one computer. Right now, for
example, those pupils over by the computer are getting out a
newsletter.

MR. NEWMAN:  That requires a printer, doesn't it? How did you manage that?

MS. OLDHAND:  I learned about a program of small grants to teachers and
applied for one of the grants so now I have a printer and software for basic word processing, graphics, and spreadsheets. My
pupils were ecstatic.

MR. NEWMAN:  I'm beginning to understand that there's more to teaching
than I thought.

MS. OLDHAND:  We old-timers have learned to stay on the lookout for ways to
get resources for our classrooms.

MR. NEWMAN:  Now that you have it, what are the children doing with it?

MS. OLDHAND:  That's a good question. Go over and talk to the children who
are using the computer now and they'll tell you.

Mr. Newman learned that, when Ms. Oldhand received the printer and software
and explained to her pupils some of the things that could be done, they decided
to produce a class newsletter to distribute in the school and to parents. Ms.
Oldhand divided them into four groups of six pupils each, being careful to have
mixed groups in terms of gender, ethnicity, ability, and any other variables
among the pupils in her class. She had received the equipment in January so she
had assigned each group to one of the months remaining in the school year.

The tasks of producing a newsletter were divided up, and each group was
told that they would have time to work on this project, when it was their turn,
while other pupils were engaged in other activities. The whole class decided,
after much discussion, what the basic layout of the newsletter would be, but
each month's content was left up to the group responsible for that issue. Ms.
Oldhand found that some of her pupils were already adept on the computer and
that they caught on very quickly to how to use the software. These children
were able to teach others, and, with some initial instruction and continuous
monitoring, all groups produced newsletters that surprised both themselves and
Ms. Oldhand.

Ms. Oldhand had several purposes in mind when she encouraged her pupils
to produce a newsletter. It would require them to organize their ideas, their
materials, and their time, abilities that are needed in all subject areas. Ms. Oldhand also had science in mind; as the pupils worked on the newsletter they

learned, almost incidentally, to use spreadsheets and to make graphs. By learning that they could use computer tools to represent what they knew, they were developing skills they could also use in science. As they collected data in their science investigations throughout the remainder of the year, each cooperative group had a computer file, and the groups took turns using the computer to enter the group's data. Some children suggested writing lab reports on the computer, but Ms. Oldhand explained that that was impractical with only one computer and, more important, she believed that the children derived many benefits from keeping their science workbooks.

Over the course of two decades computers have moved from being a novelty to becoming standard equipment in elementary schools. Computers have also become enormously more powerful and can be used in ways that were not possible when they were first introduced. As with any new technology, their uses, implications, and consequences, both intended and unintended, become clear only with continued use over time. We as teachers are still trying to discover what kinds of things computers can do to help us meet curriculum goals that cannot be done by other means. This experimentation is particularly true for teaching science in the elementary school.

High school science teachers use computers routinely in laboratories for data collection and analysis, for simulations, and in other ways. Middle school science teachers also use many computer applications, including data collection and analysis. The situation in elementary school is more complex. The youngest children can learn to use computers. In fact, many of them are using computers at home from the age of 3, but in school they need firsthand experiences in science that cannot be obtained from a computer. Older children, too, need firsthand experiences, but computers can enhance learning for them if used thoughtfully.

## LEARNING *WITH* COMPUTERS VERSUS
## LEARNING *FROM* COMPUTERS

The first use of computers in schools was to support drill and practice or rote learning, called *computer-assisted instruction* (CAI). The novelty of using a computer kept children interested longer than they might have been with a workbook, but it was still rote learning based on principles of behaviorism. Tutorials, the next development, went one step beyond the drill and practice programs by correcting incorrect answers that learners gave and repeating the information in another form, followed by a question. In both cases the computer held information, showed it to the learner, and asked for recall.

The constructivist approach rejects this way of teaching. It does not accept the idea that learning is transfer of information from either the teacher or a computer to the brain of the learner. Knowledge of a subject is not obtained by memorization but by connecting what is known from personal experience with information from other sources and making sense of it all by thinking about it. The question for science educators and for you as a science teacher is to find ways that the computer can be used creatively and productively in that process.

An early proponent of using computers in education, Seymour Papert (1980b), wrote, "I believe with Dewey, Montessori and Piaget that children learn by doing and by thinking about what they do. And so the fundamental ingredients of education must be better things to do and better ways to think about oneself doing these things" (p. 161). Papert developed Logo, a computer language that was used to control, at first, a stylus that moved about on a large piece of paper on the floor and, later, an object on a computer screen. Logo is simple enough for children to learn quickly and was designed as a way for children to develop logical thinking through understanding the consequences of their actions on an object. Papert argued that the microcomputer had opened the door for earlier and more advanced mental growth than had been possible before. Logo is seldom used now, but Papert's ideas as presented in his book *Mindstorms* (Papert, 1980a) are still relevant.

Learning *with* computers, rather than learning *from* computers or learning *about* computers means to use computers as tools for learning. When computers are used as tools Jonassen (2000) calls them *mindtools,* defined as "computer-based tools and learning environments that . . . function as intellectual partners with the learner in order to engage and facilitate critical thinking and higher order learning" (p. 9). Linn and Hsi (2000) call the computer a *learning partner.*

Computers cannot take the place of active engagement in the kinds of investigations and other science experiences described in previous chapters. These remain the experiential basis on which children construct knowledge in science. What computers can do is to help children use these experiences to construct knowledge. That happens when pupils use computers to reorganize and represent knowledge, to serve as a stimulus for reflective thinking, and to use symbols to promote new ways of thinking. When used this way, the computer becomes a tool.

## USING COMPUTERS TO MEET CURRICULUM OBJECTIVES

When you're contemplating using computers in a lesson, you should ask yourself two questions.

1. Will the use of this computer application support the objectives of the lesson?

Supporting lesson objectives should be your first consideration in deciding what materials to use in a lesson or a unit. The purpose of using computers or any other technology is to aid in reaching the curriculum objectives. The use of computers in business and in personal lives is now so widespread that a teacher who isn't using computers all the time can feel out of step. Resist that thought and use computers only when they contribute to meeting the lesson's objectives.

2. Will the computer be able to do something that cannot be done another way or that cannot be done as well another way?

Computers can do some things that cannot be done by any other means. They can make lightning-fast calculations, turn charts into graphs with a click of the mouse, save and store enormous amounts of data, and facilitate almost instantaneous communication throughout the world. But reading a page on a computer is no improvement over reading a page from a book. In fact, many people would say that reading from a book is a better experience. Use the computer only when it offers an advantage over other ways of accomplishing your objectives.

# CONTENT-RELATED SOFTWARE

Content-related software is designed to teach a concept and/or process and isn't a general tool of the kind Jonassen refers to as a *mindtool*. These programs nevertheless have a place in a constructivist science program.

## Simulations

Simulations provide vicarious experiences that the pupil would not be able to experience directly. An example of the use of a simulation is Ms. Oldhand's use of *Sky Travel*, a software program that simulates the position and movement of stars and planets. She integrated the simulation into a unit that included actual observation of the night sky and comparisons of what was observed with what was in the computer simulation.

> **Resource Materials Note.**
> Sources for all computer programs cited in this chapter are listed in the Appendix.

■ **MS. OLDHAND'S UNIT ON STARS**

### NSE Standard
Objects in the sky: The sun, moon, and stars all have properties, locations, and movements that can be observed and described (NRC, 1996, p. 134).

### Grade Levels: 4–5

### Objectives
Ms. Oldhand took the following cognitive objectives from *Benchmarks* (American Association for the Advancement of Science [AAAS], 1993, p. 63):

1. Know that the pattern of stars in the sky stays the same, although they appear to move across the sky nightly and different stars can be seen in different seasons.
2. Know that stars are like the sun, some being smaller and some larger, but so far away that they look like points of light.
   Ms. Oldhand added an affective objective of her own:
3. Develop awareness of the vastness and mystery of the universe beyond our solar system.

## Materials
*Sky Travel,* a software program

Ms. Oldhand's pupils had had experience in earlier grades of observing the moon at night and in the daytime. They had learned that the earth travels around the sun and that the moon travels around the earth, and they had learned something about the planets. This unit was designed to take the pupils beyond the earth's solar system and into the universe beyond.

Ms. Oldhand asked how many pupils had looked at the stars at night and what they thought about as they looked up into the night sky. She asked them to imagine that they were all on an island, with no other land in sight and no communication with the rest of the world except for radio messages. The messages had predictable patterns, but they were otherwise unintelligible. No one knew where they came from or what they meant. She explained that this situation was not unlike that of people long ago as they looked up at the stars and wondered what they were, where they were, and what they meant.

Ms. Oldhand led a discussion about what could be learned by just looking up at the night sky. Pupils said that they could see that some stars are brighter than others and that stars are in different places at different times. Some pupils could find the North Star and knew that it was always in the same place, near the Big Dipper. They talked about the invention of the telescope and the more recent Hubble telescope.

After this discussion, the pupils did a series of hands-on activities to help them understand, first, that the movement of the earth makes it appear that the stars are traveling across the sky and, second, how scientists measure distances in space. They also learned that some objects that appear to be stars are actually planets in the earth's solar system and how to distinguish planets from stars. Finally, they used sky maps to identify constellations, and each group chose a constellation to study and draw.

Now it was time to get ready for a special star-gazing field trip that Ms. Oldhand had planned with the pupils' parents. Before the children arrived, Ms. Oldhand connected the computer to an LCD panel and loaded *Sky Travel* into the computer. This program has many features, but the one that Ms. Oldhand brought up on the screen was Sky Window, a module that charts hundreds of stars and shows dozens of constellations, depicting the heavens at any chosen time and place. Ms. Oldhand had chosen the time and place of the field trip and used Sky Window to show on the screen what the children would see when they looked up at the night sky. Ms. Oldhand brought first one and then another constellation into the center of the screen. When she chose one star in a constellation, the computer gave information about that star. As Ms. Oldhand had made sure that the groups chose a constellation that would be visible at the designated time and place, all the children could check their information and maps against what they saw on the screen. At the end of the period, Ms. Oldhand told them that she would leave the program on the computer and keep a flexible schedule for the 2 days remaining before the field trip so that groups could use the program in between their other work.

They were lucky to have good weather on the night of the field trip, and all the groups were able to find their constellations and identify the stars that they had studied. They found that they could see much more in the sky than they had seen before because now they knew what to look for.

Ms. Oldhand knew that she had barely touched the surface of *Sky Travel*, and she made a note to herself to tell other teachers how easy it was to use and how much the children had learned from it. She also decided that she would find additional uses for this software in the future.

Now that she had a computer in her classroom and had used one piece of software successfully, her thoughts raced to other curriculum-related software that she could integrate into the units that she would teach on electricity, ecosystems, and weather. She had also heard of a software simulation of the dissection of a frog, *Operation Frog,* that might be a good choice for her sixth graders. She had a lot of homework to do to find software that would make her science program more meaningful for her pupils.

## Other Content-Related Software

Programs are available that present problems on topics in science and that are also more open ended than older programs. For example, *Botanical Garden* lets pupils experiment with environmental conditions to find the conditions that a particular plant needs for maximum growth. With *Build a Circuit,* pupils can put together the elements of a circuit and the computer will tell them whether the circuit will work.

Some useful programs pose a problem for the pupil to solve in the context of an adventure or expedition, with many factors to take into account. *The Oregon Trail,* an early example designed for social studies, posed problems that learners had to solve successfully in order for their party of settlers to survive the ordeal of crossing the continent. Designed for grades 4 through 8, *Ecosystems* focuses on science and also poses the problem of survival, but in a different context. Students are challenged to survive on an island, using only the resources available on the island and without disrupting the island's ecosystem. Both programs are interactive, forcing the user to make decisions, and each decision has consequences for survival.

## COMPUTER-BASED TOOLS

Think for a moment about the tools you use in your life. A pen or pencil is a tool for writing, a hammer is a tool for driving a nail, and a hair dryer is a tool for drying your hair. A tool is a device that makes it easier for you to do something or makes it possible for you to do something that you couldn't do otherwise.

The software programs just described are instructional materials, sources of information about specific topics. They take the place of a textbook or a teachers' explanation or, in some cases, a hands-on experience. In contrast to those programs are software programs that are used as tools, referred to earlier in this chapter as *mindtools*. These computer programs can be used across the curriculum, not only in science but in all subjects.

To understand the concept of a computer-based tool, think of making a graph representing data you have collected. You draw the two axes on a sheet of graph paper, find the first point, mark it on the paper, find the second point, mark it, and continue until you have plotted all the points. Then you draw a line through the points, making a smooth curve. With a computer and the needed software, all of this can be done with the click of a mouse. Software programs that can be used as tools in teaching science, and ways to use them, are described in the rest of this chapter.

## Spreadsheets and Graphs

A spreadsheet is a ledger sheet with rows and columns into which data can be entered and stored. Numbers, words, or a combination can be entered. Each cell in the grid can be located by reference to the letter designating its column and the number designating its row. The numbers of columns and rows can be adjusted to suit the data to be entered. With a few clicks of the mouse, numerical data from a spreadsheet can be converted to a bar graph, a line graph, or a pie graph. Spreadsheets can also be used for solving problems and performing other functions but the most common use in elementary school is data entry and storage.

An example of the use of a spreadsheet is the production of Table 12.2 and Figure 12.5 in Investigation 12.7. Each week students took temperature readings of the air above a creek and at the surface of the water. The temperature readings were averaged and entered into a spreadsheet at the end of each month. Thus the data were recorded and safely stored in the computer. Table 12.2 shows data from the investigation printed from a spreadsheet. At the end of the school year a click of the mouse produced the graph shown in Figure 12.5. The same data could also have produced the graph shown in Figure 13.1.

In both graphs data have been represented in a form that makes it easy for pupils to see relationships between the variables and to ask questions that can be answered by reference to the data. In this way, the spreadsheet, and the table and graphs generated from it, have become objects that help pupils analyze and make sense of the data they collected and thus understand this part of their study of the creek. When a spreadsheet is used in this way it becomes a *mindtool* or a tool for thinking.

## Databases

Banks, hospitals, governments, and almost all other institutions in the United States now store information in databases. A database is a system that stores information in files, each of which contains information on one topic. Conceptually, it is similar to the contents of a filing cabinet. Databases can be used as tools for thinking in many ways.

Creating a database requires gathering information, analyzing it, categorizing it, and organizing it. The pupils who carried out the group investigations of trees in Chapter 6 could have created a database, using information about the trees in their neighborhood. One way to do so would be to use a field guide to identify each species of tree, collect the same information about each species, and create a file for each species. Information that might be entered would be the average height at

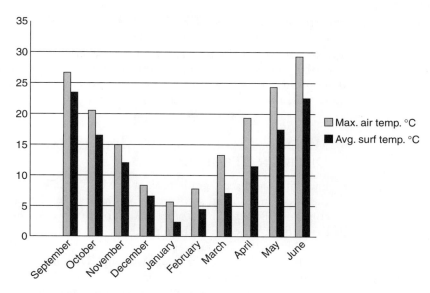

**FIGURE 13.1   Air and Water Surface Temperature**

maturity, rate of growth, kind of leaf, size of leaf, deciduous or evergreen, and other characteristics that pupils could suggest. These data would be collected by observation, searching books or other sources of information, analysis, and organization. Once the database had been created, pupils could use it to answer questions such as:

What is the relationship, if any, between the size of the leaves and the height of a tree?

What are the fastest growing trees in this area? What do they have in common?

Pupils may also build databases by exchanging data over the Internet with pupils in other locations. For example, pupils in six locations from east to west or north to south in a state could use data they collected on weather or trees or birds in their areas to build a database that could be accessed by all of them. This database could then be used to answer questions generated by the teacher and the pupils and would be an authentic resource for integrating science, geography, and history. Information can also be taken from an already established database to answer questions. Some of the information in the database on trees—say, the average height of trees—might well have come from searching the World Wide Web.

## Microcomputer-Based Laboratory (MBL)

Combinations of hardware and software, such as *The Bank Street Laboratory,* are now available for elementary-school children to collect data on temperature, sound, light, and pressure and to see the data displayed on the computer screen. Data are collected by means of sensors, or probes, connected to the computer via an interface box that fits into a computer port. These devices aren't available in most elementary schools, but they are frequently used in middle schools and high schools where each pair of students works at a computer in a laboratory setting. The following lesson description shows how one teacher took advantage of an opportunity to use this apparatus, although he had only one computer.

## ■ MR. NICOLA'S LESSON ON MIXING WATER AT DIFFERENT TEMPERATURES

Each fifth- and sixth-grade teacher at Mr. Nicola's school had one computer for a classroom and shared software. When it was Mr. Nicola's turn to have the Micro-computer Based Laboratory (MBL) for two weeks, he designed an experiment that required the use of the temperature probe (thermistor).

He installed the software in the computer, attached the interface box, and tried it to be sure that everything was working. Then he introduced MBL to the class by using an LCD panel with the computer to teach a modified direct instruction lesson on the use of the equipment to measure temperature. His demonstration included putting the thermistor first into a beaker of hot tap water and then into a beaker of cold water. He had individual pupils come to the computer and take readings, which were then displayed on the screen. He then asked and answered questions.

He explained that he would place the computer with the MBL in the science learning center and each cooperative group would have directions for carrying out an investigation and a series of questions to answer. Groups would circulate through the center as their work permitted over the following week. He placed the following materials at the learning center:

Three beakers, one set in a styrofoam jacket
A graduated cylinder
A stirring rod
A timer
Access to hot and cold water
(Hot tap water can be used, or a hot plate, set on low, can be used to keep water moderately hot.)

The directions called for pupils to (a) measure a specified volume of cold water, pour it into one beaker, and use the probe take the temperature; (b) measure a specified volume of hot water, pour it into a beaker, and take the temperature; (c) carefully pour the water from the two beakers into the third beaker (the one insulated by the styrofoam jacket), place the probe in the beaker, and watch the computer screen as the temperature changes; (d) wait until the temperature stops changing (reaches equilibrium); and (e) note the temperature and the time required for the water to reach that temperature.

Each group had directions to mix different volumes of water; for example, one group mixed 20 ml of cold water with 40 ml of hot water, and another group mixed 30 ml of cold water with 30 ml of hot water. When all the groups had completed the assignment, Mr. Nicola put all the data together, displayed it to the class, and asked whether they could see any patterns. With skillful questioning and allowing time for the pupils to think, he led them to the conclusions that, when water of two temperatures is mixed,

- the final temperature is somewhere in between the starting temperatures, and
- the final temperature is determined by two variables: (a) the beginning temperatures and (b) the volumes of the hot and cold water.

Mr. Nicola didn't introduce the terms *heat capacity* and *heat energy* and didn't explain that the mass rather than the volume is the operating variable. Rather, he used this lesson as an introduction to a concept that the class would study later. *Benchmarks* (AAAS, 1993) supports this approach by recommending that

> students need not come out of this grade span [3–5] understanding heat or its difference from temperature. . . . Computer labware probes and graphic displays that detect small changes in temperature and plot them can be used by students to examine many instances of heat exchange. (pp. 83–84)

The advantage of using MBL devices is that pupils are not hampered by their own awkwardness and inexperience in handling laboratory equipment and thus are able to collect data, see the plotted results, and think about the meaning of the

*A teacher makes good use of one computer in her classroom.*

experiment. In a traditional experiment, children are often so involved in collecting data and trying to make a graph that they don't get the point of what they've done.

## Other Computer-Based Tools

Word processing is primarily a production tool but can also promote the thinking processes that accompany any form of writing that isn't simply copying. The children in Ms. Oldhand's room who were putting out a newsletter were using word processing as they thought about their work and organized their thoughts. Modeling programs, visualization tools, communication tools, and search tools can all be used as tools for thinking. It is up to the science teacher to create problems, questions, and activities that use these potential tools to enhance learning in science.

## The World Wide Web

The World Wide Web (WWW, or the Web) is a source of information rather than a tool, but planning and carrying out a search demands some of the thinking processes that have been mentioned. If you plan to have your pupils use the Web as a source of information, take the time to teach them how to do it; otherwise they may lose a great deal of time wandering about in hyperspace. The following steps are suggested by Jonassen (2000, p. 186).

1. Make a plan: What do you want to find? Why do you want it?
2. Use strategies to search the Web: Identify key terms and subsidiary terms.
3. Evaluate the usability of the information you find: Does the site have the information that you're seeking? Look for links to other sources.
4. Critically evaluate the information: Who put it on the Web? How can you check the sources?
5. Collect the information and attribute its authorship as you would something taken from a book or newspaper: How can you best use it for your purpose?
6. Reflect on the search: Did you find what you needed? Was this a good way to get that information or could you have gotten it more quickly and easily from another source?

Used in this way the World Wide Web can promote organization, analysis, and reflection.

# MANAGING YOUR RESOURCES

There is still wide variability among schools in the number and kinds of computers they have and how they are distributed within the schools. In some schools all computers are in one "computer lab"; in others computers are in classrooms or are on carts that can be wheeled from classroom to classroom. In this section you will find some suggestions for ways to adapt to whatever circumstances you find yourself in.

## The One-Computer Classroom

A teacher with 25 pupils and one computer may think that little can be done except to let children take turns playing games as a reward for finishing their work or assigning a low-achieving pupil to a drill-and-practice program. Dublin, Pressman, Barnett, Corcoran, and Woldman (1994) suggest a number of practical ways to take advantage of just one computer in your classroom. Some of their suggestions are as follows:

- By using an LCD screen with the overhead projector or by connecting the computer to a television monitor, you can display the computer screen to the whole class. You can run software as a way to introduce a new topic or to present information and ideas that pupils will use in subsequent activities. You can demonstrate how to use tool software such as word processing as you would in a direct instruction lesson.

- If your classroom has a number of learning centers, you can add a computer center, cycling small groups of students through a computer center while the rest of the class is engaged in other activities. If your class is doing independent investigations, several groups may use the computer to their advantage. Those groups can take turns using the one computer, or you might have one period each day in which groups of children carry out assignments at various learning centers.

- A single computer can be used as a peer tutoring tool. Children who have had an opportunity outside of class to learn how to use particular software can help classmates acquire the new skill. Having teams of two students introduce other teams of two students to new software provides benefits to both teams.

- If your school has a collection of computers in a central place, such as a resource center or a computer lab, you can introduce a topic or a skill to the whole class on your classroom computer. Then your students are ready to work on their own, in pairs, or in groups when they go to the computer center. Pupils can ask questions, clear up confusion, perhaps come up to the computer, and make entries that everyone can see. They can then use their time on the computers to best advantage, which is important because time on the computers is always limited for any one class.

- If your computer is connected to the Internet, you are in luck. This opens up the possibility for your pupils to send and receive messages from children all over the country as well as other parts of the world. Your pupils can become part of exciting scientific investigations as they collect data and share it with other pupils elsewhere.

## The Multiple-Computer Classroom

The ideas suggested for the single-computer classroom are applicable to a classroom that has two or three computers, but it becomes easier to integrate computers into your teaching as more become available. Suggestions for use include the following:

- If the classroom has three computers and 24 pupils, it's possible for everyone to get time on the computer in one period. In groups of four, half the class works at the computers for half the period, then they switch with the other half who have been working on some other activity.

- Two computers, with different software installed, can be used to set up two computer centers, perhaps one for math and one for science. A computer in a learning center can be moved and connected to an LCD panel or television monitor and used for whole-class teaching whenever the teacher wants to use it in that way.

## Computers in a Resource Center or Computer Lab

In many schools individual classrooms do not have computers, with all computers installed in a resource center or computer lab. Some administrators are now recognizing the difficulty of true integration of computers into the curriculum when all the computers are down the hall somewhere and teachers can only take pupils at certain times that have to be negotiated. The following are some suggestions for maximizing benefits of this arrangement:

- Plan ahead so that the software you need is available when you need it.

- Assign cooperative groups of two to four children to each computer. Make the assignments in your homeroom to avoid confusion when you get to the computer lab.

- Monitor the class carefully to keep pupils on task. There are many distractions and attractions in a resource center or computer lab.

## COOPERATIVE LEARNING ON THE COMPUTER

Cooperative group work is as beneficial and effective when pupils are using computers as it is in other kinds of classroom activities. A child sitting alone in front of a computer may feel isolated and become frustrated; when a problem arises, there is no one to turn to for help, and a child's attention span may be very short. When children work in cooperative groups on a computer, the benefits are both social and cognitive. They learn to share an object that they all want to get their hands on, and they learn from each other as they work together to solve problems or produce a product.

A very practical reason for teaching students to cooperate is that you will not have enough computers for children to work on alone, even if that were advisable. It has

*Children learn to use the computer cooperatively.*

been suggested that at some time in the future all children will have a computer at their desks; however, that isn't likely to happen, and it's probably not a good idea.

Setting up cooperative groups to work on a computer is similar to setting up such groups for other activities, as explained in Chapter 6. In assigning pupils to groups, try to compose groups that include children of different abilities and experience. If your pupils have already worked in cooperative groups, remind them that

- an individual is successful only if the group is successful;

- each child is responsible to help others learn, and pupils should ask for help from the group when needed so that they will learn;

- they will receive guidelines and help in developing the social skills needed for group work; and

- each child will be assigned a specific role—for example, one pupil will read the problem and try to explain it to the others, one will control the mouse (and/or use the keyboard), one will remind everyone to stay on task when they go off on tangents, and one may be a recorder—and will alternate among roles.

As in other situations, you will have to monitor the group and be available for help if needed. You will probably also be needed elsewhere, so you may have to rearrange the group members if one or more groups seem particularly contentious or nonproductive.

# MAKING THE COMPUTER WORK FOR YOU

What most teachers look forward to least is averaging grades at the end of a marking period. Now you can make this chore a thing of the past by setting up a spreadsheet for each subject or for each class if you are a special science teacher and teach different classes. Once you have set up the spreadsheet, enter a grade for each pupil every time you give a quiz or a test or assess a project or portfolio. Grades can be weighted by entering one grade more than once; that is, a project grade will count more than a short quiz, so weight the grade appropriately. The computer will average the grades. If you need to change a grade, the computer will give you a new average immediately. The spreadsheet lets you know when a pupil is falling behind and gives you a basis for feedback to pupils and their parents at any time. Programs with special features for teachers are available, but any spreadsheet program will work.

The computer can help you plan units and lessons, either with special software designed for teachers or with a more general program. You can create a template for lesson plans that makes planning simpler. As ideas for lessons and units come to mind, you can file and retrieve them much more easily and confidently than you can with notebooks, file cards, and manila folders. As you explore the possibilities, you will become more aware of the power and utility of the computer to help you with creative planning and with paperwork.

## ■ CASE STUDY

### THE COMPUTER AS LEARNING PARTNER

An interesting and instructive long-term project, *Computer as Learning Partner,* has been reported by Linn and Hsi (2000). This project included many of the elements of science teaching that you have encountered in earlier chapters. The group based its work on constructivist principles, used authentic assessment, sought to develop autonomous learners, and carried out the project as a true investigation. As you read about this project, try to project yourself into the future as a teacher and think about how you might use this model to form or become part of a team to continue learning about how pupils learn and how you can become a better teacher.

The project was a systematic study of how computers could be used to improve middle school students' knowledge and understanding of the concepts of heat and temperature and, as a broader goal, to promote autonomous learning so that the students would become lifelong learners. A team composed of scientists, science educators, science teachers, and others was assembled. As the project continued for 15 years, there were many changes in personnel; graduate students came and went, as did visiting scientists and others. At the center of the team was a creative middle school teacher who was committed to his own continued learning and the learning of his pupils. He wanted to know how computers could be used to foster better understanding of science.

The team worked by designing curriculum, developing assessment, experimenting, refining curriculum on the basis of results, reporting results to others, and continuing the process. In the beginning the team members found that students didn't connect what they had learned in class to anything in their lives outside of class. They also found that textbook treatments of heat and temperature were confusing and misleading. Then, most surprising of all, they found that college graduates with majors in science couldn't give commonsense explanations of the concepts of heat and temperature or connect them to everyday phenomena. These "experts" were unable to say why a metal table feels colder than a wooden table in the same room or whether aluminum foil or wool will keep a bottle of soda colder. They weren't much better than middle school students at confronting authentic, real-world problems.

After many problems and frustrations with technology, the team designed and stabilized a curriculum that used both real-time data collection (i.e., probes or sensors) and simulations. Both types of computer applications were assessed and both were found to make science concepts more accessible to pupils. As each version of the curriculum was tried and assessed, and as pupil understanding continued to improve, the team also worked to design a curriculum to improve understanding of science and to promote autonomous learning.

Linn and Hsi concluded that their

> experience with the CPL partnership underscored our belief that a science curriculum is most successful when it is developed and regularly refined by people with diverse interests and different areas of expertise—classroom teachers, scientists, educational researchers, computer specialists *et alia*—who come together in a sort of mutual respect to fulfill a common goal. (p. 355)

## ■ SUMMARY

Computers have become an important, almost essential, tool for teaching. The challenge to teachers is to use them to help meet instructional goals rather than as something extra that isn't integrated into the curriculum. In an inquiry-based science program learning *from* computers is replaced by learning *with* computers.

Both content-related software and tool software can be used in a constructivist science curriculum. Simulations can be used when the actual experience isn't possible and should be treated in lesson planning in the same way that the actual experience would be treated. Tool software, which is not specific to any area or content, can be used to promote the cognitive processes of organizing, analyzing, and representing information and ideas. Spreadsheets, databases, and microcomputer-based laboratories are examples of ways that the computer functions as a tool. The Internet, especially the World Wide Web, can also stimulate cognitive processes in some applications.

Although teachers may have little choice in the kind and number of computers available to them, they can decide how to use what there is. Options for integrating the computer into instruction are available whether the teacher has a one-computer classroom, a multiple-computer classroom, or is in a school where all the computers are concentrated in one location. In all these situations, assigning cooperative learning groups to work together on the computer is preferable to having children work individually.

The computer can work for teachers as well as for pupils by serving as an automated grade book that averages grades and as a means of making planning easier and more systematic.

The chapter closes with an account of Computer as Learning Partner, a project conducted by Linn and others over a 15-year period. This project included many of the elements of science teaching that you have encountered in earlier chapters and shows what can be done with computers when a group of teachers and others work together to improve teaching and learning.

## ■ ACTIVITIES FOR THE READER

1. Obtain a catalog from a company that specializes in computer software and choose a program to preview without charge. Use the software to develop a lesson plan.

2. Develop a database that you can use when you begin your career as a teacher. You are free to include anything that you think will be useful.

3. Make a list of WWW addresses that will be useful to you in the future and exchange it with other students.

## ■ QUESTIONS FOR DISCUSSION

1. Discuss the advantages and disadvantages of having all the school's computers in one place instead of having them in the classrooms.

2. How can you use a computer to meet the special needs of children with hearing disabilities, sight disabilities, or emotional problems?

3. What can a teacher do to compensate for the fact that some children have computers at home but that others have no access to a computer?

## ■ REFERENCES

American Association for the Advancement of Science. (1993). *Benchmarks for science literacy.* New York: Oxford University Press.

Dublin, P., Pressman, H., Barnett, E., Corcoran, A., & Woldman, E. (1994) *Integrating Computers in your Classroom. Elementary education.* New York: HarperCollins.

Jonassen, D. (2000). *Computers as mindtools for school*. Columbus. OH: Merrill/Prentice Hall.

Linn, M. & Hsi, S. (2000). *Computers, teachers, peers. Science learning partners*. Mahway, NJ: Lawrence Erlbaum.

National Research Council. (1996). *National science education standards*. Washington, DC: National Academy Press.

Papert, S. (1980a). *Mindstorms*. New York: Basic Books.

Papert, S. (1980b). Teaching children thinking. In R. P. Taylor (Ed.), *The computer in the classroom: Tutor, tool, tutee*. New York: Teachers College Press.

# *Appendix*

## SOURCES OF MATERIALS
### Comprehensive Curriculum Programs

These are modular programs that include teacher manuals and student workbooks or worksheets and may also include all the equipment and supplies needed for each module. Most of these programs were developed with funds from the National Science Foundation and/or other agencies and foundations. When a school system adopts one of these programs, it buys all the necessary print materials and equipment as a package and teachers receive training specifically related to the adopted program. Some districts choose modules from more than one program to meet their own curriculum goals. Information and catalogs can be obtained without charge from the addresses given.

### *Science and Technology for Children (STC)*

Inquiry-based curriculum materials produced by the National Science Resource Center to provide a full science program for Grades 1–6. For each grade level there are four units, covering earth science, life science, physical science, and technological design. Also available is a booklet that shows how the units are linked to the *National Science Education Standards.* Activities for children, teachers' guides, and kits of materials are available from Carolina Biological Supply Company in Burlington, NC 27215-3398.[1-800-227-1150: on-line at www.carolina.com]

### *Science Curriculum Improvement Study (SCIS 3+ )*

K–6 core curriculum program consisting of one unit for kindergarten and two units for each of the other grades. Half the year is spent on a physical science unit and the other half on a life science unit. Each unit has a teacher's guide and a kit of materials needed to carry out the activities. Available from Delta Education, 80 Northwest Boulevard, Nashua, NH 03063 [1-800-258-1302; on-line at www.delta-ed.com]

### Full Option Science System (FOSS)

Series of modules each of which has a teacher's guide, an equipment kit, and an interactive Web site for topics in life, physical and earth sciences, and technology. Other components are a measurement module, teacher preparation videos, reading resources, and FOSS science stories. FOSS provides materials for a complete K–6 science program, but components may be purchased separately. It was developed at the Lawrence Hall of Science, University of California at Berkeley and is distributed by Delta Education at the address previously given.

## Curriculum Units

These are collections of teacher guides for individual units or a series of lessons on one topic. Most of these programs have guides or directions for all the basic topics presented in the elementary-school science curriculum and provide for a more flexible program than the modules previously described.

### Great Explorations in Math and Science (GEMS)

A program practical for teachers who are on their own in developing a science curriculum or need additional ideas to meet curriculum requirements. Teacher's guides, consisting of a series of lessons built around a central concept, have been developed for more than 60 science and math units for grades K–8. The materials may be used to construct an entire curriculum or as separate units that fulfill specific curriculum requirements. The guides are inexpensive, indicate appropriate grade level, contain complete directions, and suggest the use of materials that are widely available. Two of the units, *Treasure Boxes* and *Schoolyard Ecology*, were referred to in this textbook. A catalog is available from the Lawrence Hall of Science, University of California, Berkeley, CA 94720. [415-642-7771; on-line at www.lhs.berkeley.edu/GEMS]

### Activities Integrating Mathematics and Science (AIMS)

Teachers who have to develop their own curriculums will find this program useful. A wide variety of products are available, including activity books, a magazine, multimedia resources, specialty labs, lab components, manipulatives, games, and materials for technology projects. A catalogue can be ordered from AIMS Education Foundation, Fresno, CA 93747-8120. [1-888-733-2467; on-line at www.AIMSedu.org]

### National Geographic Kids Network

A computer-based program that provides the tools necessary for children to construct and use a database on such topics as acid rain and insect populations. Children gather observational data on one topic for a period of weeks, add it to a database shared by children at other sites, and use the combined data to compare sites, search for patterns, and find relationships. Available from Educational Services, National Geographic Society, P.O. Box 98018, Washington, DC 20090-8018.

**Resource Materials Note.** Women's Educational Equity Act (WEEA) Equity Resource Center, Education Development Center, Inc., 55 Chapel Street, Newton, MA 02458. DO-IT (Disabilities, Opportunities, Internetworking and Technology). University of Washington, Box 354842, Room 206, Seattle, WA 98195. On-line at doit@u.washington.edu.

# Books and Periodicals

### *Schoolground Science. Activities for Elementary and Middle Schools*

A collection of ideas for projects that can be carried out on the school grounds by children from kindergarten through ninth grade. Written by C. Roth, C. Cervoni, T. Wellnitz, and E. Arms and available from the Massachusetts Audubon Society, South Great Road, Lincoln, MA 01733.

### *Science for Children: Resources for Teachers*

A comprehensive annotated list of available materials in all areas of the elementary science curriculum. Available from National Science Resources Center. National Academy Press. Washington, DC.

### *Science Activities*

A magazine containing practical classroom projects and curriculum ideas written by and for teachers of all grade levels. Published quarterly by Heldref Publications, 1319 Eighteenth Street, NW, Washington, DC 20036.

### *Teaching Tolerance*

A magazine of articles, stories, art work, and curriculum ideas devoted to promoting acceptance of people of all races, religions, ethnic backgrounds, and sexual orientation. Published twice a year and sent free upon request to educators by the Southern Poverty Law Center, 400 Washington Avenue, Montgomery, AL 36104. [On-line at www.teachingtolerance.org]

### *Publications of the National Science Teachers Association (NSTA)*

Magazines, books, and booklets on a wide range of topics for all grade levels are published by this organization. *Science and Children* is a magazine for elementary teachers that contains articles of general interest, curriculum ideas, and news of interest to teachers and children. For a list of available titles and prices, contact the National Science Teachers Association, 1840 Wilson Boulevard, Arlington, VA 22201. [On-line at www.nsta.org]

## Equipment and Apparatus

Many items needed for a hands-on science program can be found at a local hardware store, office supply store, or drugstore. Most merchants will give discounts for items purchased for use by school children. School supply stores also carry some items that may be useful.

The following companies specialize in science equipment for schools, including equipment for elementary science. In addition to the comprehensive science programs with kits previously mentioned these companies supply individual pieces of equipment, such as balances, magnets, magnifying glasses, glassware, and many other items. Some items not listed in their regular catalogs may be listed as replacement parts for science kits and can be purchased individually.

Carolina Biological Supply Company, 2700 York Road, Burlington, NC 27215. [1-800-227-1150; on-line at www.carolina.com]

Delta Education, 80 Northwest Boulevard, Nashua, NH 03063. [1-800-258-1302; on-line at www.delta-ed.com]

A company that doesn't specialize in science but has been recommended by a science teacher is Lakeshore Learning Materials, P.O.Box 6261, Carson, CA 90749. [1-800-421-5354; on-line at www. lakeshore@lakeshorelearning.com]

## Computer Resources

### Software

Two useful sources are the following.

Scholastic, Inc., P.O. Box 7502, Jefferson City, MO 65102 [1-800-724-6527; on-line at www.scholastic.com], publishes *Scholastic Technology Guide,* a source of information about a large number of companies that provide software programs. Scholastic, Inc., also publishes software for elementary science.

Sunburst Communications, 101 Castleton Street, P.O. Box 10, Pleasantville, NY 10570 [800-321-7511]. *Botanical Garden, Build a Circuit, The Bank Street Laboratory,* and *The Voyage of the Mimi* are but a few of the software packages available from this source.

### Internet

There are too many Web sites even to begin to list them. A good place to start on-line is *The Science Learning Network.* Search by name or use www.sln.org, which will lead you to other sites. Searching for one or two key words will usually lead you to the information you need.

# Index